Why *Not* Me?

Mandy McMillan

with Lesley Roberts

hachette
SCOTLAND

First published in 2010 by
HACHETTE SCOTLAND, an imprint of Hachette UK

1

Cataloguing in Publication Data is available from the British Library

ISBN 978 0 7553 6058 1

Typeset in Dante and Foundry Sans Light by Avon DataSet Ltd,
Bidford-on-Avon, Warwickshire

Printed and bound in the UK by
CPI Mackays, Chatham ME5 8TD

Hachette Scotland's policy is to use papers that are natural, renewable and
recyclable products and made from wood grown in sustainable forests.
The logging and manufacturing processes are expected to conform to the
environmental regulations of the country of origin.

HACHETTE SCOTLAND
An Hachette UK Company
338 Euston Road
London NW1 3BH

www.hachettescotland.co.uk
www.hachette.co.uk

MANDY McMILLAN is a hairdr[...] job is in a small but busy salon in Glasgow. Her full-time job is fighting cancer. She lives with her husband, Scott, [...]

For Holly.

The names of some of the people, as well as some physical descriptions, have been changed to protect the privacy of the individuals concerned.

Acknowledgements

This book is dedicated to my loving husband, Scott, who has stood by me through good times and bad times; to my wonderful mum and dad who give constant love and support; but especially to my beautiful daughter, Holly, who puts a smile on my face every day.

I'd also like to acknowledge the other special people who're very much part of my life story, even if they don't realise it.

My brother, Joseph, and his family; Scott's mum and dad, who've been through so much with me.

Liz who has never failed to lift my spirits and Jackie for the countless hours she's spent listening to my secret fears. And Yvonne for becoming such a good friend.

Esther, for always being there and going out of her way to do anything for me; Lorna, for all the times she's cheered me up with a good night out; Sharon, for always being there when I need to talk. And Dawn, for the inspiration.

To Vicky and all the staff at the Beatson; to Aileen and Helen at Stobhill Hospital and to all the NHS doctors and nurses who've given me such fantastic care. Special thanks to my oncologist for all you have done for me.

To Lesley Roberts, without whose encouragement and patience my story would never have been told. And to Bob and Wendy who took a chance on us.

To the rest of my friends and family, too many to mention. Thank you, all of you, for everything.

Foreword

I'm writing this while in the midst of my fifth course of chemotherapy. I'm sporting a ridiculous headband to cover the missing parts of my hair, I'm wearing my 'fat' clothes because I'm so bloated, and I'm exhausted. All in, truth be told, I'm feeling pretty crappy.

But my three-year-old daughter, Holly, is tucked up in bed, fast asleep and dreaming about the fun we'll have tomorrow. Things will be better tomorrow.

Holly, you're my miracle drug.

Chapter 1

'Hurry up – the cars will be here in a minute.'

I was trying my best to help fellow bridesmaid Dawn into her bodice, but I was fumbling with the laces at the back and she was losing her patience.

'Pull them a bit tighter, Mandy. Don't worry – you're not hurting me.'

I was all fingers and thumbs. 'I'm sorry,' I muttered, still concentrating on straightening and pulling the laces, while Dawn held the front section in place over her boobs. 'I'm terrified it's going to press too hard on your sore bits,' I said through gritted teeth, struggling to tie a bow.

There. That would hold everything in position. Done.

'How do you feel?' I asked, taking a few steps back to admire her.

'I'm fine,' she said, smoothing her skirt and giving me a look of exasperation. 'Never mind that. How do I look?'

She was gorgeous. The aubergine-coloured outfits our pal Catherine – the bride – had chosen for us were slim-fitting and sexy, with boned bodices resting on narrow skirts.

'Can you see anything?' Dawn asked, nodding in the direction of her chest. 'No scars on show?'

None.

'Watch me walk,' she said, turning away to parade up and down a bit.

She was very slightly stooped, but I would never have told her.

'Great,' I said.

'And how's my hair?' she went on.

'Dawn, you look amazing.' I sighed with exasperation of my own. 'No one would know a thing.'

Finally the three of us were ready and standing nervously in Catherine's living room. Catherine was radiant. Dawn and I had scrubbed up well. The cars had arrived. This was it.

As we walked down the aisle, I could see my fiancé, Scott, standing a few rows behind the groom and grinning at me proudly. He was an usher, and looked particularly handsome in his kilt. It would be our turn next. Our wedding was booked for the following year. Catherine's was to be our practice run. It was exciting.

I glanced at Dawn, smiling beside me, and felt a jolt of pride. She'd made it after all.

It's a perfect day, I thought. I hope we're as lucky.

It was May 2001, a little over a month since Dawn had been diagnosed with breast cancer. She'd had a mastectomy and simultaneous reconstructive surgery, and the wounds were still raw in so many ways. She'd barely opened her eyes after the operation before she was fretting about how she was going to look at Catherine's wedding.

'I might have to use a walking stick to get down the aisle,' she'd grumbled, as she lay hunched in her hospital bed. 'Imagine how that's going to look! I can't even straighten up at the moment and the wedding's four weeks away.'

Catherine and I had popped in to see her on our way out for a Saturday night on the town. We were dressed up in our glad rags; she was propped up on a pile of pillows and attached to all sorts of machines.

'What if I've still got these big dressings on?' she continued. 'They'll stick out of the top of the bridesmaid's dress.'

'Rubbish – you're not going to have bandages by that time,' I tutted, without having any clue whether it was true. I thought it sounded reassuring, though.

'At least my hair should be all right,' she added. 'I don't start chemo until two weeks after the wedding. What a relief.'

Catherine and I sat at her bedside listening quietly and feeling totally inadequate. We didn't really understand any of the treatment she'd just had and the best we could muster was a bit of sympathy and a lot of encouragement.

'You'll be out of here in no time,' I told her. 'You're looking great already.'

I had no idea what I was talking about. It was such new territory for all of us.

Dawn was thirty-three, a single mum to a lovely eight-year-old daughter called Stephanie and, as far as anyone had known, perfectly healthy.

I'd joined her little gang of friends through our mutual pal, Catherine, and we slotted together beautifully. A group of five of us met every Tuesday night to share a takeaway and a few drinks while putting the world to rights. We were pretty ordinary girls: Dawn had a job in Asda, Catherine was a florist, Dawn's sister-in-law, Joy, and her pal, May, both worked for the Inland Revenue, and I, the baby of the group, was – and still am – a hairdresser in a little salon called Clippers in Glasgow, where I take care of the grooming needs of males young and old.

When Dawn had announced, during one of our soirées, that she'd found a lump in her breast and had decided to have it removed, I don't think any of us appreciated for a second just how serious it could be. She made it sound so casual, like she had some say in whether or not to take the thing out.

'I'm sure it will turn out to be a cyst,' I'd said, taking another sip of wine. 'They're really common, especially in younger women. My mum has had loads of them over the years.'

I did know that much. Mum had suffered from lumpy breasts for a long time and regularly had to have cysts drained. She still occasionally found new lumps in her boobs, but she'd learned not to panic at every one. That said, I'd gone with her a couple of months before for a nerve-jangling appointment at Glasgow's Royal Infirmary. She'd been referred by her GP after finding yet another lump, and the doctor was determined she should have this one investigated further.

Mum thought this a total waste of time. 'It'll be the same as usual,' she'd insisted as we drove to the hospital. 'There's no point getting another biopsy done.'

We arrived at around 9 a.m., expecting to be free by 10 a.m. to get started on some shopping. When 1 p.m. came and went and we were the only people left in the waiting area, we were both agitated. She'd had all sorts of tests – a mammogram, an X-ray and a biopsy – and still they kept us hanging on.

'There must be something wrong,' Mum kept saying. 'I wouldn't be here this length of time if everything was all right.'

I was way out of my depth. I wasn't prepared for there to be a problem. I was only meant to be keeping her company, not offering counselling.

'You know what the NHS is like,' I said. 'They'll just be running behind schedule. The consultant is probably away for his lunch.'

But nothing put Mum's mind at rest and her anxiety was infectious. We were both sitting wringing our hands when her name was finally called.

'It's a cyst again, Mrs Russell,' the doctor said. 'Still, you've done the right thing, having it checked out.'

'I wouldn't have been half as worried if I hadn't bothered having it checked out,' Mum huffed, as we made our way to the car.

Sadly, Dawn's news, when it came, wasn't so good.

Catherine phoned me at home.

'Dawn's test results have come back,' she said. 'It's bad. She's got breast cancer.'

I couldn't believe it. Thirty-three-year-olds didn't get breast cancer. Old ladies got it, everyone knew that, not vibrant young women with jobs and kids and their whole lives ahead of them. I knew I should pick up the phone right away and call her, but I couldn't. I didn't know what to say.

'If that happened to me, I don't think I would ever be able to leave the house again,' I told Scott over dinner that night. 'I'd just stay in crying all the time. People avoid you after something like this, and I'd hate that.'

Scott agreed. 'Her life has changed for ever now,' he said, chewing thoughtfully on a mouthful of food. 'Even once she gets through all the treatment, she'll probably always be worried about it coming back.'

In a few sentences we'd blithely described Dawn's fate

as we saw it: hiding away, nursing her own anguish, scared to see anyone or let them see her. In our charmed world, cancer was unthinkable. It was the end.

Seven months later those words came back to haunt us.

Chapter 2

Saturday, 10 November 2001 was my twenty-seventh birthday. I woke up before Scott and snuggled into his back, whispering, 'Wakey, wakey . . . It's my birthday,' until he eventually began to stir.

'Mmm . . . Happy birthday,' he groaned drowsily, without actually opening his eyes.

'Where are my presents?' I cooed.

I've always enjoyed birthdays – I'm a bit of a kid that way. I love surprises, though I'm terrible at springing them myself because I just can't keep a secret. Scott always pandered to me on my birthday and made a real fuss – except first thing in the morning, that is, and particularly if it interfered with a weekend lie-in.

'They're downstairs,' he mumbled. 'I'll get them in a minute, Mandy. Let me wake up a bit first.'

I had to be at work at 9 a.m. and the salon was bound to be busy, so there would be no lie-in for either of us. I bounded downstairs and found a pile of neatly wrapped gifts and pretty boxes sitting on the couch. Scott never bought just one present – he always shelled out for loads of extra things – and he'd clearly tried really hard to make them all look gorgeous.

'Oh, I love this jacket!' I shrieked, charging back upstairs clutching the contents of the largest parcel – a fabulous leather jacket I'd lingered over while shopping in Oasis the week before. 'I knew you'd get it for me.'

Scott was sitting up in bed, shaking his head as I pranced around the room admiring myself.

'Open the rest of them,' he laughed. So we went back downstairs to work through the remainder of his gifts: slippers, perfume and a leather purse.

'I love them all,' I grinned. 'You're too good to me.'

I went off to work full of the joys. On Saturdays the shop was mobbed from the minute we opened the door, but it was always fun on birthdays. The girls at work had a card and a bottle of vodka for me, which came with the strict instruction that it was to be shared with them one night. The day passed quickly and I couldn't wait to get home to start titivating myself for a night on the tiles.

Scott and I were supposed to be going out to celebrate with a bit of a dance at some of my favourite clubs, but the sudden onset of unbearable toothache changed his mind.

'You go with one of your pals,' he said. 'I'll get a DVD and stay in. I don't want you to miss out, but my mouth is absolutely killing me.'

He was rubbing his jaw to emphasise the point, but I

could see he was suffering. I didn't *think* it was just an attempt to avoid being dragged around a dance floor. He would wince every few minutes as pain stabbed his gum, and he refused any dinner.

'I don't think I could chew,' he groaned, as I busied about in the kitchen making my own.

Anyway, I wasn't too bothered that he couldn't make it, if I'm being brutally honest. I knew some of my friends were planning to go clubbing, so I'd join them instead. It was my birthday, after all. I couldn't be expected to sit at home babysitting my fiancé.

'Don't worry about it,' I told Scott, giving his hair a quick rub. 'You just stay home. We'll go out another night.'

I arranged to join Nicky, one of my fellow barmaids at the Muirhead Inn, the local pub where I worked part-time. I'd only taken the job at the end of February to earn a bit of extra money for our wedding, the cost of which seemed to be growing at the rate of Third World debt. I hadn't expected to enjoy it so much. The other bar staff were fun, all different ages but up for a laugh, and they really helped me settle in. I'd been thrown in at the deep end, mind you, working a St Patrick's Day party on one of my first shifts there – long before I'd perfected the delicate art of pouring a pint of Guinness. The place was packed and I was stressed up to the eyeballs as I tried to juggle serving and pouring and smiling and working out the bill while I waited for the drink to settle, then pouring again and smiling and using the till. Somehow I muddled through with Nicky on hand to show me the ropes. The two of us had hit it off right away. We'd started socialising outside work too, so I knew I could join her for a night of mad celebration at a club in nearby Cumbernauld – super-cheesy but always a giggle.

'I'm off to get ready,' I declared as soon as I got the last forkful of dinner down my throat. 'Nicky is picking me up in a taxi at half past eight.'

I switched on some music and pondered over the contents of my wardrobe till I'd chosen a suitably fabulous birthday outfit – tight jeans, a strappy black top and some killer heels – then I streaked from the bedroom to the bathroom. In the shower, I was singing along to the music, which I could still faintly hear, as I squirted a little shower gel on to my hand and began to lather myself. In one quick swipe across my left breast, my fingers touched something hard.

What was that? I thought.

I brushed my hand back over the same breast. My fingertips found it again. It felt like a lump.

I carried on washing, staying clear of my breasts this time and trying not to overreact.

No, it wasn't a lump. I was just being extra-sensitive because of Dawn.

I shampooed my hair, pulling my eyes away from my

left breast and forcing my mind back to the excitement of my birthday.

I couldn't help myself, though. Was something protruding from my skin? I had to touch it again, just to be sure I wasn't imagining things. I was already squeamish about what I might feel, so very gingerly, as if I was inching my hand through the bars of a lion's cage, I put my fingers directly on the spot. It was about halfway up my left breast, above my nipple. It felt slightly raised, thicker than the rest of the breast, and it seemed to be about the size of a ten-pence piece. I snatched my hand away. Bloody hell. I couldn't get out of the shower fast enough.

Don't panic. Just don't panic, I was telling myself as I rushed to dry myself and get downstairs to ask Scott's opinion. It's probably just a cyst. Mum had lots of cysts in her breasts when she was younger. I'm getting the same thing, that's all.

I wrapped my hair in a towel, pulled on my dressing gown and ran downstairs to where Scott was engrossed in some international football match on Sky. I stood watching him for a few seconds, shifting from foot to foot, desperately thinking about how to word what I was about to say.

'Can you do me a favour, Scott?' I said, trying hard to sound completely cool. 'I was just in the shower and, well, I thought I felt a lump in my breast.'

He turned to look at me. I was in a flap, chewing my lip and clutching the dressing gown high at my neck as if to keep the offending area covered.

'Oh . . . right,' he said, clearly waiting for what was coming next.

'Could you have a feel and see if I'm imagining it?'

Slowly he got up from the couch. I kept waiting for a dismissive wave of his hand or some loud objection that he was watching the game and didn't want to be interrupted by his neurotic girlfriend, but he said nothing.

I directed his fingers to the area I'd identified. For a few seconds he concentrated on what he was feeling.

'I'm not sure it's any different to the rest of your breast,' he said eventually.

'Oh really?' I sighed with relief. 'Thank God for that. It's probably nothing, then. Just me being—'

'But now you come to mention it,' Scott interrupted. 'Last week I think it was, when we were messing about, for some reason you bumped against me at one point and I thought I felt something.'

I couldn't believe what I was hearing.

He went on, 'I mean, it didn't really register as a lump at that point, but it did feel a bit, well, unusual.'

What on earth was he talking about? He'd felt a lump in my breast and hadn't said anything about it? What in God's name was happening?

'Scott, why didn't you tell me?' I was beginning to panic. 'With all that's been happening to Dawn, you didn't think you should tell me that you thought you'd felt a lump in my breast!' I was pacing the living-room floor.

'I honestly didn't think any more about it after that moment,' Scott was protesting. 'It's only come back to mind now because of what you're saying.'

This could not be real.

You're too young for breast cancer. It's not cancer, I was repeating to myself, but then Dawn's face would float into my head. God, help me. I was supposed to be going out to celebrate my birthday in an hour's time and I couldn't think straight.

My mum would know what to do. She was used to this kind of thing. She would know what a cyst felt like. She would give me an honest appraisal of what I'd just found. Mum and Dad lived in the next street to us, just round the corner, so she wouldn't mind coming along for a few minutes.

I phoned her and stammered through the problem: 'M-mum, I found a l-lump in my breast while I was in the shower and I'm a bit w-worried about it.'

She was utterly calm. 'Och, it'll be nothing. It's probably just a cyst. I'm sure they're hereditary.'

I was frightened, though, and she could hear it in my voice. 'Honestly, Mum, I'm not sure about this. I've asked Scott and he thinks there might be something, but he really doesn't know about things like this. Can you please just come round and have a look at it?'

'OK, OK,' she said. 'It's not a problem. I'll come round right now.'

Five minutes later I was standing in the dining room while Mum cautiously felt around the upper part of my breast. She was very serious, but she didn't seem scared.

'Yes, there's definitely a lump there,' she said. 'You'd better phone the doctor on Monday morning and get it checked out.'

I really, really didn't want to hear that.

'Look, I don't think for a minute it's sinister,' she went on. 'You're probably being a bit paranoid because of Dawn's illness. But if you're going to suffer with a lot of cysts the way I have, you'd better see the doctor about it.'

She was right. Of course I was being paranoid. Dawn's cancer had shocked us all so much. I hadn't realised how badly I'd been affected and it was hardly surprising that I was putting myself in her position. If it could happen to her, it could happen to any of us, after all. There but for the grace of God go I, and all that.

Nevertheless I had to snap out of it for my own peace of mind, get things into perspective.

'Right, I'm going to get ready,' I declared. 'Thanks for coming round, Mum. I'm fine now,' and off I went to put on my party gear. Crisis averted thanks to some straight-talking from Mum, the voice of reason.

Scott was back on the couch watching a DVD about vampires by the time the taxi arrived to pick me up. He looked a bit sheepish, but I kissed him good-bye and said, 'Don't worry, I'm fine . . . and don't wait up.'

Nicky was waiting in the cab when I bundled in and I poured out the events of the past hour as we sped through the night to the exotic nightspots of Cumbernauld.

'There's nothing I can do about it till Monday so I'm not even going to think about it any more tonight,' I told her as we arrived at a nightclub called Sax.

'Good,' she said. 'Get the drinks in, then.'

We had a great night, dancing and laughing and fielding the amorous advances of a few lecherous drunks, though every now and again a little bubble of doubt would pop in my brain. What if it was cancerous? No, no, I am not going to think like that, I resolved every time. It was my birthday and I was going to enjoy it.

By 3 a.m., however, after a few drinks, my emotions were frazzled. Nicky and I climbed into a homeward-bound taxi, the tears already pricking my eyes.

'I can't believe I've found a lump,' I sobbed, my head resting on her shoulder. 'I hope it's nothing. Do you think it's nothing? Surely it's nothing.'

Nicky must have been asleep through most of this boozy babbling because after a few garbled words, which I think were meant to be reassuring, she started snoring.

Tired and emotional, the only way to end a night out in Cumbernauld.

It was Monday morning before I gave any serious thought to the breast lump again. Throughout my hangover on Sunday I'd completely ignored it. Scott hadn't mentioned it, and I'd managed to shower without even washing that breast. When I arrived at the salon on Monday, however, I knew I was going to tell my pals Liz and Jackie about it. I'd worked with the pair of them in Clippers for eight years by that point – after joining when I was nineteen – and they'd become my surrogate elder sisters. They both came from big families – Liz had four sisters, and Jackie had five – so they were used to dealing with problems of a girly nature. In my family there was only me and my older brother, Joseph, and though we were always close, I kind of missed a sisterly connection. Liz and Jackie knew me better than anyone, and I trusted them completely. We told each other everything. Honestly, if the walls had ears in that salon, what tales they could tell.

So in a quiet moment that morning, before any customers had arrived, I dragged them into the back and relayed the trauma of the weekend as they listened, wide-eyed. I was desperate for them to tell me there was definitely no cause for concern, that I was getting my knickers in a twist for no reason.

'Would you mind touching it to see if you feel

anything?' I asked tentatively, aware that this was a bit of a strange request with which to start the week.

Liz agreed straight away: 'Let me see,' she said, direct as ever, and I pulled my bra aside just enough to let her reach the suspect lump. I wasn't quite brave enough to reveal my whole boob, which seems silly now that I'm so used to baring all to strangers. My modesty has vanished completely in the years since.

'Just see if you can feel anything unusual,' I told her, trying to keep an eye on the salon door in case anyone came in.

She couldn't feel the lump at first, so I took her hand and guided her fingers around the spot until she said, 'Oh, yes, I think it does feel a bit different.'

Another confirmation, then.

Jackie was grimacing. 'I'm not sure I'm very good with lumps,' she said cautiously, but she stepped forward nonetheless.

She felt it right away. Surely all the opinion I needed.

'But it's not going to be something scary,' she said. 'You've not been ill at all. You feel OK, don't you? Loads of women get lumps in their breasts that aren't cancer, you know.'

Still, I phoned the GP immediately. The receptionist was busy telling me there were no available appointments that week; in fact, the earliest would be in eight days' time.

'No, you don't understand,' I said. 'I've found a lump in my breast and I'm really worried about it. I want to be seen as quickly as possible.'

Maybe I over-egged the urgency a little, but it worked: 'We'll squeeze you in tomorrow if you come at about five thirty,' she said.

Other people were taking me seriously. Every time they did, it ratcheted up my stress levels by another few points.

I was fidgety and flushed as I sat in the surgery waiting room the following afternoon, and my nervous tummy wasn't helped when Dr McNeill walked out and called my name.

Oh, no, I thought. I don't want to be seen by a male doctor.

I always requested a female doctor for potentially embarrassing appointments like smear tests. Revealing my boobs to a virtual stranger certainly counted as potentially embarrassing.

Into the bargain, I suspected Dr McNeill was thoroughly fed up with me waving poisoned fingers under his nose. They're an occupational hazard for hairdressers because the tiniest shaving of hair can work its way under your fingernail and cause a painful infection. He probably found that a rather trivial complaint. Well, he was in for a shock. It wasn't a boring old finger I was about to show him.

Oh, what if he thinks I'm wasting his time with some

other nonsense? I thought to myself as I followed him into the consulting room. And I'm still going to have to let him see my boobs. Nightmare.

I took a deep breath and launched into a scattergun explanation that couldn't have been easy to follow. 'I've found this lump in my breast, and I know it's probably nothing – because I know I'm too young for it to be serious – but I've got a friend who's just been diagnosed with breast cancer at thirty-three, and I'm probably being over-cautious because I know what she's been through, yet my mum suffered a lot with breast cysts when she was younger, so I know you're probably going to tell me that's what it could be, but I'm actually just starting to get a bit worried.'

He listened thoughtfully to all of this and somehow understood enough to tell me to nip behind the curtain and get undressed from the waist up. I sat on the examination bed, feeling all exposed and vulnerable, while he read through some notes.

Thank God I put on one of my good bras this morning, I thought, looking at the white lacy Marks & Spencer one lying on top of my small pile of clothes. If it had been one of my work bras, it would be covered in hair and I'd have been totally mortified.

Dr McNeill pulled back the curtain enough to venture inside and found me with my arms crossed defensively across my chest. I didn't know where to look.

'Just lie back and raise your right arm above your head,' he said.

He began pressing round and round my right breast, very methodically working his way from large outer circles to smaller ones that wrapped round my nipple. Then he started moving out towards my armpit, pressing firmly all round and inside it.

What have my underarms got to do with it? I thought. I'm here about my breast – and not even the one he's working on at the moment, for that matter.

He didn't say a word, just moved on to the left boob and started the same process, but he quickly found the area I was worried about. Backwards and forwards he went over the same bit. I glanced down and he was looking at it closely. Then he directed his attention to my armpit again. He spent a lot more time working on my left breast.

I was red-faced and tense when he finally said, 'OK, you can get dressed now. Come and have a seat at my desk.'

'Did you feel the lump I'm talking about?' I called over the curtain as I was putting myself back together again.

'Yes, I did,' he said.

I waited for him to continue with 'There's nothing to worry about', but he didn't say anything else. My hands were shaking as I tried to get my bra back on again.

He can't possibly know it's cancer after a quick

examination like that, I was telling myself. I mean, it's not like he's a specialist.

I sat down at Dr McNeill's desk. He was typing something into his computer and I shifted uncomfortably in the chair. He turned to look at me, and his opening sentence made me freeze to the spot.

'Well, there's definitely some kind of lump there and I am concerned about it,' he said.

My head started to spin, my mouth suddenly too dry to speak, so when Dr McNeill started asking me questions, I had trouble answering.

'Try not to worry,' he was saying now. 'Please don't get too far ahead of yourself. We do like to get suspicious lumps checked out, but that doesn't mean it's anything serious.' I noticed his face had softened and he was speaking slowly, patiently, with concern in his voice. 'Do you know if you have any history of breast cancer in your family?' he went on. 'Does your mum have any history of it? Any sisters or aunts experienced problems?'

Why had we suddenly started talking about breast cancer? Hadn't we bypassed a conversation about cysts or hormone changes or infection or whatever else that could possibly cause a lump? Why had we gone straight to breast cancer?

Maybe this is just standard procedure, I thought to myself. This is probably what he says to everyone who finds a lump.

I could hear myself begin to ramble, as if I could talk him out of thinking I might have something nasty. 'I know I'm being affected by my friend who has breast cancer,' I was saying. 'I know I'm far too young to have it myself,' and though he was nodding slowly, I clearly wasn't persuading Dr McNeill that he was worrying needlessly and that we really didn't have to bother with more examinations.

'I'm writing you a referral letter for the breast clinic at Stobhill Hospital,' he went on, 'and I'm asking for an appointment as soon as possible. I'll phone you tomorrow with the details.'

An appointment as soon as possible? Was this an emergency? A cyst is not an emergency. I felt sick all of a sudden, unable to take in the information. I wanted to go home and forget this had ever happened. I wished I'd never said anything, never even found the lump. I wished I'd stayed in with Scott and his toothache on my birthday. I certainly didn't want to go to Stobhill Hospital and have more tests done.

'Now do try not to worry,' said Dr McNeill as he led me out. 'It's just best to be on the safe side.'

I'm sure he knew, as he watched me leave, what the results would be. I've often wondered how different my life would have been if he hadn't taken me so seriously that day.

I went straight round to Mum and Dad's house and let

myself in through the back door. My brother, Joseph – who's two years older than me – was leaning against the radiator in the kitchen, idly flicking through the *Daily Record*. He lived nearby with his partner, Natalie, and their eighteen-month-old daughter, Olivia, and he was in the habit of popping into Mum and Dad's on the way home from work.

Mum was making dinner. 'Oh, how did you get on?' she asked when she saw me.

'He's referring me to the breast clinic at Stobhill,' I said. 'I think he's treating it as an emergency.'

Mum didn't flinch. She immediately had an explanation for the referral. It was protocol to send patients for further examination, she insisted. GPs have to cover every eventuality. 'They want you to get every single test done just to be absolutely certain,' she said. 'Isn't that right, Joseph?'

Joseph hadn't raised his head throughout the discussion. I knew he was trying to keep out of it. He didn't particularly want to hear about his little sister's breast problems after a hard day at work. He was an electrician. What did he know about boobs? Or rather, what did he know about boobs that could be of any conceivable help to me?

'Eh, I'm sure that's right,' he said. 'Er, it's probably nothing.'

By the time Scott got home, and I broke the news, I'd

calmed down enough to start believing the follow-on appointment was merely routine. Dr McNeill was simply being thorough. In bed that night, though, I lay turning things over in my head for hours on end.

What if I did have it? I'd never be able to go through what Dawn had been through. I wasn't brave enough.

Oops

'Mandy, I cannot find any other published cases of women in your situation who've become pregnant.' My oncologist, Dr Sarah Hendry, was wearing an expression so stern I was in no doubt just how concerned she was by my predicament. 'I've spoken to the Herceptin manufacturers and they're aware of twelve documented cases in the world but there's no published information on any of them.'

I must have looked like a mischievous schoolgirl, gnawing on my bottom lip and shrugging my shoulders like I'd just been caught doing something incredibly naughty. Oops.

Beside me, Scott was focused on Dr Hendry, who was looking more grim than ever.

'So it's impossible to say how many of those pregnancies progressed to healthy babies,' she went on. She seemed to think two had miscarried and one was stillborn but that was the extent of the detail.

I shrugged again and glanced at Scott. He ignored me. 'What are the pregnancy hormones doing to Mandy's cancer?' he asked curtly. 'Is pregnancy making it worse?'

Dr Hendry frowned. 'Well, that's something else we just don't know, I'm afraid.'

Chapter 3

The appointment for the breast clinic at Stobhill Hospital, in the north of Glasgow, was to be on Thursday, just two days after I'd seen the GP. By NHS standards, that was unbelievably fast.

'Another bad sign,' I said gloomily.

'Rubbish,' said Mum. 'They always see breast cases really quickly. Just go along and get it over and done with. Nine times out of ten these lumps turn out to be nothing.'

Scott took the afternoon off work to come with me. Within a few minutes of our arrival I was flat on my back in another examination room, naked from the waist up again, with my arms raised above my head in 'surrender' as another middle-aged man had a look at – and a feel of – my boobs.

This would be the first of many appointments with specialist breast surgeon Douglas Hansell over the years. I've grown to like him and his good-natured approach, but at the time I just wanted to get out of that room and away from him as quickly as humanly possible. He was friendly and cheerful, chatting away breezily as if he was about to examine my in-growing toenail, not some terrifying breast lump. His examination was similar to the GP's, firmly pressing all round my breasts with the pads of his fingers and checking under my arms, which made me think that there was definitely some significance in the condition of my armpits.

'I can feel the lump you're talking about,' he said finally.

I jumped in immediately. 'So do you think it's just a cyst, then?'

He smiled. 'Well, I don't know for sure, but the good thing is you're very young, so it's unlikely to be something sinister. All the same, I'd like to get a wee biopsy done on it.'

He said it so calmly – like it was the most natural thing in the world – that I really didn't feel very worried about the procedure. Mr Hansell was relaxed, he wasn't alarmed, and that settled my nerves a little too.

'Is it going to be sore?' I asked.

He gave a little sympathetic scowl. 'It will be a little uncomfortable because I'll have to put a fine needle into the lump and draw off a bit of fluid.'

'That sounds horrendous,' I shivered. 'Can Scott come in, please?'

Scott had been sitting outside the curtained area, probably hoping I'd let him stay there because he has a mortal fear of needles and the doctor was clutching a syringe with the longest needle I'd ever seen in my life.

The nurse sat rubbing my hand and trying to make small talk: 'Now, just concentrate on taking deep breaths, Mandy,' she said, but that was easier said than done while a great big needle was being shoved into my left boob. 'And how did you get here?' she went on. 'Did your husband drive you? What were the roads like?'

I knew she was trying to distract my attention, but I really wished she would bloody shut up. My body was turning to stone and she kept wittering on about 'relaxing'. Somehow I suppressed the urge to yell at her, 'How relaxed would you be?'

It was over quickly. Mr Hansell placed a tiny round plaster over the jab site and we were sent off to have a coffee while the sample was analysed.

'If you want to go down to the tearoom, someone will come along and get you in about an hour,' the nurse said.

After an hour we were still sitting there, nursing our drinks, and feeling a little confused.

'Let's go back up to the department in case they're looking for us,' Scott said.

They weren't looking for us, so we sat in the waiting area watching the clock again. After nearly an hour more the nurse came back to speak to us.

'We still haven't got your results, I'm afraid,' she said. 'Do you want to go back to the tearoom for half an hour?'

If I had been concerned before, by now I was all but having palpitations.

'Why haven't they got these results, Scott?' I kept asking him, as if he had some inside track. 'I mean, how can it possibly be taking this long? Do you think there's something wrong?'

The nurse had insisted the lab was swamped with work and running a bit behind, but I couldn't help feeling we were being fobbed off.

After thirty minutes we returned to the department. The results still weren't ready. Another half-hour passed, still nothing.

'There is no way on earth they're running this far behind,' I said. My mind was blank now, afraid to think of anything too deeply. This was the way Mum had felt earlier in the year as we sat waiting for the results of her breast biopsy. The best I had offered her was, 'They're probably just running late.' Some help I'd been.

Finally a breast-care nurse called Margaret showed us into a side room. 'The biopsy has shown up some abnormal cells,' she said.

Abnormal cells? What was wrong with them?

'Does that mean breast cancer or not?' I broke in. The words stuck in my throat as I tried to say them. No one here had actually mentioned breast cancer. I could be jumping the gun by giving it a presence in the room.

'We don't know what's there at the moment,' she went

on, again avoiding the term, 'so we want to do a mammogram to see if we can find out anything else. We don't
usually do them in women under thirty because the
breast tissue is too dense, but we would like to try it.'

I began to shake uncontrollably. Scott had to keep me
upright as we made our way to the X-ray department.
Normality was spiralling away from me.

Minutes later I was wrapped in a surgical gown, my
clothes in a plastic basket at my feet, waiting to have my
sore breast compressed between a couple of metal plates
by yet another nurse, one who was less than sensitive to
my feelings. The tears were running down my face as I
pleaded with her to be a bit gentler.

'I've just had a biopsy,' I protested.

'I know, I know,' she said, 'but I have to bring this plate
down really low if we're going to get a clear picture.'

Despite the most torturous procedure, the mammogram was no more enlightening than the biopsy, so we
were back to square one.

'We'd like you to come back tomorrow and have a
core biopsy,' Margaret explained. 'That lets us get further
into the lump and extract some more cells out of it.'

The doctor would use a needle to take some tissue
samples from the lump, which sounded pretty awful, but
she promised me I'd get some local anaesthetic this time.

'We'd also like to arrange for you to have the lump
removed altogether,' Margaret added. 'We've got a date

for that in two weeks' time if that's OK with you.'

I no longer had the energy to react. I felt as if I'd been tied to the front of a juggernaut that was out of control and picking up speed all the time. I'd walked into the hospital feeling scared but optimistic. I was leaving in a state of abject terror. Five days ago it was my birthday and everything was well with the world. All of a sudden nothing was the way it should be.

'I don't want to come back here tomorrow,' I whined as I clung to Scott. 'This is too much for me, Scott.'

How was I ever going to cope with this? I wasn't strong like Dawn. She was raising a daughter on her own and still managed to hold down a full-time job. Dawn was resilient and capable and impressive. I was just 'Wee' Mandy, the local hairdresser, who fainted at the sight of blood and couldn't bear to look at anyone else's bumps or scrapes.

At home that night, Scott and I barely spoke. We just stared at the telly hoping to be distracted by some soaps and a bit of sitcom, but when did *EastEnders* ever cheer anyone up? Mum phoned to say she was taking the day off work so she could come to the hospital with me for the core biopsy. She'd called her boss at the bookies where she worked as a cashier and he'd totally understood. Though I tried half-heartedly to talk her out of it, I was pleased she could come. Scott was becoming more stressed than I was, I could tell, and I really didn't want to subject him to a second day sitting around helplessly while someone poked and prodded my breast. He'd be much better off just going to work and immersing himself in some financial calculations for a while. He was an assistant manager for a credit company in Glasgow, arranging and keeping track of loans, and it was work that required concentration. If he was thinking about money, he wouldn't be worrying about me and my boob problems.

'I'll come if you want me to,' he volunteered bravely, but Mum was better prepared. She'd understand a lot of what went on.

'Are you worried?' she ventured, as we sat outside ward 7B in Stobhill Hospital, awaiting my turn in the queue.

I gave a little snort. 'Well, I'm worried about how sore it's going to be,' I said, 'and I'm worried about how well the anaesthetic will work, and I'm worried about whether I'll make it back to work this afternoon.' What I pointedly didn't say was, 'I'm absolutely bloomin' terrified that I've got breast cancer.' I didn't think she'd appreciate that kind of honesty.

We were led into a small, dingy room with a frosted-glass window. It was all prepared for my arrival, but they hadn't exactly rolled out the red carpet. I didn't expect five-star luxury, but it might have been nice if someone had bothered to rehang the tatty curtain where it had been pulled off its hooks. There was a trolley-bed with a strip of green paper towel running down the middle and a little table sat beside it, laden with packets of dressings and needles.

'The doctor will only be a few minutes,' said the nurse. 'Just take your upper clothing off and get yourself up on the bed.'

I lay there wondering whether I should have taken off my shoes.

Oh God, I should have shaved my legs, I thought, as I glanced down at my feet and noticed an area of exposed skin where my trousers had crept up my leg. I hope the doctor doesn't notice.

Thankfully she didn't seem bothered by my unshaven legs. She explained she would be working round the breast lump, with a device that looked eerily like a pistol, removing tiny areas of tissue, and that these biopsies would be sent away for analysis. 'I'll give you some local anaesthetic first of all, so you won't feel a thing,' she smiled.

What a whopper that was. By the time she was on the sixth anaesthetic injection she practically had to scrape me off the ceiling, but soon my breast was entirely numb. All I could feel as she worked was some tugging at my boob, but I could hear jars being opened and closed. Mum sat at the head of my bed, maintaining a steady stream of chat to keep my mind – and my eyes – diverted from the work going on a few inches south. Within about twenty minutes it was all over.

'Well done, Mandy,' the doctor said. 'That went really well. We've put some Steri-Strips over the wounds and you can take them off in the morning. You'll probably get a bit of pain once the anaesthetic wears off, so just take some paracetamol.'

Well, it hadn't been as bad as I'd feared.

Then she said, 'We'll go ahead and do the lumpectomy as planned on the twenty-seventh of this month.'

That would mean taking the whole lump away – including a margin of healthy tissue around it – which would definitely leave me with a scar, the doctor conceded, but it wouldn't be a big one, a couple of inches at most. So long as everything was OK, that should be the end of it. So long as everything was OK.

'But the results from this core biopsy should give us a lot more information to work with,' she added. 'We'll phone you with them in about ten days' time.'

'Ten days!' I moaned at Mum as she drove me to work. 'That's ages to wait for results like that, don't you think? I'll worry myself into a frenzy.'

Mum was trying to be a steadying influence. 'You'll just have to put it out of your mind for a while. There's nothing you can do anyway. Try and forget about it for the next week or so.'

But I couldn't forget about it and started calling the hospital practically every day, just in case they'd heard any news.

'No, no word back from pathology yet,' Margaret would say patiently, before reminding me, 'It usually takes around ten days.'

Just five days after the core biopsy, however, I got a surprise call from Margaret. I was startled when I recognised her voice. It could only mean bad news if she was phoning me this early.

'This really isn't official, but I know how worried you've been, so I thought I would just let you know that it seems they're pretty confident what they've found is a fatty deposit.'

Preliminary tests on the tissue samples were clear, apparently. What did that mean? Not cancerous, then? They couldn't know for sure at this stage, but to my ears it sounded hopeful.

'I can't give you a one hundred per cent guarantee,' she went on. 'Obviously they won't be able to confirm it until they've taken out the whole lump and sent it to pathology, but it seems to be just a bit of fatty tissue.'

I wanted to kiss her. I could hardly speak clearly enough to thank her. She'd taken time out of her day to phone me and try to put my mind at rest. I'd sensed her sympathy after the initial needle biopsy and she'd thought enough about me to make a call like that. I was so, so grateful, so relieved that I wanted to lie down for a while and recover. Instead, I started calling everyone to tell them my good news.

Scott was overcome: 'Oh, Mandy, that's brilliant,' he sighed. 'I knew you'd be OK, but it's such a relief that it's over.'

Mum tried her best to play it down, because she'd known it would be nothing all along of course, but I'm sure she was blubbing by the time she hung up. She's not very good at hiding her feelings.

So that was it. I was all right. There was no need to fear the lumpectomy. I was simply having a lump removed from my breast, not a tumour, just some fatty tissue. I could handle that. I had another week to wait before the surgery, but I didn't sweat about it. The terror had gone.

Scott came to the hospital with me that morning – Tuesday, 27 November. I was in theatre for about an hour and they kept me in overnight to make sure I didn't react badly to the general anaesthetic as it was the first time I'd ever been knocked out.

'I'm just glad that this is the end of treatment,' I told Scott, as I lay in bed afterwards feeling decidedly groggy. 'I am totally sick of being in hospital. How do people go through this all the time? It must drive you crazy.'

I'd been left with a two-inch scar midway up my left breast. At the time I thought it the biggest, ugliest scar I had ever seen.

'I won't be able to wear a bikini ever again,' I moaned to Scott. 'I'm damaged goods now.'

I'd organised a trip to Dublin for Mum and me, flying

out at the start of December, to do a spot of Christmas shopping. It had started off as a surprise, but I got too excited to keep the information to myself, so I'd ended up blabbing and we were both really looking forward to it. We liked to go on 'girls' adventures' every now and again, and we both felt we could do with some retail therapy after the strain of the past few weeks. With days left before we were due to go, however, I realised I still hadn't heard anything to confirm the pathology tests on the lump.

'Don't worry about it,' Mum said. 'No news is good news. If they had anything to tell you, they'd have phoned before now.'

Still, I knew I would feel better on our trip if all the loose ends were tied up, so I called Margaret and asked if she'd had an update.

'No, I haven't heard anything,' she said, 'but as soon as I know, you'll know.'

At work the next day, I excused myself from the teenage boy whose hair I was trimming (a number one all over) and went to check my mobile phone for a message I was expecting from Scott. Instead the screen showed a missed call from Margaret.

Oh, this is *the* phone call at last, then, I thought to myself before I hit the 'return call' button.

'Hi, Margaret,' I chirped when she answered. 'It's Mandy. I don't want to sound paranoid or anything, but I noticed I missed a call from you and you haven't left a message. I take it everything is OK?'

She sidestepped my question, but I didn't notice.

'We've got your results,' she said quietly.

'Uh-huh,' I said. 'So everything is fine, yes?'

'I wonder if you can come up and see us,' she said, and I began to realise this wasn't the way the conversation should be going. 'And is there someone you could bring with you?'

Chapter 4

The boy's mum was staring at me. Her son's hair was half shaved. I was rigid, unblinking, ghostly white. I knew instantly what Margaret meant. There was no good news. After everything she'd said. I was numb.

Liz was suddenly beside me. 'Look, just go,' she was saying. 'Whatever it is, just go. I'll finish the haircut.'

I'd never had a panic attack before, but I couldn't breathe and I couldn't speak and suddenly I couldn't stop shaking.

Yet I'd been so calm while speaking to Margaret, asking her time and time again to tell me exactly why they had to see me in person. It didn't seem real while I was talking to her, just a disjointed conversation about some vague problem she didn't really want to discuss.

'Would you rather I came to see you?' she'd said, as I floundered.

She was prepared to come all that way to see me face-to-face. What more did I need to know?

'No, I'll be up in half an hour,' I'd told her.

Then she'd hung up, and reality swept me off my feet

with the force of a tsunami. That soft tone she'd used, more gentle than she had ever sounded. Sympathetic, concerned . . . like she was speaking to the bereaved at a funeral. I've heard that same type of voice from the lips of so many breast-cancer nurses since then, every time they've got bad news to tell me. I think they must practise it at college.

Liz kept saying, 'Don't worry. Whatever's happening, try not to worry.'

Jackie had abandoned her customer too and was holding my hand. They'd heard enough of my side of the conversation to put the rest together in their minds. The ironic thing was, we'd been joking about the 'dreaded phone call' for days. Every time the salon phone rang, we jumped out of our skins.

'I wish that bloody hospital would hurry up and call,' Liz would laugh, clutching a hand to her heart. 'This is driving us all crazy.'

We thought the call was a formality. I was merely waiting for the official all-clear; that's why it was funny. I didn't expect this: a voice on the phone telling me the worst without actually articulating it. I hadn't even taken myself off to make the call somewhere quiet and private. Now I was falling apart in full view of strangers.

The world seemed to be going crazy around me, while I was totally incapable of responding. Finally, with the instinct of a lost child, I called my mum.

'Margaret has just phoned. They want me to go up right away.' There was no disguising my panic.

Mum didn't speak for a few moments. Then she said, 'I'll grab my coat and come with you.'

I told her to wait for me, I'd pick her up. Then I phoned Scott at work. I heard his intake of breath. I pictured him slumping in his chair.

'I'm leaving right now,' he said eventually. 'I'll meet you in the hospital car park.'

I drove along the motorway at 100 miles an hour while blinded by my own tears, which somehow didn't seem particularly risky at the time. I was sweating and struggled to unbutton my jacket and unravel my scarf while trying to control the car. I left the motorway to swing past Mum's house and collect her, but Dad nearly jumped out of his skin when I walked into the kitchen. My niece, little Olivia, was clinging to his leg.

'What are you doing here?' he said. 'Your mum went to go and meet you.' She'd set off for the hospital already, in such a state that she'd bungled my instructions.

'Oh, Dad, I told her to wait,' I wailed.

'Mandy, just calm down,' he said, patting my arm reassuringly. 'Everything is going to be OK. Just stay calm. I wish I could come with you, but I've got Olivia. Phone as soon as you get out.'

I fled to my car and took the back road, through bleak open countryside, to Stobhill Hospital. It's a desolate, lonely route, and though I've driven it countless times since, every time I do I recall that first trip, vomit and panic mingling at the back of my throat, perspiration soaking my top, my hands gripping the wheel for all they were worth, nothing but emptiness around me. Scott and Mum were standing together in the car park when I arrived, both of them composed, but Mum's face was badly tear-stained and Scott's was grey.

I can't go to pieces here, I thought, walking towards them. They're hardly holding it together at the moment. If I lose it, they won't be able to cope.

I was nervous and trembling, but my legs held. I had to be strong for them. We linked arms, me in the middle, and made our way in. Scott pulled me close as we waited in the outpatients department. Then my name was called and we were directed into a small side room. If I hadn't already guessed I was in line for the worst possible news, I would have twigged as soon as I walked through that door.

It was a family room, not a treatment room. The kind of place you see unsuspecting relatives being led into on *Casualty* or *Holby City*, just before a kindly doctor tells them their loved one has passed away in gory circumstances. There was a sofa, a coffee table, a television in the corner, a couple of pot plants, some magazines strewn about and lots and lots of leaflets on cancer. Scott sat on one side of me, Mum on the other, and we waited for what seemed like ages for Margaret to arrive. When she did, she didn't bother pulling up a chair or sitting on the sofa with us; she perched on the coffee table, directly in front of me. She looked sombre, her eyes slightly lowered, and when she spoke, she was still using that same quiet voice.

'We've had your results back, Mandy,' she said, 'and I'm afraid it is breast cancer.'

Mum and Scott dissolved. They fell on me, crying so hard the pain seemed to be bursting out of them. I didn't dare look at them and kept my eyes firmly on Margaret. I seemed to be the only one who was calm.

I took a deep breath. 'Right, what happens now?' I said, focusing on her face.

Margaret explained that my tumour was categorised as grade three and that I would be booked in immediately for a mastectomy and simultaneous reconstruction. I didn't know what she meant by grade three. I had no idea it was the worst grade out there, that it indicated a particularly aggressive tumour that could easily spread. For some reason, I didn't even question her about that. Instead I heard myself asking what she meant by mastectomy, even though I knew exactly what it would entail. Dawn had just had one, for heaven's sake. Total removal of my breast. Horrendous surgery. Deformity. I could feel hot tears sliding down my face, but I was still in control. I was coping. My brain just wasn't working properly; my mouth wasn't saying the right things.

'I've made an appointment for you to go to Canniesburn Hospital tomorrow and meet the plastic surgeon who'll be doing your reconstruction,' Margaret said, before launching into detail about some X-rays and blood tests she wanted to carry out.

I couldn't understand what she was saying any more. She hadn't mentioned a thing about the reassuring phone call. What did it matter anyway?

Just let me out of here, I was thinking. I don't want to be here for a minute longer.

I'd had enough. I wasn't going to hang about for more tests. I asked if we could go, and with Scott and Mum propping me up, we made our way back to the cars. I don't know who was supporting whom.

Choices

Rightly or wrongly I felt she was very gently steering me towards a termination. Not pushing me, but directing me that way.

'Mandy, you have secondary breast cancer,' she said. 'And you've probably been taking Herceptin through the key developmental stage of your pregnancy. We are in uncharted waters.'

In my head the choices were slotting into place. I had three of them. I could stop taking Herceptin and continue with the pregnancy without any further cancer treatment. Clearly that was a 'cross your fingers and hope for the best' scenario.

'We don't know how your cancer would behave if you stop Herceptin,' Dr Hendry invaded my thoughts. 'If we take you off the drug, there's a chance the tumour could grow rapidly.'

Second, I could continue with the pregnancy AND Herceptin, another leap in the dark.

'There just haven't been enough births to see how it might affect you or the baby,' Dr Hendry interjected again.

Or there was the third choice, the unspoken one: terminate the pregnancy and get on with our lives. Get rid of the only good thing that had grown in my body. Lose my only chance of being a mother. Look after myself.

'I'm not going to risk losing you,' Scott whispered. 'Not for anything.'

Chapter 5

None of us was capable of driving. Scott, Mum and I stood in the car park of Stobhill Hospital, staring at our cars, dazed to immobility. People talk about being in shock over all sorts of trivial, everyday things; goodness knows I did it myself. I could be 'shocked' by terrible weather or the price of groceries. I'd watched the Twin Towers of the World Trade Center fall to the ground just a few months before, thinking I'd never been as shocked by anything in my life. But I hadn't known real stupefying, debilitating shock until my own world began to crumble. We had no idea what to do.

'Come to our house,' Mum said at last. 'We'll have to tell your dad,' but she couldn't possibly negotiate the road home on her own. She'd have to abandon her car and travel with Scott.

I'd drive myself. I needed to think. Trouble was, the diagnosis was clanging around my head all the way home, so loudly that I couldn't hear my own thoughts and I wanted to close my eyes till it went away. The journey was a blur, but I was the first to arrive, which meant I had to break the news. Olivia was sitting in her highchair, beaming at me, Dad standing beside her, willing me to speak.

'It's breast cancer,' I managed before breaking down.

My poor dad. He was still hugging me when Mum and Scott got back.

'It's early days,' he was saying, smoothing my hair like I was his little girl again. 'You don't know an awful lot about it at the moment. Once you know a bit more, it will be easier to deal with.'

I called Joseph on his mobile and I could hear the crash and rattle of a building site behind him when he answered, the sound of people getting on with their lives without knowing the world had stopped. For a while after I told him my results, the bustle of the site was the only noise on the line.

'I'll phone you later tonight,' he said, before adding, 'Mandy . . . I'm sorry . . . I can't believe it.'

We sat in the lounge, Olivia playing around our feet with her toys, while we stared into space.

Dad began to try to talk me round: 'Come on, Mandy, think about Dawn. Look how well she's doing,' he was saying. 'I mean, she's been through a lot, but she's back on her feet and putting it behind her. And you'll do that too.' He started prattling on about staying positive and strong, but I knew he was filling time, saying anything in the hope of saying the right thing. Dad was a man's man, proud, straight-talking and hard-working. He didn't let things stand in his way, and he knew how to take care of his family. Anything his kids needed, he got it for them. When both Joseph and I were buying our first homes, Dad paid the deposits. When I needed a new bathroom, Dad installed it. If Joseph's car broke down, Dad fixed it. Now he was trying to find a way to fix this mess, to sort me out, and he didn't know how. Maybe he thought if he kept talking long enough, he'd think of something. Mum began phoning her closest friends to break the news and I could hear her, her voice usually so strong and confident now quiet and fractured, and she was talking about me. It was surreal. I had to leave them to their pain for a while. I realised they couldn't let it out while I was there. Couldn't and wouldn't.

Back at our house, Scott and I were lost in our own living room. He had no idea what to say to me and I didn't know what to say to him.

'I'd better go phone my mum and dad,' he said, and disappeared upstairs to speak to them in private. I didn't want to hear myself discussed again.

'Let's go out,' I said, when he came back down. 'I can't sit in the house. Let's go to the shops or something to clear our heads a bit.'

So we went to the shopping centre at nearby Cumbernauld and walked around aimlessly, meandering into shop after shop, wandering past rails and shelves without looking at anything, then winding our way back out again, dazed and bewildered. Why did I imagine I would be so easily distracted from the whirlwind of worries in my head?

The news was starting to sink in, and I was beginning to pile up all the questions I should have asked Margaret: what is a grade-three tumour? Can you cure it? How do you treat it? What happens if it has spread? Am I going to die? Am I going to die? Am I going to die?

Scott's sister, Nicky, worked in the children's shop Adams in Cumbernauld, but we couldn't find her and were on the point of leaving when she emerged from the back carrying a pile of clothes. When we caught her eye, she flashed an easy smile that told me news hadn't yet reached her.

'Hi, you two,' she grinned. 'What you doing out here on a school day?'

'Er . . . erm . . . Mandy got the results of her tests today,' Scott stumbled. 'It's breast cancer.'

Nicky stopped in her tracks. 'Oh, no,' she said. 'I'm so sorry.'

I nodded, shuffled, took her hand as she reached out to me. 'If there's anything I can do to help, anything at all, just let me know,' she said.

If I had a penny for every time someone has told me that, I could be paying for private healthcare by now, but what else could she do, accosted at her work with news like that? That's exactly what I would have said in her position.

'Let's just go home,' Scott said finally. 'There's no point doing this.'

We drove back in silence, then sat in silence staring at the TV, feeling strangely strained and uncomfortable with each other. As the hours passed, I grew more and more annoyed with Scott and his apparent inability to offer any words of consolation or wisdom. This wasn't bloody happening to him, after all. I had good reason to be stunned to silence; he didn't. Why couldn't he think of something to say to make me feel better?

'Are you all right?' he'd ask every now and again.

Was I all right? Did he think I was all right? Did I look all right? Whenever I articulated one of my own thoughts – 'How long do you think I'll be in hospital?' or 'How bad do you think the operation will be?' – he'd just shrug and turn away. 'I don't know,' he'd say meekly. 'You'll have to ask the doctor.' It was impossible. My mind was swirling with a confusion of fear and self-pity, and Scott was giving me no way to release it.

'Do you think we'll have to cancel the wedding?' I ventured. I'd been scared to mention it, afraid of even introducing the possibility it might not go ahead, but everyone else must have been thinking the same way. The whole thing was booked for the following year – Saturday, 29 June 2002 to be precise. I'd even chosen my wedding dress. But I might not be well enough to wear it.

'I don't know, Mandy,' said Scott tersely. 'We'll just need to wait and see.'

What did that mean? Did he want to cancel? Did he want to run a mile from all of this? I wanted to scream at him, pummel his chest, shake him until he told me what he really, truly felt and convinced me that everything was going to be OK. Instead he went off to make the dinner.

'Could you manage some spaghetti Bolognese?' he asked, as he retreated to the kitchen.

We ate it without speaking, stared at some mindless TV for a while longer, then went to bed. And that's where it hit me.

'Please just let me sleep,' I begged the demons in my head as I stared into the blackness of the room.

Beside me, Scott's shallow breathing had become rhythmic and steady, but I couldn't bring mine under control. I was breathless and beginning to feel sick.

'Scott?' I whispered. 'Are you asleep?'

No reply.

I eased out of bed, crept downstairs and slumped on to the sofa. My two beautiful Siamese cats – Coco and Kia – were delighted to have an unexpected night-time companion and they followed me downstairs, jumping on to my lap as I switched on the telly to let its lights chase some of the darkness away. I cuddled the cats close like teddy bears as my self-control abandoned me and I wept and wept till my head throbbed and my eyes ached. On some satellite channel or other, someone was telling Oprah all their worries. At home in Glasgow, I was choking on mine.

If Scott heard me, he didn't respond. Now that I know better the way he deals with grief and pain, I suspect he was upstairs doing exactly the same as me, except on his own and quietly. It took a good couple of hours of torrential tears before I could begin to force myself to focus, blink my thoughts clear and really try to concentrate on what to do next.

It's ridiculously straightforward, I realised in a moment of searing clarity.

'I've two choices here: sink or swim,' I told Coco and Kia as they purred their encouragement. 'I can give in to this and just admit that I'm not strong enough to fight it, or I can put up a battle.'

The treatment was going to be hard, extremely hard, I knew that. Dawn's dark hair was just growing back after her chemotherapy, and I knew how much she had struggled with being bald. I'd never even seen her without the short brunette wig she bought just before starting chemo. No one had, not even her family. She wouldn't allow it.

'I am never going out without this wig on,' she'd declared right from the start. 'I look ridiculous without it.'

Her wig was shorter than her usual style, and lacked the highlights she had in her natural hair, but it made her feel better about herself.

'I don't want to look like someone with cancer,' she'd explained. 'And that's what you look like when you're bald.'

Every time I thought about my hair falling out, I felt ill. How typical – I was a hairdresser with all sorts of products and gadgets at my disposal, but I couldn't do anything if I had nothing to work with. I'd be a hairdresser with no hair, and who wants one of those? I'd be like a diet coach with a weight problem. Less than inspiring.

By morning I'd managed a couple of hours' sleep on the couch. I felt a bit stronger. I was bleary-eyed and weary, but somewhere within I was beginning to feel the first cautious stirrings of determination, which, I have to admit, surprised me a little. I didn't know I could rally myself – I'd never had to before – but the more I thought about it, the more psyched-up I became. This disease could threaten everything I had. I couldn't let it beat me. Dad hated to row with me because I always had to have the last word. That was me, his 'nippy sweetie' of a daughter. I had to be that person. I had to have the last word against cancer.

Scott looked pained and uncertain. The prospect of my appointment with the plastic surgeon was weighing heavily on his mind and I really wanted to cut him some slack.

'Look, why don't you just go to work today and Mum will come with me to the hospital?' I said as he blankly stirred his mug of coffee. 'You're too busy to take time off and Mum is determined that she wants to come,' I added. 'I don't want all three of us sitting there.' Plus there was no point using up valuable days off at this stage. He'd have to rely on his boss's good nature soon enough, once the real treatment started.

'No, no, I'll come with you,' Scott protested loyally, but I knew he wasn't up to it.

'Honestly, I don't mind,' I said, slipping my arms round his waist. 'It's not like I'm going for any treatment. It's just to discuss what's going to happen. If there's anything I need to talk to you about quickly, I'll give you a phone. Promise.'

With the understanding I would call him as soon as I came out of the hospital, he finally agreed. 'I'll probably be more useful at work than I am to you,' he said flatly.

He knew Mum would be a better support. Scott's way of handling stress was to retreat, back off from the problem in case he made it worse by interfering, but he knew how much I wanted to talk and I could talk to Mum.

*

Canniesburn, on the west side of Glasgow, was such a gloomy place. It was in the process of being wound down, in preparation for a move to brand-new premises, and it was so old and worn out that it did nothing to lift our spirits as Mum and I made our way through to the department.

'It's so depressing, isn't it?' I muttered. 'Not exactly helping cheer me up. I just hope we're not in for very long. I want to get out of here already.'

I was introduced to consultant plastic surgeon Arup Ray, who would be performing the reconstruction, and to the breast-cancer nurse Diane, who would be in charge of my care, and they smiled kindly as they began talking me through the surgery that lay ahead.

Good God, it was horrendous. I struggled to take everything in. It all seemed to be happening so quickly and the procedure sounded enormous. I couldn't see how I could possibly recover.

'I would guess that the tumour has been there quite a while,' Mr Ray was saying as he looked at my notes. 'It is quite large.'

No one had mentioned that before. Is that what they meant by a grade-three tumour?

'Well, we have a grading system for cancerous growths,' Diane explained. 'Grade three means it's a particularly aggressive tumour.'

I could feel Mum's eyes on me.

'Younger women who get breast cancer tend to develop faster-growing, aggressive tumours. That's why you'll also have the lymph nodes removed from under your left arm. We want to be certain the cancer hasn't spread.'

Things were getting worse by the minute. Clearly there was a chance it had spread.

'You are scheduled to have a course of chemotherapy after your surgery,' Diane added. 'You might need radiotherapy too, but the oncologist will decide on that later.'

Mr Hansell, the doctor who'd originally examined me, would perform the mastectomy part of the operation, while Mr Ray's role would be to build a new boob for me using parts of my own body, so when I woke up, I'd still have a breast of sorts.

'Well, there's not enough fat on your back to use that for reconstruction,' he said, feeling around my shoulder blades and down towards my waist. 'But there's a bit more tissue around your tummy, so we will be able to use that.'

What a cheek. I didn't have that much of a belly.

I'm only a size ten, I thought indignantly. If I'd known what was going to happen, I'd have enjoyed putting on a bit of weight.

Mr Ray continued, pointing to the relevant areas of me as he went along, 'We'll take this section of your tummy, mostly under your belly button, so you'll have a scar running from hip to hip, but at bikini level, so it won't be too obvious. We'll connect the tissue and muscle to the blood supply in your chest, so it should settle down nicely. Have you any family history of breast cancer?' Mr Ray went on.

I was about to say, 'No,' but Mum got in first.

'I had an operation to remove a breast lump at twenty-seven,' she said, 'and I did have to sign some documents to give permission to take the breast away if the lump had been malignant.'

Sorry? Say that again. I was speechless. She'd had a lumpectomy at the same age as I was now and she'd never said anything.

'But it was nothing,' she carried on. 'It turned out to be benign.'

I was astonished.

'You've never told me that, Mum,' I said accusingly. 'Why haven't you mentioned it before now?'

Mum was quickly defensive. 'Because I didn't think there was any point. It wasn't cancerous. Just a lump.'

Mr Ray cleared his throat, obviously bemused by our squabble. 'Do you have any other questions, Mandy?' he asked.

My head was in turmoil. It sounded like I'd be on the operating table for a week.

'Could I die during this surgery?' I asked, flicking a look at Mum, who had her hand over her mouth.

'Well, every surgery comes with risk,' Mr Ray replied, 'but we do a lot of these operations. We're quite used to them, and it's straightforward enough. Now, would you like to see some patients who've been through it? I have some videos that may help.'

I wasn't terribly keen. The morning had been pretty overwhelming already, but Diane seemed to think it would be a good idea to see what the scarring from reconstruction surgery looked like.

'It's not as shocking as it sounds,' she said, showing Mum and me into the television room.

Another patient – a smartly dressed woman in her late thirties – was sitting with her husband, and smiled empathetically at us as we walked in. So we sat watching films about scarring and stitching and the problems of finding comfortable underwear in the weeks immediately following breast reconstruction surgery. Not exactly what I'd choose to watch on the telly.

'This is totally bizarre,' I whispered to Mum. 'I'm not sure I want to see this. And I still can't believe you never told me about your lumpectomy.'

'Oh, hush, Mandy,' she said, keeping her eyes firmly on the screen.

I had only been home a few minutes when Dawn phoned.

'Hi there,' she said. 'How did you get on at the hospital?'

I hesitated before I started to tell her. I hadn't really wanted Dawn to know much about what was happening – she had enough on her plate – but Catherine had told her some of the detail and Dawn had been a bit wounded that she hadn't been kept in the loop from the start.

'I don't want you to keep anything to yourself because you don't think I can cope with it,' she'd said. 'I can cope just fine, and we should be able to help one another.'

What seemed to hurt her most was the fact that a second member of our wee gang had been struck. Maybe she thought the rest of us would be spared if she got it. If I'm honest, I kind of thought so too. I remembered reading in a newspaper article that the risk of any woman getting breast cancer in her lifetime is one in nine but the NHS had produced information that said the chances of getting it while aged under forty were one in 200. In our group of five under-forties, two of us had got it. How could that be? I was under thirty and the chance of someone my age developing it was around one in 1,900. Dawn and I had both beaten incredible odds to get breast cancer. What kind of cruel coincidence was that? It must have been hard for Dawn to get her head round things, but, true to style, she offered any amount of help I needed and the kind of words of understanding I'd been longing for.

'I know what you're going through and I know it seems terrifying, but it will be OK,' she told me. 'You'll be able to cope with it, believe me. Look at me, I'm already getting back to normal.'

That was true. Her hair was growing back, she was starting to look like her old self again, and she was getting out and about, socialising with the girls. Mr Ray had operated on Dawn too, so I was keen to know if she was impressed by his handiwork.

'Do you want to see my reconstruction?' she asked one night, when we were all gathered in Catherine's kitchen for one of our weekly get-togethers.

'Oh, I don't know,' I stalled. 'I'm too scared.'

'Don't be daft,' she snapped, and she led me into another room before lifting up her T-shirt and loosening the sports bra she wore to help keep everything in shape.

'Wow – you've still got a lot of your natural breast,' I said, amazed to see that only an elongated oval section had been removed from the centre of her breast. 'I thought they would have to take the whole thing off.'

It wasn't anything like as bad as I'd expected. It just looked a little weird, largely because there was no nipple.

'They're going to make me a new one,' Dawn explained proudly. 'They'll do a skin graft to make it. Then they'll tattoo round it in the right colour to match my other one.'

It was unbelievably complicated, though I couldn't help but be impressed. The surgeons seemed to have thought of everything.

'You'll get a new belly button too,' she said, showing me hers. 'The old one goes when they take your tummy for the reconstruction.'

Oh, stop it. No. Stop.

'Don't tell me any more,' I cringed. For some reason, I've always had a belly-button phobia. 'I can't even look at my belly button. The thought of someone touching it . . . Yuck, yuck, yuck.'

Dawn was pulling her clothes back into position. 'The two of us will be just fine, won't we?' she said, suddenly serious. She was demanding a positive answer of me, nothing vague or downbeat.

'Yes, Dawn, we'll be fine,' I obliged, and we both laughed at the unspoken understanding that we would have to inspire one another. I realised I'd be letting her down if I gave up. Neither of us could throw in the towel. We were in it together.

Mr Ray suggested I have the operation before Christmas, to get it over and done with, but I vetoed that idea right away. Lying in hospital, recovering from horrific surgery that may or may not save my life was not the way I wanted to spend the festive period, and it wouldn't be fair on my family either.

'I'll book you in for the first day back after New Year, then,' he said. 'That means you'll come in to hospital on the second of January and we'll operate on the third.'

Four weeks. I had four weeks to tie myself up in knots

with worry. Four weeks left of the body I'd been born with. I wasn't sure how I was supposed to get through it.

The Christmas shopping trip I'd arranged no longer seemed particularly appealing. Mum and I were due to leave for Dublin in a couple of days and neither of us felt up to it.

'I think we should cancel,' Mum said. 'We're not going to enjoy ourselves, are we? Besides, it's probably not fair to leave Scott on his own.'

I was certainly worried about leaving him. Scott already seemed to be avoiding me. We usually went to bed at the same time, but he'd taken to staying up late watching TV while I went upstairs on my own. When I'd told him the details of the operation, he'd said nothing. Now I can see what he was doing – he was trying to avoid saying anything that might upset me – but at the time his refusal to offer an opinion was driving me mad and would become the source of so many arguments. During one particularly explosive row I threw a dagger of a comment at him: 'You don't think about any of this, do you? You'd rather sit and watch the telly.'

He slammed one right back at me: 'What do you think I'm doing when I'm sitting up late in the living room? I'm thinking about you. All I do is think about you. Don't you realise that?'

I deserved that. It has taken a long time, but I understand Scott's feelings and behaviour pretty well now.

He was adamant that Mum and I should go to Dublin and enjoy ourselves, just as we'd planned. He was going to work the whole time we were away. He had a weekend job delivering Chinese meals to keep some money coming in for the wedding, so he would be busy enough anyway.

'You shouldn't go changing your plans,' he said. 'You need to try and be as normal as possible.'

It was only a long weekend, I reasoned, a cheap-flight package from Prestwick Airport, so if we really weren't enjoying ourselves, we could always hop on a plane home.

Dublin was heaving with as many tourists as Irish natives. Mum and I fought our way through the shoppers, going through the motions of searching for Christmas bargains but not actually buying anything. In truth, we couldn't really be bothered. To strangers, we must have looked like a happy mum and daughter caught up in the festivities, but in reality we'd simply surrendered ourselves to the crowds. One afternoon we went for lunch in a typical Irish pub where a raucous folk band was playing and some happy drunks were dancing. Mum and I had to shout our conversation, but I guessed what she was saying by the way her eyes kept filling up.

'I need to get away from this,' I yelled over the music.

Mum nodded and we ambled back to the hotel, arm in arm, weeping all the way.

At night I'd fall asleep quickly, eased on my way by a couple of large vodkas, but I'd sleep fitfully and wake countless times. Each time I did, Mum was sitting in a chair, wide awake and watching me. She didn't sleep the whole weekend. I don't think she's had a full night's sleep since. Mum and I have always been best of friends, joined at the hip. 'Thick as thieves,' my dad would say. She's young at heart and fun to be around; my friends become her friends and hers become mine. If Dad is a fixer, Mum is a comforter, always ready to bundle me in for a cuddle, always ready to help anyone, in fact. Mum loves to be needed and I needed her more than ever. But when the lights were out and all distractions were gone, she couldn't sleep for worrying. She still can't.

'We're having a great time,' I'd tell Scott cheerily, whenever I called home. 'It's a great place. We should come here together.'

When Mum and I stepped off the plane on Monday afternoon, however, safely back on Scottish soil, neither of us could wait to get home.

I returned to work the next day, glad of some genuine normality. The customers, even my regulars, had no idea what was happening and it felt good to have a few hours of chat without hearing or mentioning the word 'cancer'. Trouble was, the only chat they did have was about Christmas and New Year. Have you done all your Christmas shopping? Where are you having Christmas dinner? What are you doing for Hogmanay? I could hardly say, 'I'm not thinking about Christmas because I've got cancer, so I might not live to see another one, and I'm not thinking about Hogmanay because the next day I'm going into hospital to have my left breast removed.' I just smiled and made up some story or other.

For the first time in the twelve years Scott and I had been together, my family and his joined up for Christmas. Usually we took turns in going to each other's parents' for traditional Christmas dinners – mine one year, his the next – but someone, I've never found out who, decided to book a table at a local Chinese restaurant that one of Mum's friends had recommended. I'm the fussiest eater, and a few of our group were quite hard to please, but we all adored Chinese food, so it seemed like an option that would suit everyone. I assume it was mainly a show of solidarity for my benefit, and it was a nice thought, though I did wish the ground could have opened up and swallowed me when Scott's dad stood and proposed a toast. 'I think we just want to wish Mandy all the best and say we hope everything goes well next year,' he announced, raising a glass of wine in the air.

'To Mandy,' they all chimed in.

Well, that was a bit of a conversation-stopper, I thought, though I was touched by the sentiment. I just wished I'd been a bit more tipsy first.

We were stuffed by the time we left, all complaining

about how full we felt. I knew my tummy would soon be put to good use and wondered if my huge Chinese meal would give Mr Ray a little something extra to work with. Happy to oblige.

The countdown from Christmas to New Year was an ordeal. While everyone else was planning which party to go to, I could only think of my date with the operating table, and while they were choosing their festive outfits, I was packing my hospital bag. I had a selection of sports bras in various sizes, bigger ones to hold the reconstruction in place while it was swollen immediately after surgery, smaller ones for when the swelling began to subside. Sports bras would hold everything firmly, supporting and shaping the new breast as it healed, and because they didn't have underwiring, they were kinder on sore bits. The pressure of the tight fit would help reduce the swelling too. I'd also been told to take a bra extender, an elasticated device that attaches to the back clips to relieve the tension a little.

'It's important that your bras are not too tight,' Margaret had told me. 'You will be very tender for a few weeks after the surgery, so your breast will need protection as much as support.'

I had a couple of pairs of pyjamas, some soft sportswear for sitting around in hospital, packets of sandwiches and lots of crisps – cheese and onion Squares to be precise.

'I need to keep my strength up,' I protested as Scott watched me make room for yet another bag of my favourites.

Lastly I put in my little good-luck charms. People had started buying me things, small cards or teddies or lucky tokens, and I found them incredibly comforting. It felt as if I was being surrounded by positive thoughts. I liked the angels best of all, grateful for the idea of someone watching over me.

I'll take all of them, I thought to myself. I need all the luck I can get.

On Hogmanay my boss, Anne, closed the salon early, but no one really wanted to go home. Liz, Jackie and I sat inside talking for ages. Closing up for the last time that year was so final and I didn't want to leave, too scared to go in case I never actually made it back.

'Do you mind sitting a while?' I asked the girls. 'I'm not ready to go home yet.'

They felt the same. 'I can't be bothered with New Year anyway,' Liz said. 'I wish it was all past.'

I knew what she meant. This was painful for all of us. It felt like the end, and it was in a way. It was certainly the end of the carefree life I'd had. Sitting in that salon, where we had laughed our heads off so many times at one of our jokes or some hilarious story, we were crying our eyes out. For all their bluster and banter, Liz and Jackie were as soft as butter. Jackie was applying for college courses to study social care. Liz was planning to take on some part-time work as a communicator for people who were both deaf and blind. They were natural-born carers, but I didn't want them to become my carers. I just wanted to be their pal, Wee Mandy. I didn't want things to change, yet nothing would be the same again and we were all aware of that.

I was worried about money too. I'd only be eligible for statutory sick pay during my six months off, which amounted to around £60 a week. How were we supposed to save for a wedding on that kind of cash? I would have sat there all night, if I could have, praying I could turn back the clock to better times, postponing the inevitable.

'You're going to beat this, you know,' Jackie said, wrapping an arm round my shoulder. 'You're a wee fighter.'

I don't know how she'd worked that out. I had never fought anything more serious than a cold in my entire life. I'd only had the occasional sick day; now I was facing at least half a year without work, without money, and that was my best-case scenario. Scott and I were supposed to be getting married in six months' time. All the arrangements – the venue, the cars, the cake – were still in place. Though I couldn't bring myself to cancel them, I couldn't even think about walking down the aisle. My life had ground to a halt.

For four years in a row Scott and I had spent the first

week in January sunning ourselves in the Canaries. We were on the verge of booking a trip when I'd found the lump. Those plans had been shelved too.

'Scott and I should be getting ready to go to Tenerife right now,' I sobbed. 'I don't know if I'll ever go there again. I don't know if we'll ever go anywhere . . .'

When the bells finally rang out that horrible old year, I was stuck in a strange limbo, too scared of what lay ahead in 2002 to be glad to see the back of 2001.

Mine

'Mandy, think about this sensibly,' Scott was saying. Well, he was shouting. We'd barely uttered a word to one another for so long that the dam had to burst eventually.

At least we waited till we got home. We had plenty of rooms to storm in and out of.

He raved on a bit more. 'All I'm saying is, I don't know if it's the right thing to carry on with the pregnancy. What happens if you fall ill a few months down the line and you can't get chemo? What happens if the baby is born deformed?'

OK, OK, I totally got the point, but he was failing to get mine. This was a chance worth taking. The unexpected opportunity to hold my own baby in my arms! It was irresistible. I couldn't contain my excitement any more. I might have been trying to appear rational and detached, but I'd known from the second I'd seen the pink dot in the 'pregnant' window of the test stick: I was going to have this baby.

'I'm sorry, Scott, but I will do this on my own if I have to,' I said.

Chapter 6

Lying on a bed in Canniesburn Hospital, on a bitterly cold January evening, I was watching Mr Ray draw all over my chest and stomach, quickly marking out the areas to be cut away for the mastectomy and reconstruction the following morning. It was 2 January 2002. Happy New Year.

Mr Ray was concentrating hard as he marked me with a black felt-tip pen, peering closely, then stepping back, like an artist putting the finishing touches to a masterpiece. A nick here, remove this, lift this up, stitches there. If only I would be a work of art afterwards.

'This will probably look pretty bad, so I don't want you to panic,' he said when he'd finished.

I looked down at his scribblings in horror. I was a roadmap of dotted and solid lines that seemed to take in every inch of my chest and stomach. A thick black line went right round my breast and continued out under my left arm, clearly tracing an area that would be removed altogether, except it was far larger than I'd imagined it would be. I thought of Dawn's neat eye-shaped scar as I looked at my gaping circular outline and began to wonder exactly why they felt they had to take so much of me away. On my tummy he'd drawn a shape that looked like an open mouth, stretching from hip to hip.

'This is the area of fat and tissue I'll use for your reconstruction,' he said.

I knew they needed a substantial amount to work with, but seeing it sketched out on my own skin was something else altogether. Mr Ray had told me it would be at bikini level, which essentially it was, but it would need a monster bikini to cover this. Were big pants making a comeback?

Scott was sitting just outside the curtain that Mr Ray had closed around me, but he might as well have been a million miles away. I had never in my life felt so utterly alone.

This is just going to be about me, I thought. I relied on everyone else so much, but none of them could get me through this, not Mum and Dad, not Scott. I was going to have to do it on my own.

I'd felt it as soon as I'd walked into the ward. In the weeks since the diagnosis I'd been surrounded by people who loved me, who felt my anguish, people who would do anything for me, give anything to make me well again, but I suddenly realised this was as far as they could go with me. They couldn't go into the operating theatre. They'd held my hand through it all up till now, but they would have to let go. I'm an only daughter. Mum and Dad had always been there to pick me up and give me a cuddle, to put a plaster on my cuts and gently rub my bruises better. Even as I grew older, I'd never got out of the habit of running to them at the first sign of trouble or pain or fear, and they'd protected me from it all. Not now. They were weaker than I was. If I felt helpless, how must they feel?

Dad had called the night before. A long-distance lorry driver, he's never been prone to overblown displays of affection, but I knew he was hurting. He was thousands of miles away – driving through France, in fact – while his little girl was undergoing the worst ordeal of her life. I'd made him set off on the trip, because I didn't want him sitting around worrying, and he'd bowed to my wishes as he always did, but as I listened to him speak that night, and pictured him sitting in his cab in some desolate service station, I wished I'd let him stay at home. He needed to be around his family, not sleeping in his lorry with only his fears for company.

'You'll be all right,' he had said. 'You're young and you're strong – you'll get through this. I'll be back by Friday, if all goes according to plan, and I'll be right up to see you.'

I'd never heard him cry before. Dad was always the strong one. I knew to expect tears from Mum, but not Dad. We said our goodbyes and I hung up, and wept for him.

Then there was Mum. She had come to hospital shortly after Scott and I arrived, to check I was OK and wish me good luck. She was smiling and upbeat as we played out an awkward 'normality' ritual, all three of us perched on hard chairs in the dismal downstairs waiting area, discussing any humdrum nonsense from New Year TV programmes to the state of the paintwork, and trying to ignore the massive cancer ghoul sitting between us.

I knew she was forcing herself to be calm, and she pulled it off fairly well, until she stood up to leave.

She grasped both my hands in hers. 'It's just a year out of your life,' she said. 'Try and remember that.' She'd worked out that it would take that long to recover from the surgery, get through the six months of chemo and grow a little replacement hair. 'This time next year it will all be behind you and you'll be getting back to normal,' she added. She held on to me for ages. 'Try not to worry too much, and make sure you ask a nurse for something to help you sleep tonight.' She looked at me so tenderly my heart was breaking for her. 'I'll let you and Scott have some time on your own,' she said, giving me a last kiss.

I knew she would be alone at home, awake the whole night, with Dad so far away. What was I putting them through?

Mr Ray explained the operation would take at least eight hours and I winced at the very thought.

'Don't think about it in those terms,' he said. 'Thousands upon thousands of women have already been through this. It's a pretty common procedure.'

Not for me it wasn't.

'And just to let you know,' he added, 'Mr Hansell won't be able to perform the mastectomy after all. He's got an emergency on his hands, so it will be another surgeon, I'm afraid.'

Oh great. So I was getting some stand-in to do the operation. Lucky me.

After Mr Ray left, Scott and I whiled away our remaining few hours together, trying to find anything to say that didn't require the word 'cancer'.

'I hope we're not stinking out the ward with this,' Scott said, munching into the Chinese takeaway he'd brought for us so I didn't have to eat appalling hospital food for dinner. I wouldn't be allowed anything to eat or drink after midnight, in preparation for the anaesthetic, so I was grateful for a decent meal. My very own last supper.

'I don't care,' I replied. 'If I have to go through all that tomorrow, I'm going to make sure I enjoy this.'

By the time we'd polished off the last of the fried rice, our conversation was stalling. 'Are you all right? Do you want anything else?' Scott kept asking. We'd run clean out of idle chit-chat, so he'd started to fill any lulls by asking how I felt and it was getting on my nerves. God knows what he'd have said if I'd given him the honest answer: 'Please don't leave me here. Take me with you. Don't abandon me.' He was trying as hard as I was to be brave – I could see it in his face, and I see it even now, after everything that has happened. His blue eyes are slightly altered, tinged with something almost imperceptible, which I have come to recognise as fear. It has been there since the moment Margaret sat us down and confirmed the lump was malignant, and it tells its own story, even though he finds it difficult to talk about how he's feeling. Scott hadn't discussed his emotions with anyone, not his parents, his sister, his friends and certainly not with me. Whatever was going on in his head remained there, bottled up tightly. Maybe it will never be released, but a lot of it is there in his eyes.

By the end of visiting time we could drag it out no further. Scott had to go. I went with him through the corridors and in the lift, escorting him right to the front doors of the hospital. I wanted to throw myself at his ankles and hang on tight. I wanted to run for the hills and never come back, but we just stood there hugging and whispering our love.

'Before you know it you'll be out and back home and we'll just be getting on with our lives,' he said quietly in my ear, and I squeezed him tightly to show I believed him. I had to believe it.

He waved and smiled as he walked away, and I stood watching him, feeling like a prisoner locked up for the night and sentenced to a day of torture before my release. Damn it, there was no getting away now. Nothing between me and the operating table but a few hours' restless sleep.

The two women sharing my ward could see I was upset when I returned and they fussed around my bed. 'This is the worst part,' said one of them. 'The waiting is awful. Once the surgery is past, though, you can just concentrate on getting better.'

Joan and Mary had had the same surgery the week before and were now well enough to be out of the high-dependency unit and back in ordinary care, preparing for freedom. I recognised Joan immediately. She was the woman with whom we'd sat watching the video nasty of reconstruction surgery. She was an attractive lady, with short brown hair and a lovely warm smile, and we whiled away a little more time chatting about our families, our jobs and the diagnoses that brought us together.

'I thought the lump in my breast was a blocked milk duct,' she told me. 'I'd just had my son, my second baby. I didn't think for a minute it would end up like this.'

There I was, thinking myself the worst hard-luck case in the world, while Joan had a newborn baby to worry about. She was having breast-cancer treatment during what should have been the happiest time of her life. I was horrified.

'Oh, that's terrible,' I said. 'You must be so worried about him.'

We were interrupted by the nurse, who'd arrived with some drugs for me.

'Mandy, I need to give you some instructions for tomorrow morning,' she said.

That dragged me back to the isolation of my own problems.

'Good luck,' Joan smiled as she went back to her own bed. 'You'll be fine.'

'I'll wake you at about six-thirty,' the nurse said. 'Here's some antibacterial shower gel. You need to use it on your body and your hair. Be sure to remove all make-up, jewellery and nail varnish. Then put on these two hospital gowns. The first one should go on back to front and the next should go on top of that like a dressing gown. Is that all clear?'

Very. So vivid in my mind, in fact, that I would have had no chance of sleep at all had she not also given me a sleeping tablet, which took about ten minutes to wipe me out cold and I lapsed into a deep, dreamless sleep before being gently shaken back to consciousness before dawn the next morning.

I examined my naked reflection in the mirror in the shower room, moistening my finger, then tentatively rubbing small areas of the inked-on lines to make sure they didn't wash away.

How would the surgeon know what to do if this all came off in the shower? I pondered. Maybe they wouldn't go ahead with the surgery.

But the lines resisted my rubbing and stayed

stubbornly in place. Permanent marker – they'd thought of everything.

I gazed at my left breast, which was covered in black ink. It was the last time I'd ever see it. I expected to feel sad for it, but I didn't. I was afraid of it. Something awful was going on inside there, something threatening. It had to go. The quicker the better.

The antibacterial gel smelled like Toilet Duck, which upset my already nervous tummy. I couldn't keep away from the loo. A nurse struggled to roll a pair of ultra-tight surgical stockings on to my legs, to keep my circulation going while I was under the anaesthetic. Another one arrived clutching a clipboard and read through a checklist. Did I have any caps, crowns or loose teeth? Any jewellery or body piercings? Any make-up on? Hair been washed? Then someone else appeared with some pre-med drugs and suddenly I was so drowsy that everyone around me seemed to be moving through a dream. I heard someone say, 'The porters are here for you now,' and I was slid on to a trolley and covered with a blanket. I must have slipped into sleep as the bed started to glide out of the ward and into the corridor, but I opened my eyes as I was being lifted on to the operating table, dazzling theatre lights directly above me, shiny silver equipment all around. This wasn't right.

'They haven't given you enough anaesthetic,' said a panicked voice inside my head. 'This is wrong. You're going to feel everything.' Then the general anaesthetic tightened its powerful grip on my system and I closed my eyes for ever on the Mandy I had been before.

Back home, Scott was carrying out the plans he'd made on how to pass time while I was in surgery.

'There's no point in waiting around all day,' I'd told him. 'Just go into the office and get stuck into some work.'

He had dismissed me angrily. 'Do you really think I'll be able to concentrate on anything else knowing that you're in theatre?' he'd said. 'Just let me handle it my own way. I'm going to do some work in the garden.'

On 3 January, with the ground frozen solid, he spent hours pottering about outdoors. I have no clue what he found to do there, but I suspect he was staying as far away as possible from the phone, which didn't stop ringing. Everyone we knew seemed to be waiting for news. Mum invited him to wait with her, even offering a cooked breakfast as an incentive. Dad had made it back from France that morning. They could all wait together. 'Thanks, but I'm better being on my own,' Scott told Mum. 'The garden will keep me busy.'

At 4 p.m. Scott called the hospital. He'd been told I should be out of surgery by then and they'd be able to tell him how it had gone.

'Sorry, but she's still in theatre,' he was informed.

He called back at 5 p.m. Still no sign of my return. He phoned again at 6 p.m. and 7 p.m. and each time the news was the same: there's nothing to report yet. The surgery was ongoing. His nerve went. Scott was snapping like a fiend at every well-meaning relative who called to see how I was.

'Has something happened?' they kept asking him.

'How would I know?' he would bark. 'I don't know anything. There is no news.'

Finally, at 8.30 p.m. – exactly twelve hours after I'd been wheeled into theatre – the hospital called to say I was in the recovery room and the surgery had gone well, despite taking a little longer than anticipated. Apparently they'd had a bit of trouble connecting up the blood supplies, but everything had worked out well in the end. Scott all but passed out with relief.

'Can I see her?' he asked the ward sister.

'Just for five minutes,' she replied. 'Don't expect much, though. She's still rather out of it.'

I was lying in a darkened room in the high-dependency unit. Before Scott, Mum, Dad and Joseph were led in, they were warned I was connected to lots of machines, so there would be several tubes coming out of my body. They were told not to worry about that, yet from somewhere in the depths of my stupor I thought I heard my mum's cries. She seemed to be screaming, and almost hysterical, as if she just couldn't bear the sight that met her eyes. Machines blinked and whirred all around the bed and I lay, unrecognisable and motionless, in the midst of it all, a messy tangle of bandages and wiring. I had an oxygen mask on, a central line emerged from my neck, two drains came out of my chest and two from my stomach wound. I had intravenous lines inserted in both arms, was wired up to a morphine pump and had been fitted with a catheter. There were four pillows under my knees to try and ease the strain on my tummy scars. I couldn't speak, and though I was having brief periods of shallow consciousness, my visitors weren't aware of it. I clearly remember Scott holding one of my hands, while Dad held the other. I looked like a car crash, but at least they had me back again in some form.

And so began the longest night of my life. I woke every fifteen minutes convinced I'd been asleep for hours.

Please let it be morning, I thought each time I opened my eyes. Please let there be daylight.

Even in my fuzzy-headed state I wished for light. Things always seemed so much more bearable in daytime. The darkness and silence of the old hospital at night made everything appear so bleak, and they were bleak enough already. A nurse was checking my condition every quarter of an hour, monitoring my temperature and blood pressure.

'What time is it now?' I'd ask whenever she appeared at my bedside.

'Fifteen minutes after the last time you asked,' she started answering.

I must have been driving her crackers. By the time she told me it was 4 a.m., I could take the agony no longer. My chest and stomach were tight and uncomfortable, but the pain of the surgery itself hadn't yet crossed the morphine barrier. It was my stiff back that was killing me. The only part of my body that I could move was my head and the rest of me had seized into tight spasm after hours of immobility on the operating table. I couldn't turn or stretch to relieve the pain because I was pinned down by tubes, wires and the remnants of the anaesthetic.

'Why are my ankles so sore?' I wondered aloud hazily.

'It was probably the way they were manoeuvring you on the operating table,' the nurse explained. 'It will ease off soon.'

Nevertheless the pain in my back became so unbearable that I finally begged her to help me get up and move about to loosen off my spine.

She looked at me in horror. 'Are you crazy?' she said. 'You've just had major surgery. You can't get up and walk yet.'

Undeterred, I pleaded: 'Please help me get up for a little while. It's so painful. I can't take lying here any longer. Please . . . just for a minute or two.'

She called a colleague over and they spent a few minutes shaking their heads and muttering incredulously.

'OK,' she said eventually. 'We must be as mad as you, but we'll give it a try. If you feel you want to stop at any point, say so.'

They started disconnecting me from the various pipes and potions that were keeping me on an even keel. It took a while. Each line was carefully capped so they would remember to put it back in again. Then they lowered the bed as close to the floor as it would go and sat on either side of me, careful not to press on raw areas, before tentatively easing me to the edge. The blood rushed from my head as soon as they started pulling me upwards off the pile of pillows and the dizziness made me feel instantly nauseous. I thought I might faint.

'Take your time,' they kept saying. 'Take it easy.' I was hardly in a position to move too quickly for them.

Gradually they tipped me forward on to my feet. I looked like the stooped little figure you see on road signs warning of elderly people crossing, but I was up.

'Try and take a few steps,' said one of the nurses.

I attempted to move my feet, but I don't think anyone could accurately describe it as walking. They had me wedged between them, each with one hand cupping an elbow and the other grasping an upper arm, so my feet seemed to skim the floor in more of a drag than a stroll.

The nurses were amazed that I was even moving.

'I have never seen anything like this,' said one of them. 'A patient who's just been through what you've been through and you're up a couple of hours afterwards. This is incredible.'

Every movement took the most monumental effort and I was desperately trying to breathe evenly as we made our slow progress down the corridor past the other sleeping patients. The central line was dragging heavily on my neck, and when I looked down, I could see that my stomach and chest were swollen and bloated, thick dressings making them protrude even further. The nurses were as exhausted as I was after a few minutes and they steered me back to my bed to begin hooking me up to my electronic support system again. I felt rather proud of myself.

I'm back on my feet already, I thought to myself. I was not going to lie down to it a minute longer than necessary. I would show them.

A few hours later I awoke to find another nurse at my bedside preparing to give me my first bed bath. That brought me crashing back down to earth.

'Do I have to get it done?' I asked weakly, but it wasn't as if I could wash myself. I couldn't even raise my arms. The wounds round my chest and underarm were restricting my movement, and the tight scar across my stomach seemed to object to the merest twitch.

'It won't take long,' said the stony-faced nurse, and in a few embarrassing minutes she washed away the euphoria of my post-surgery walking trip and left me to face the stark truth. I wasn't superhuman, I wasn't about to make a miraculous recovery, and there would be no escaping the same indignities everyone else had to go through.

By the time I had my second bed bath, the following day, I was determined it would be the last.

Tomorrow I will have a shower, I thought to myself, as I lay grinding my teeth and trying to ignore the intrusive wiping of my body. No stranger is going to wash me again.

The next day I insisted on being taken into the shower room in a wheelchair, accompanied by a nurse to help me.

'Would you like to see your breast?' the nurse said. 'I think you should. It will probably be easier to see it now rather than later.'

I didn't want to. The appearance of my new breast wasn't important. I didn't wake up from the op wondering what it would be like. After all, it wasn't my real breast – I would never think of it like that – it was just something to fill a space. In my mind, it was a sideshow to the main event of the life-saving surgery. And what if it looked truly horrendous? It would make me feel worse; it would be a setback in my recovery. I didn't want to risk that. As far as I was concerned, the surgery was over and the bandages were on. I would face it in time, when I felt a little stronger. The dressings were waterproof. I could shower without removing them – the nurses had told me that already.

'No, just leave the dressings on,' I said. 'I'd rather not look at it right now.'

The nurse had other ideas. 'Well, it's not a good idea to put it off,' she said, 'and it's probably not as bad you think.' She clearly had me marked as a coward.

She helped me take off my pyjamas and I could quite clearly see the huge, angry wound across my tummy where the tissue for the reconstruction had been removed. A long, transparent Steri-Strip had been stuck over it, protecting a vicious-looking line of staples that resembled a piece of barbed wire wrapped round my body. Glancing downwards probably didn't give me a particularly good perspective, but at that moment the hip-to-hip scar I had been promised actually looked like I'd been cut in two.

OK, I thought, immediately looking away, that's pretty disgusting. I'll not bother looking at it again for a while.

The nurse was already unhooking the sports bra that was holding my chest dressings in position. I could have stopped her, but she'd made me feel a bit of a wuss for protesting. 'Now, do you want to look or don't you?' she said, like she was a gameshow hostess about to reveal the hidden prize.

'All right,' I said reluctantly. 'Let me have a look.'

She carefully peeled back the dressings to reveal a familiar mound underneath. It wasn't my breast, but it was a breast, albeit a black-and-blue one, encircled with stitches and staples and swollen out of all relation to the other. There was no nipple – just as Dawn had warned me – and it seemed rather misshapen, but it filled the space quite adequately. It wasn't attractive by any stretch of the imagination, but it had potential.

'Actually, you're right – it's not that bad,' I said eventually. 'It'll look better when it starts to heal. Maybe once I've got a bra on, the scarred bits will be covered up. Yes, I think I can live with this. Can we get out of the shower now, please?'

My new breast began to take on a life of its own. It received a great deal of individual medical attention. I was merely an appendage. Nurses checked it every half-hour to make sure it was warm enough and pink enough. 'We have to be sure there's a good blood supply to the breast,' one of them explained. 'If it starts going cold or it changes colour, there may be a problem with the blood flow.'

Colour change? What kind of colour change?

'Well, if it starts looking a bit black, it could be a sign of a problem. But that is very, very rare.'

What? There was a chance my new breast could turn black? I didn't know that was even a remote possibility. No one had mentioned a risk of failure. As if I didn't have enough to worry about, I was suddenly concerned about my new boob turning black and dropping off.

Scott and Joseph were my first visitors. I'm sure they

must have rehearsed their routine beforehand because they launched into a comedy double-act, making jokes about how good I looked and what a lovely room I had. They brought me crisps and sweets and made me laugh at my own plight. Then they started discussing football over my bed, as if I wasn't there. For a few minutes, at least, I could have closed my eyes and thought I was at home. It was nice.

'You're looking better all the time,' Mum declared at every one of her twice-daily visits.

'I'm feeling much better,' I'd respond, no matter how I actually felt. She looked so relieved every time she walked into my room and found me awake, alert and, well, alive, I couldn't ruin her optimism. I had no end of visitors – Scott's mum and dad, Catherine, Dawn, Liz and Jackie, all my relatives – and they did a great job of making me feel human again, but when they left, my emotions were all over the place. Dull hours in high-dependency, mainly stuck in a reclining chair, were doing little for my state of mind. The days were long and boring, leaving me with far too much time to brood. Mum and Dad brought me magazines and newspapers, but I wasn't in the mood to concentrate on anything and I would cast them aside after a cursory glance. I didn't have the strength to get up and wander around, and I didn't even have a TV in my room to fill the empty hours, so I spent an inordinate amount of time contemplating my ordeal. I looked awful, I felt awful, and I was thoroughly fed up sitting in that hospital chair in my pyjamas.

All I've got to look forward to is starting chemotherapy, I thought. I'll lose my hair, I'll have to start wearing a wig, and I'll probably feel even worse.

One anxiety troubled me more than any other: what if all of this just doesn't work?

I was desperate for a full night's sleep, but I couldn't get comfortable in bed because my back was still so stiff and sore. On the fourth night after the op, I thought I'd try sleeping in my reclining chair instead. With the chair tilted backwards as far as it would go and my knees propped up with cushions, it was reasonably comfy – until my back started spasming again.

'I need help to move,' I groaned, fumbling for the buzzer that would summon the nurse. I dropped the stupid thing on the floor. I could see it, lying close to the leg of the bed, but there was no way I could stretch down to reach it. I started wriggling around, moving myself backwards and forwards with the chair's remote control, trying to find a position that might let my hand fall close to the buzzer. Then I dropped the remote control for the chair. Everything I needed lay on the floor, goading me. I was furious.

I am going to pick those bloody things up, I thought, twisting and turning with whatever limited movement I could muster. I didn't even notice that I was winding the tubes from my drip right round my neck until I was slowly strangling myself. What a way to go after all this.

'Help, help,' I rasped, but my throat was still dry and painful from the breathing tube used during surgery, so my voice was as weak as I felt. Nobody heard.

I started to sob and it built rapidly until I was taking great gulps of air and the tears had begun to drip on to my pyjamas. One dropped hospital buzzer opened the floodgates. It all came tumbling forth: the terror and grief and self-pity I'd been dodging for so long. Guilt too, terrible guilt for what I was putting Scott through.

Why would he want to marry me in this state? I thought. How could I expect him to look at me and want me when there were lots of beautiful young women around with two normal breasts and a reasonable chance of survival? We had such a good little life together and I had gone and got breast cancer. What twenty-seven-year-old gets breast cancer? Trust me to be the one.

I knew I should let him go off and have a better life with someone else, but I didn't want him to. I wanted him to stay and go through all this rubbish with me, and I desperately wanted to marry him. How could I be so unfair, so cruel?

Just then a passing nurse noticed me. 'Oh, for goodness' sake, what has happened to you?' she said, and quickly began untwisting my garrote. 'What a state you've got yourself into.'

While she tidied me up, and untangled all my lines, I sat weeping like a baby.

'You just have a good cry, love,' she said. 'It's better out than in, that's for sure. Sometimes you've just got to let it go. Shall I give you a wee tablet to help you sleep?'

The next morning I woke up feeling like I'd turned a corner. It was time for some straight-talking . . . to myself.

Right, it's about time you started getting back to normal, Mandy, I told myself. You need to be yourself again if you're going to get through this.

I found my make-up bag in my bedside locker and started putting a bit of colour on my face.

'I'm going to blow-dry my hair this morning,' I told the nurse who came to see if I needed any help getting ready. 'I'll see if I can do it without lifting my arm.'

I declared I no longer needed a catheter, nor did I require my regular chaperone in the shower. I could cope perfectly well on my own. I decided to get dressed too, swapping my pyjamas for the tracksuit Scott had bought me for Christmas. I even slipped my feet into a pair of trainers instead of slippers, and I felt pretty damn proud of myself, though as I edged around the ward, supporting myself with two drip-stands and with chest drain pouches dangling like shoulder bags at either side of my body, you could never have mistaken me for someone straight from an aerobics class.

'I'll walk you to the door,' I told my visitors as they prepared to leave that day, but it took me fifteen minutes to shuffle the short distance to the lifts. They could have been halfway home by the time I had escorted them all the way to the exit. No one objected, though.

Eight days after I walked in, I stood at the hospital doors, bent double but breathing in the winter air with a sense of release. I was getting out at last. I'd been told to expect to be in hospital for a fortnight. They were discharging me six days early because I was doing so well, and Mum had arrived to take me home.

'I've brought a pillow,' she said, as she helped me into the passenger seat. 'Put it underneath the seatbelt so it doesn't press into your tender bits.'

She drove all the way home at a steady twenty-five miles an hour, much to the annoyance of our fellow drivers on the motorway.

'Ouch – watch the bumps!' I yelled every time she ran over so much as a hairline crack in the road.

I'd been through things that I still hadn't managed to tell anyone about in great detail, but talking could wait. I wanted to savour my own belongings in my own environment for a while. I felt like I'd woken up from a terrible dream, shell-shocked and troubled but relieved to sit in the peace of my home to recoup my thoughts. Coco and Kia leaped up beside me as I rested on the sofa, gently nestling their elegant heads against me to welcome me home. I always said they knew how I was feeling, those clever cats; they seemed to sense when I was down. I'd had them since they were kittens – Coco, a male with chocolate-coloured flashes to his fur, and Kia, his sister, who had lilac ears and paws. I'd developed an allergy to their luxurious coats and had to use an asthma inhaler to control the wheezing they brought on, but I'd totally ignored Scott's suggestion that maybe we should give them away. How could I? They were my babies. On that day, just back from hospital, they made me feel warm and safe and so glad to be home. That was until I saw the mess Scott had left the place in and I just had to start tidying up.

'Put that down!' Mum shouted, snatching the brush from my hands as I tried to sweep the dining-room floor. 'Can't you just sit down for a while?'

But I'd been away for over a week and Scott's attempts at keeping the house in some semblance of order didn't exactly meet my standards.

'It's not doing any harm, Mum,' I protested. 'I'd rather be doing normal things anyway. I'm fed up with not being normal.'

When her back was turned, I sneaked upstairs to do a little cleaning. 'I bet he hasn't even made the bed,' I muttered as I made my way up.

Pinned on a message board in our spare bedroom, I found a picture of Scott and me, a photo of us sitting in a restaurant in Benidorm, smiling and happy, me with my arms round his neck.

He must have put this up while I was in hospital, I thought, as I took it down to get a closer look.

I was wearing a strappy blue dress that I'd bought in the Dorothy Perkins sale and I looked great, even if I do say so myself. It had been taken three months before I found the lump and we looked so youthful and optimistic. Scott's smile was clear and confident. He looked ten years younger, but there was something else. No fear in his eyes.

This must be the last photo of me with my left breast intact, I thought suddenly.

I stared at it, looking for signs I might have missed then. There I was, posing for the camera without a care in the world, when a bomb was about to explode under my life – our lives – and I was carrying it around with me like an innocent stooge. Why didn't I realise what was going on inside my own body? My boobs were on display a lot during that holiday. I never was one for topless sunbathing, but my 34Ds were on show every day, encased in bikinis. You'd think I would have noticed something.

I probably should have gone topless while I could, I thought ruefully.

The worst I'd suffered on that trip was a bit of sunburn. My shoulders were fried and my nose glowed like a beacon, but as far as I was concerned, I was as fit as a slightly singed flea. Yet, as I looked at the photo, a niggling thought began to crystallise in my mind. The dress I was wearing had been bought a full year before. I'd never worn it because it was just a little neat. I found it languishing at the back of my wardrobe while packing for Benidorm and thought I'd try it on to see if it was worth taking. I was pleasantly surprised that it fitted me nicely.

'I think I've lost a bit of weight,' I told Scott triumphantly. 'This dress didn't fit me last year, but it's fine now.'

He grunted an acknowledgement and I shoved the dress in the case with the rest of my stuff.

Now that I thought about it, a few items were slightly looser on me that holiday. I hadn't been trying to diet, because I've never really had to – and because there's no way that I would voluntarily deprive myself of food – but I had a vague recollection of people remarking that I looked slimmer.

'It's probably because I'm working every hour,' I told them. 'I'm full-time at the salon and part-time in the pub. I haven't got a minute to myself.'

I didn't give the loss of a few inches a second thought. Knowing me, I probably seized the opportunity to snack a bit more while I was away. If it was a warning sign, I had well and truly missed it.

This is the way I'll remember my left breast, I thought. Not covered in a surgeon's black ink.

Miracle

'I'm going to work!' Scott threw back at me, slamming the door behind him as he went.

'Good,' I shouted after his disappearing form.

Nothing had come close to breaking us before. Since the cancer started, we'd been rock solid through ordeals that would have split weaker couples. Now the one thing that should have brought us even closer, the prospect of becoming parents, was driving a wedge between us. I was prepared to go it alone.

For days we'd been at pains to accommodate one another.

'This has to be a joint decision,' Scott had said, right at the start. 'We both have to agree on the right thing to do.'

'Absolutely,' I'd replied eagerly.

But this was only going to be a joint decision if Scott came down on my side. He had his whole life to have kids. He could have them with someone else if I wasn't around.

This was it for me. My one piece of good news. My one miracle.

Chapter 7

I was dreading the 'big reveal', as they say on those make-over programmes on the telly. I knew there would be no hiding my appearance from Scott when I was home because I'd need his help with bathing and dressing. We had always been so open with each other, and I'd never been self-conscious about my naked body before. Scott would never, ever say anything remotely critical, I had complete confidence in that, but his expression would betray him.

'Are you ready to look at this now?' I asked nervously, as he ran me a bath the next morning.

'Yeah, of course,' he replied, trying really hard to sound completely undaunted, though suddenly he was very preoccupied with the taps.

My eyes never left his face as I gradually opened my dressing gown and his gaze wandered over my chest. I didn't pick up any trace of disgust, curiosity maybe and certainly a little surprise, but no horror.

Phew, I thought. He doesn't seem to want to throw a towel over me and run screaming from the room.

'It looks OK, actually,' he mused. 'It's much better than I thought it would be.'

I tore my stare from him to the mirror. The new boob wasn't a great shape. The swelling had gone down and the scars were healing, but there was definitely too much flesh under my arm, which made it appear rather lopsided.

'I think with my bra on and a T-shirt over it, it will look all right,' I said, attempting to convince myself more than Scott.

There was no denying that, in all its unclothed glory, my new breast lacked the smooth, even curves of a real one. In fact, it looked a bit weird.

Scott insisted he didn't care. 'This is the way you are now, and that's fine by me,' he said, leaning forward to kiss my forehead. 'I think it looks OK now and the doctors told you it will get better with time. You just have to give yourself a chance to get used to it.'

He was probably being kind, holding back his shock, but he managed it and I loved him for that. My lack of a breast really didn't make that much difference to him. How amazing. My belief in Scott hasn't wavered much from that little exchange between us, standing in the bathroom in those earliest of days, nervously exposing myself. He took my hand and helped me ease into the bath, then gently washed my back and shampooed my hair as I sat, helpless as a baby – a very demanding baby, mind you.

'You're not rinsing my hair properly,' I complained. 'There will be no shine on it if you don't rinse it with clean water.'

He tutted. 'Typical – I get to wash a hairdresser's hair. I was never going to get it right, was I?'

We laughed and it felt like we were a couple reunited.

'It's so good to be home, Scott,' I told him.

'It's good to have you back,' he smiled.

For some inexplicable reason, I vanished from the radar of Canniesburn Hospital the minute I left the building. They sent me away with some painkillers and plenty of leaflets on how to massage moisturiser into my reconstructed breast but no forwarding appointments, no instructions on having my dressings changed and no indication of when I should return to have the staples and stitches taken out.

'I'm getting a little worried that these dressings haven't been changed in four days,' I told Scott, as I examined the edges of the chest bandages. 'Maybe I'm supposed to be doing it myself, but I haven't got a clue what to do.' I'd been in such a hurry to leave hospital I hadn't concerned myself with such matters.

'Get on the phone to them right now,' said Scott. 'It just can't be right that no one has come near you in days.'

I wasn't exactly in pain, but I was slightly uncomfortable. I'd been having a bath every day since I got home and the dressings were becoming a bit damp.

A horrified breast-care nurse agreed with Scott when I phoned the hospital to check. 'A district nurse is supposed to be calling on you every day,' she gasped. 'They're meant to be changing your dressings and checking you for infection. You'll need to have a thorough examination before starting chemotherapy.'

That was scheduled for 5 February – about five weeks after my surgery.

'Don't worry, Mandy,' she added. 'I'll get someone out to you right away.'

I might have been grateful if I'd contracted an infection and had to push chemo back a little, but I was getting stronger by the day thanks to my own recuperation regime, gently pushing myself through physiotherapy and gradually straightening my back to stretch out my scars.

Scott and I were sleeping in separate beds. 'Don't take it personally, but neither of us will sleep if we're in the same bed,' I assured him when he baulked at my idea. 'I mean, there's barely enough room for me once I've got all my support pillows in place. You'd be hanging on to a couple of inches of space.' I had to sleep on my back, with three pillows under each knee to minimise the drag on my tummy wounds. Plus I was scared Scott would bump into my sore bits while he slept. 'I'll move into the spare room for the time being,' I volunteered, 'but don't get used to having our bed to yourself. This is not a permanent arrangement.'

With bitter irony, I was really starting to feel better when it was time to begin chemotherapy. I had tried to prepare myself psychologically, with some gentle coaching from Dawn, but I knew I was going to lose my hair and I couldn't get my mind round that at all. Dawn insisted that crushing lethargy was the worst of the side effects.

'You can stick on a wig and you don't look bald any more,' she said, 'but there's nothing you can do to stop yourself feeling so exhausted. You just have to lie down to it.'

She wasn't persuading me, though. Whatever else it did to me, chemotherapy was going to make me look sick, even if it was only in my own mirror.

I sat with Mum at the Beatson Oncology Centre in Glasgow as a nurse laid six syringes of vivid red liquid on a table beside me. Epirubicin chemotherapy: it was the colour of a raspberry alcopop. The nurse ran through all the possible side effects: tiredness, mouth ulcers, nausea, diarrhoea.

'Whatever you experience, we've got something to help it,' she said, 'so don't suffer without letting us know. You might get some of the symptoms, and you might not get any. Just keep us posted on what you're experiencing.'

Mum held one of my hands as the nurse attached a huge syringe to a needle in the back of the other. Then she slowly started to push the liquid through. My vein seemed to glow scarlet as the drug seeped in; then a cold sensation spread up my arm as it began its journey through my body. There was no turning back. I couldn't stop the tears that fell silently as I watched the chemo's slow progress.

For such a poisonous, powerful treatment the whole process was ridiculously easy and painless. It took only about twenty minutes to give me four big syringes plus two smaller ones.

'Usually hair starts to fall out about ten days after treatment,' the nurse recounted in matter-of-fact fashion. 'You'll probably have lost it by the time you come for your next chemo in three weeks' time. See you then,' she said brightly, handing me some steroids and anti-sickness tablets to tackle any nausea. 'That was all right,' I assured Mum. 'I feel fine at the moment. I might be the type of person who doesn't get any side effects from chemo.'

My course was to include eight treatments in all – four with epirubicin and four with a type called CMF, which was a mixture of three chemo drugs. It sounded daunting, but I was still planning to get on with everyday life between sessions.

'Well, that's one down and seven to go,' said Mum, as we prepared to head home. 'They'll go past in no time.'

'I'll just nip to the toilet before we set off,' I told her. 'You carry on and I'll meet you at the front door.' But I nearly keeled over in the cubicle. My pee was scarlet, bright pillar-box red. Perhaps my body wasn't coping so well after all.

Nausea hit me like a sledgehammer while we were driving home. Suddenly I could hardly keep my eyes open and there was a hollow sensation in my stomach, sickness welling upwards. It didn't feel like a tummy bug – it wasn't sore or spasmodic – it just worsened gradually until my stomach churned with every sensation from smell to movement.

'What is that terrible smell?' I said, collapsing on to the couch at home. 'Scott, you'll really have to get rid of those air-fresheners. They're making me feel sick.'

I forced myself to try to make dinner, but the scent of the washing-up liquid from dishes washed hours before was enough to make me gag. The aroma of food was unbearable.

'I can't face anything,' I said. 'I'm just going to bed.'

Though all I wanted to do was sleep, nausea would wake me every couple of hours.

The next day Dawn called and asked if I felt up to going to the cinema with her and Catherine.

'If you're not feeling well, we'll just come home again,' she said.

I thought I'd make myself go, if only to get out of the

house for a while. I knew she was trying to give me a distraction and I appreciated the gesture.

We stopped at a snack bar on the way, where the girls got something to eat, but it was the worst thing we could have done. To me, the smells were nauseating.

'Are you all right, Mandy?' Dawn asked. 'Do you want to forget about this?'

But I was determined to get to the movies. 'I'll be OK when I get a seat,' I said, forcing a laugh, and I made it through the film, though I can't claim to have watched much of it. My eyelids felt like lead. All I wanted to see on screen were the words 'The End'.

'I think I'll have to go home now,' I told them sleepily as soon as the final credits began to roll, and they helped me back to the car.

Over the next day or so I began developing mouth ulcers, which spread all round my mouth and tongue until it was agony to talk. Then the diarrhoea started, so I couldn't stray too far from the toilet even if I'd had the energy to go anywhere or do anything, which I didn't. For four days I was totally wiped out, but by day five I started to feel a little less exhausted, and as the days wore on, I began to regain my strength.

'I feel a bit better today,' I told Scott a week after the treatment. 'I'm getting over this quite well.'

I'd fought my way through every one of the symptoms the nurse had discussed . . . except one.

Then, bang on cue, exactly ten days after the chemo, I noticed my scalp was becoming painful, like my long hair was a heavy weight stitched on to my head and pulling on the skin. I noticed it while I was decorating the living room.

'I need to do something to pass the time,' I'd told a dumbstruck Scott that morning when I called him at work to ask where he'd put the paintbrushes. 'I'm feeling much better and I'm going crazy with boredom,' I'd insisted.

'I really don't think you're up to painting the place on your own,' he'd said patiently. 'Why don't you wait till I come home and we'll do it together?'

But I couldn't bear another day of sitting around doing nothing, and I was desperate to transform the lounge with shades of brown and cream – well, cappuccino and cookie dough to be precise.

'If I get tired, I'll stop,' I'd promised, but I had managed to do the whole room in a couple of hours. I was giving the chimney breast a second coat of cappuccino when I felt my head tingling. My ponytail seemed to be dragging the skin downwards.

Oh-oh, it's starting, I thought.

The next morning strands of dark hair were strewn across my pillow, and every time I touched my head, a small section of hair came loose from my raw scalp. I stood in the shower and watched more of it disappear down the plughole. If I ran my fingers through it, great clumps of hair would remain in my hands until it was hard to believe that there could be any left on my head at all.

I never realised I had this much hair, I thought.

It was everywhere except where it should have been. All of my body hair went, which at least saved me the bother of shaving legs, armpits and other sensitive regions. My eyelashes were thinning out too, and my eyebrows, though – thankfully – enough shaky hairs remained that I could still apply a bit of mascara to the lashes and pencil in the missing parts of my brows. You can work wonders with make-up and I especially liked to do my eyes. If nothing else they diverted attention from my ever-worsening hairdo. Yup, the hair on my head was becoming a patchy disaster area.

I called Liz. 'I need you to shave my head,' I told her. 'My hair's started to fall out. It's a total mess and I really don't want this to go on for ages till it's all gone. I'd rather just get rid of it now.'

Silence.

'I don't want to do it,' she said eventually. I could hear she was upset. 'Wouldn't it be better if you just let it come out by itself?' she added, but I had made up my mind. It would be easier to lose short, bristly hair than to keep picking up the long, silky strands that left a trail behind me wherever I went.

Twelve days after my first chemo, Scott drove me to Jackie's house, where she and Liz were waiting – in fact, where they were arguing over who was going to do the deed. Neither of them wanted to be the one.

I had arrived equipped with several packets of paper handkerchiefs and a mid-length red wig I'd bought with an NHS voucher especially for cancer victims going through chemo. Liz and Mum had helped me choose it, during a bizarre shopping trip on which they pretended I really suited the most horrendous wigs and I pretended I didn't mind trying them on. The girl in Judy Plum, a wig shop in Glasgow, was tolerant as we cast our hyper-critical eyes over the stock, and after I picked out the red one as 'the best of a bad lot', she ushered me into a little booth and sat me down in front of a mirror.

'Play around with it a bit till you get it the way you like it,' she said, giving the thing a quick comb before positioning it on my head. 'It takes a bit of time to get accustomed to a different look.' She left me alone to think about it.

Liz peeped in to find me staring vacantly back at her, my lopsided wig pulled right down to my eyes. It looked like it might be able to wander off of its own accord, given half a chance – less of a chic hairdo, more of a sleeping small animal. 'For God's sake,' she tutted, marching in and producing a tub of hairstyling fudge from her handbag. 'Here – have a go at putting some product through it.'

I worked on it until the wig actually started to resemble a proper hairstyle.

'Ooh, that's lovely,' said Mum when I finally ventured out. 'You really suit it.'

'She does, doesn't she?' Liz grinned in agreement. 'That's just what I've been trying to tell her.'

Between the two of them, Mum and Liz tried to convince me I looked so good with red hair I should go auburn when my own grew back. I'm a brunette and naturally very dark, so I wasn't convinced by this at all. I suspect they were stretching the point a little because Scott and Dad couldn't quite muster as much false enthusiasm when I tried it on for them back at home.

'It's quite nice,' said Dad.

'You'll get used to it,' added Scott.

What they didn't say was, 'Wow – you look fabulous.'

Dad's well-meaning words don't always hit the mark: 'Aye . . . it will do the purpose,' was the best he could come up with in difficult circumstances and my heart sunk to the soles of my shoes.

So the key to my new fiery-redhead look was scrunched up in a bag as Scott drove me to Jackie's house that night.

'I've got a baseball cap with me too,' I told him. 'If the wig looks too ridiculous, I'll put the hat on instead.'

For a while we sat in the lounge, feeling nervous and embarrassed, until I got fed up with the stand-off. 'Look, it doesn't matter who does it. Let's just get it over and done with.'

Jackie spread some towels over the bedroom carpet and placed a dining chair in the middle, ready to begin. She sat on the bed, gripping my hand, while Liz picked up the scissors.

'Are you ready?' she asked.

'Just do it,' I replied.

She hesitated, then lifted the first chunk of hair and lobbed a good six inches off. The hair on top of my head was still pretty thick and she had to cut away the longest parts before she could really get into my scalp with the electric clippers. Snip, snip, snip...with every slice I saw another piece of my lovely glossy hair fall, dropping limply on to the towels as Liz moved swiftly round my head. I knew she was trying to be as quick as possible. There was no point in prolonging the agony. Anyway, this was what we did every day of our lives. We were hairdressers. If anyone could handle this, we could.

Jackie started blubbering first, then Liz and then me. Liz switched on the electric clippers, but the buzzing sound they made was all but drowned out by our collective sobbing. The blades were rough on my sensitive scalp and I wanted to tell her to stop, but I knew she'd never start again so I just prayed for it to be over.

When she'd finished, we sat together amid the debris.

'I can't believe it,' Liz said. 'Trust you to suit a hairstyle like that.'

Jackie joined in. 'She's right. It's lucky you've got a nice round head.'

She passed me a mirror and I looked at the new bald Mandy, my face blotchy and swollen, a spartan fringe of lashes clinging to my red eyes. The woman staring back wasn't familiar in any way. She certainly wasn't the me I wanted to be. There wasn't even any point in trying the wig. That would have been an ordeal too far. It was never going to make me feel any better.

I pulled on the baseball cap. 'Thanks, Liz,' I said.

She nodded, closing her eyes.

Scott took my cue and we left without stopping for a drink or a cup of tea. I didn't take the cap off until we were back home and he could put his arms round me and hold me until I'd calmed down.

'My head's freezing,' I told him, as we lay in bed that night. 'I can't stop shivering.'

I mentioned that to Mum and Dad the next day and before I knew it Dad had produced two of his favourite woolly hats. He's been bald for years, so he understood my problem. 'You can wear these to bed until your hair starts to grow back,' he said. And I did.

Grocery shopping in Asda gave me my first wig-wearing outing.

'Everyone is going to stare at me,' I told Mum as we

sat in the car while I attempted to pluck up the courage to go in. 'They'll have a right good laugh at the young lassie in a wig.'

Mum was determined and she would drive me nowhere else until we'd been in the store. 'No one is even going to notice, Mandy,' she pleaded. 'You look absolutely fine.'

All round the store I tugged and pulled at the wig, trying desperately to keep it in position and afraid my side parting would slip down to my eyebrow without me noticing. I checked my reflection in every vaguely shiny surface and kept my head down to avoid making eye contact with anyone I knew.

'Will you leave it alone?' Mum ordered, as I pulled anxiously at the nape of my neck. 'You're drawing attention to it.'

'I can't help it, Mum,' I grimaced. 'It feels so weird. I'm sure it's going to fall off.'

I could imagine a shopper running over it with her trolley. It would be lying on the floor like supermarket road kill.

As the days wore on, though, I have to confess I got quite used to wearing it. Jackie cut the fringe and I started using some of my styling products to make it look a bit funky. When I wanted to alter it a little further, I'd plonk it on Scott's head and give it a trim.

He moaned at first. 'I'm sure you could do this

without me having to wear it,' he said.

'Oh, stop grumping,' I would tell him. 'You make a good dummy.'

I wore it all day every day, but I took it off as soon as I got home, tossing it casually over the end of the banister, where Coco and Kia often got their claws into it. Every now and again I'd find them in the lounge wrestling around with my wig, like it was a rival that had encroached on their territory.

'Will you two leave my hair alone!' I'd cry, and they'd dart off to hide behind some furniture while I tried to brush out the knots they'd made.

Little Olivia must have been endlessly puzzled by the strange behaviour of Auntie Mandy's hair whenever Joseph and Natalie brought her round for a visit.

'Aren't you going to wear your hair today?' she'd ask. 'Why is it hanging up outside the bathroom?'

'Ah, that's because Auntie Mandy's got special hair,' I'd tell her. 'It's magic.' And she'd look at me in wonder, trying to work out what other mystic powers I might possess.

To my surprise, I was relaxing back into an ordinary life, a different life from the way it was before, but strangely comfortable for that. At first I tried various 'tricks of the trade' to lessen the poisonous effects of the chemo in the hope of getting an easier ride, but nothing seemed to work. A nurse suggested sucking on ice lollies while having treatment because it kept the mouth cool and could help prevent mouth ulcers later.

Great idea, I thought. I love ice lollies anyway.

The chemo nurses kept a supply of raspberry and orange lollies in the departmental freezer, and I kept one in my mouth throughout each session. I'd have two in twenty minutes – occasionally three – but I still ended up with thirty-odd ulcers and I went right off lollies in the process. It would clearly take more than a few icies to beat the effects of chemo, so there was nothing else for it. I would just have to learn to live with it. I worked out a routine that let me cope with the worst side effects of the three-weekly sessions: lie low for the initial few days after treatment to let the nausea and fatigue subside, then return to work for the remainder of the time before my next treatment.

At hospital one day I bumped into my mastectomy-ward friend, Joan.

'You're looking great,' I told her. 'Although I see you've got a different hairstyle from the last time I saw you,' and we laughed at our shared baldness and our wiggy adventures.

It turned out Joan lived fairly close to me, but she was struggling a bit with transport back and forth to the Beatson for her treatment.

'I'll pick you up, if you like,' Mum volunteered. 'I'll be

bringing Mandy anyway, so I can easily collect you too.'

So on the days when our chemo coincided, we would travel together and gab for hours about our latest symptoms or the state of our reconstructions or any old stuff that came to mind. I was glad of a chemo companion. Each session flew past.

Scott and I started socialising again, having drunken nights out with our pals just as we'd done before. Apparently it was fine to have a drink or two while going through chemotherapy. As long as you didn't overdo it, it could help you relax a bit, one of the nurses had explained. It certainly helped me forget about the stresses and strains of treatment, though I did feel a little guilty when I arrived for one chemo session suffering badly from a hangover. I thought it best to keep that to myself in case the nurse gave me a telling-off.

'Will you please try and keep the wig on your head tonight,' Scott would grin as we got dressed to go out. I'd developed a party piece of whipping the thing off when least expected, then passing it round the room to let everyone else try it on. 'I know you think it's hilarious, but it might be good just to have a normal evening for once.'

On a night out with the girls, Liz gave me an over-enthusiastic embrace while we were dancing and the two of us stumbled, then keeled over in a heap on the dance floor. Liz panicked, terrified she'd hurt me, but I was laughing so much I couldn't get back on my feet. When I retreated to the toilet to sort myself out, I saw the wig had been turned entirely round the wrong way and my middle parting had become a squinty side-shed.

'Back into place,' I giggled, adjusting it brazenly while a couple of stunned girls watched. 'Yes, it is a wig,' I said, as I sashayed past them back out into the action.

I sent many a young girl scuttling off after she had innocently admired my hair while applying a bit of lippie in a nightclub toilet.

Dawn and I would even compare reconstructions during our weekly get-togethers. Sitting round the kitchen table at Catherine's house, we'd moan about the state of our newly rebuilt bodies.

'Yours is much better than mine,' I would complain, as the other girls roared with laughter. 'Mine is definitely too far over to one side. I'm jealous of your boob.'

Dawn had been left with enough of her natural breast to allow her to show a little cleavage in more revealing clothes. She could wear vest tops and still look great. I had far too much scarring to do that.

'Well, your belly button is nicer than mine,' she'd retort, and I wasn't in a position to argue as my belly-button phobia hadn't allowed me to inspect my new navel too closely.

Both Dawn and I were aware there was a danger we could turn into 'cancer bores', droning on about our illness while the others pretended to be interested. We'd both met people like that during our trips back and forth to hospitals, people who'd become so obsessed with their own treatment they couldn't think of anything else to talk about. I hated to get stuck beside one in a waiting room.

'Don't let me get like that,' I told Dawn. 'You have permission to give me a slap if I start going on about cancer all the time.'

It wouldn't have been fair to hijack the girls' nights. Who wants to hear gory details of surgery and symptoms week in, week out? Certainly not me or Dawn, and we were living with them. So we started phoning or texting one another when we wanted to talk, trying to preserve our weekly meetings as cancer-free zones. It wasn't always possible, but we tried.

Catherine and the others knew there was a connection between Dawn and me that went beyond our get-togethers. I suppose it changed the dynamic of our group a bit. Catherine was Dawn's friend initially, having been neighbours years back. Catherine and I became pals through our boyfriends. Catherine introduced me to Dawn and, in turn, to Dawn's friends Joy and May. So I was a relative newcomer, but what started as a casual friendship between Dawn and me became a special, precious bond. Breast cancer gave us that. I think the others understood.

*

Eight weeks after my surgery, I went back to work full-time. I could have gone back earlier, but I kept having an attack of cold feet every time I debated my return. The thought of having difficult conversations with my customers was putting me off, but what scared me more than anything was the prospect of being surrounded by mirrors all day, my reflection taunting me at every turn.

'OK, I'll have to grin and bear it,' I told Scott eventually. 'I can't stay in the house until my hair grows back.'

Unsuspecting female customers would regularly compliment my 'lovely red hair' and ask for details of the dye I had used. The first time was a bit awkward, and I mumbled some excuse about forgetting the colour name, but the more it happened, the funnier it got. Jackie and I invented a shade that we would discuss at great length whenever my hair was mentioned by an admiring client.

'What colour did we do my hair, Jackie?' I'd call down the salon.

'Oh, we mixed two together for that one. I can't remember exactly which ones we used. Let me think now . . .'

Occasionally I'd confide in regular customers – 'This is actually a wig. I'm going through chemotherapy' – but it's not the kind of information your hairdresser normally imparts.

'Oh, really,' they'd blush before attempting to steer the

conversation back to something altogether easier. 'Er, you going on any holidays this year?'

Sometimes customers would surprise me with their reaction to my news. One man, a regular client, immediately started telling me about a friend of his who was also going through breast-cancer treatment. He knew a lot about it, and every time he came into the shop, he'd ask about my progress and give me an update on hers.

'She's doing really well,' he'd say. 'She's having chemotherapy now,' and I'd listen and smile encouragingly, secretly a bit sad that there were obviously so many of us breast-cancer girls out there.

He never mentioned her name, and I never asked. It didn't seem important and I didn't like to pry.

Out and about at weekends, I'd taken to gazing at women with beautiful long, dark tresses, watching them enviously as their hair billowed out behind them in the breeze, lucky them.

'I'd really love a ponytail that swings when I walk,' I'd tell Scott whenever we drove past someone with exactly that hairstyle. 'I am so jealous of long, bouncy hair like that.'

'You'll have hair like that again before too long,' he'd say, 'and the first thing you'll do is decide you want a haircut.'

To be frank, my weight was becoming as much of a problem as my baldness. The steroids I was taking to control nausea made me pile on the pounds, and I shot up a dress size in a couple of weeks. My bloated body changed my image even more than my lack of hair because I couldn't disguise being fat. I certainly didn't feel ready to be the centre of attention, which was going to make it difficult to be a bride.

Our wedding was four months away, 29 June. The ceremony and reception were being held in the Sherbrooke Castle Hotel on the south side of Glasgow, with 100 guests coming along to eat, drink and dance the night away before Scott and I jetted off on honeymoon to Cyprus. I knew I was about to throw more than a year's preparation out of the window, but try as I might, I couldn't convince myself to go ahead with it. I simply had to tell the groom.

'I'm so sorry, Scott,' I sighed, as we got ready for bed one night. 'I just can't go through with the wedding.'

He knew I had been thinking about postponing. I'd mentioned it briefly before the mastectomy op, but as soon as my hair had started to fall out, the decision was made.

'I can't stand the thought of being a bald bride,' I went on. 'There's no way I'm going to be wearing a wig when I walk down the aisle. Now it looks like I'll be fat and bald. I can't do it.'

Scott wasn't fazed in the slightest, aware that I was far too vain to put myself through such a trial. 'That's OK,' he said, giving me a hug. 'We can get married anytime. How about if we put it back a year? By this time next year we'll be back to normal and we'll have the day we really want.' He started digging out the numbers of all the companies with which we'd made bookings. 'We'll just have to explain what's happened and hope they'll not try to charge us for postponing.'

Astonishingly, every one of them was pretty sympathetic to our plight and happily went along with our changes. The hotel booked us a new date – Sunday, 4 May 2003 – so we were on target again. Our future had been handed back to us, our plans simply delayed. Scott still wanted to marry me. Thank God.

I knew I was asking him to take much more than my hand in marriage. I had cancer, and even if things were beginning to look up, we were by no means out of the woods.

'I'm going to ask the doctor about having my eggs frozen,' I told Scott one night.

He almost spluttered out his dinner. We'd never actually discussed having a family together, but I knew there was a risk that chemotherapy could damage my fertility. I was scared I'd lose the opportunity to have children before we'd even got round to thinking about them.

'I know we're not planning kids at the moment,' I carried on, ignoring his popping eyes, 'but I want to make sure we've still got a chance if we decide to do it at some point. You know, once we've grown up enough ourselves.'

I'd been watching Joseph with Olivia and it was lovely. She would look up at him with her huge brown eyes, reaching out till he grabbed her and swung her high into the air, and I thought how amazing it must feel to be so important to a child. I would love to know that feeling. Not right away but in the future.

Scott laughed nervously. 'You're probably right,' he said. 'I suppose there's no harm in looking into it. So long as you're not planning on doing anything right now. I'm not sure I'm ready for it yet.'

So I found myself asking various doctors and nurses how to go about having my eggs frozen for potential use in fertility treatment. My periods had stopped pretty much as soon as chemo started, but they had returned after a few weeks, so I was quite confident my body was working normally. The response from the medics was always much the same: 'Oh, there's plenty of time to think about that later' or 'You won't have to worry about that'. I let them palm me off because it seemed like a fight I could have another day, if I actually ever wanted to fight over it. I was too busy with the here and now to worry about problems that might never arise.

By July 2002 chemo was coming to an end. The finishing line was in sight and I lumbered towards it like an exhausted athlete at the end of his worst-ever marathon. Completing our courses of treatment meant I wasn't seeing so much of Joan, which was the only negative part. I knew she was grateful she didn't have to make the journey back and forth to the Beatson any more, but I'd miss her chat.

'Keep in touch, though,' she said at her final session. 'You've got my mobile number, so keep me posted with how you're getting on.'

We did text each other, and she was always cheerful and positive, entirely back to her old self and busy with her kids, but Mum and Dad bumped into her in the supermarket one day.

'Joan didn't look very well,' Mum told me later. 'Do you think she's sick again?'

No, I didn't think so. She would have mentioned it.

'She was probably having an off day,' I said. 'It happens to us all.'

For my part, I was becoming increasingly confident in my own recovery. The worst was behind me, I was sure of that. There would be no radiotherapy as follow-up because the doctors were content the cancer had been fully contained in the removed breast. In fact, it had probably been entirely in the lump. All seventeen of the lymph nodes they removed during surgery had tested clear, so, as far as I was concerned, the life-saving part of the treatment was over. Since I no longer had cancer to worry about, I figured I could afford myself a little vanity over the reconstruction. I started seeing Mr Ray again, this time about making some cosmetic changes to the surgery sites, and he was more than happy to do a bit of tweaking to my appearance.

'I can take away this puckered section in your armpit, and we'll do a bit of liposuction on your hips,' he said.

Excess flesh hung over the tight tummy scar, making my hips look lumpy.

'I'll also do some liposuction of the reconstruction, where there's a little too much sitting under your arm,' he went on.

Great. I was desperate to get rid of that. Everything would be done before the new wedding date, which meant I'd look fantastic for my photos.

'You'll be marrying a new woman,' I told Scott. 'You might not even recognise me when I turn up on the day.'

Watch

The obstetrician, Dr Mathers, led Scott and me into an ultrasound room. 'Right, Mandy, if you can get on to the table, we'll have a look at your tummy,' he said.

My stomach was in knots and I was desperate for a wee. I'd been told to try not to go until after the examination.

Dr Mathers took a seat at the side of the bed, in front of a large monitor. He helped me slide up my jumper to reveal my swollen belly, moving the waistband of my jeans downwards a bit too.

'This will be a little cold, I'm afraid,' he said, squeezing a blob of clear gel on to my stomach.

I winced. Scott took my hand.

'Now,' he went on, 'as I explained before, if you would rather, I can turn this screen away so you don't have to see. If you haven't made a decision on what to do yet, it might be easier not to watch.'

Scott and I looked at one another.

Chapter 8

'And the theme is "sexy policewomen", Mum.' I was regaling her with the last of the details for my hen weekend in Dublin. 'So you'll need a miniskirt and some fishnets.'

I thought she was going to have a heart attack.

'There's no way I'm wandering around Dublin like that,' she objected. 'I mean, can't I just stick to a police hat and a pair of trousers?'

Liz, Jackie and I already had all our gear and we were toning it down for no one. The good denizens of Dublin would not know what hit them when my gang of saucy law-enforcers arrived.

It was Easter weekend 2003, three weeks before the wedding, and we had planned a massive blow-out to celebrate both my imminent nuptials and the reappearance of my hair. I was nine months clear of the chemo and enough of my hair had grown back to let me create a bob style that everyone seemed to like, apart from me, as I still hankered for long locks. My greatest concern was whether I'd manage to achieve something resembling the glamorous bridal hairstyles I had in mind.

Scott didn't quite get it.

'I'll be looking at my wedding photos for the rest of my life,' I attempted to explain, 'and a terrible hairdo ruins your image. You must know that by now.' I was taking the whole 'bride' thing extremely seriously, and I couldn't wait to step out in front of everyone and show them that I was back to normal, better than normal, in fact. I was determined to be fabulous.

I'd started exercise classes and went to the gym practically every night. I'd even taken up jogging. I'd lost a bit of weight – entirely deliberately this time – plus I'd had the corrective cosmetic surgery three months earlier, so I actually felt quite relaxed about the way I looked, even if I was decked up like a dodgy kiss-a-gram. With my temporary prosthetic nipple in place, glued on to my reconstructed breast, I felt practically whole again, though it did fall out of my bra quite regularly, and it was covered in tiny puncture wounds after Coco and Kia found it abandoned on my dressing table and took turns to sink their teeth into it. They would flip it up in the air like a flying saucer, the two of them fighting over who would claim it as their trophy.

'You know what, Mum?' I said, as I squashed an extra pair of shoes into my weekend bag. 'You were right. I've lost a year out of my life, but I'm OK. I finally feel that we're getting back on track. And I'm loving it.'

Mum was quite chuffed with herself. 'I only wish people would listen to me more often,' she said, smirking.

The natives of Dublin had a good laugh at us as we paraded about looking like a comedy dance troop, all except the manager of the nightclub we managed to talk our way into. He was less than amused by Liz's attempts to surreptitiously blow up a life-size inflatable 'boyfriend' for me. She'd smuggled it all the way from Scotland and waited till I was out of sight before trying to prepare her surprise. Unfortunately, Mr Inflatable took a while to get going, so she was blue in the face endeavouring to get enough air into the most crucial part of him when the stroppy manager came over.

'Let the air out of that or I'm afraid you'll have to leave the premises,' he growled.

Still, the 'boyfriend' had a smile on his face as he sat on the couch beside us and slowly crumpled. Typical man – plastic or not, they've got no staying power.

I came home still sporting the fluffy pom-pom deely-boppers that were regulation wear for the weekend. I was all partied out, hung-over beyond redemption and thoroughly looking forward to Sunday, 4 May, our wedding day.

My dress had been hanging in the bridal shop for two years, picked and paid for in the summer of 2001, and I could hardly remember what it looked like. I hadn't even gone near the shop until my hair began to grow back.

'I am terrified to try it on,' I confided in Mum. 'What if I hate it now?'

I'm notoriously fickle about my clothes at the best of times, loving something one minute and loathing it the next, and in this particular instance I had a reasonable excuse to be fearful. Two years, a mastectomy, reconstruction and chemotherapy may have changed how I looked in it and how it felt on me. There was quite a risk that the £1,300 gown that had reduced Mum to tears of joy when I'd first put it on would leave me weeping with regret.

'Just try it,' Mum said, clutching a camera to take photos of me that we could pore over later. 'Your tastes haven't changed that much, surely?'

When I opened up the dress carrier again and examined it in full detail, I knew.

'It's OK, Mum,' I called from the fitting room. 'It's still the right one.'

It was white silk-satin, with lots of silver embroidery over the boned bodice and a swathe of fabric in the skirt, which opened when I walked to reveal a panel of silver. I had chosen a full-length diamanté veil and a princess tiara to complete the ensemble. With the bodice altered to fit as tightly as possible, no one would ever have been able to tell the breasts held snugly inside weren't exactly a matching pair. My scarring was entirely covered and had healed so well that I wasn't in any pain as my boobs got manoeuvred into position.

This is perfect, I thought, swishing around the bridal shop like Scarlett O'Hara.

My wedding day was not going to be about breast cancer. I wanted people to look at me and see a beautiful bride on the most wonderful day of her life. No feeling sorry for me. No making allowances.

Two weeks before the big day, however, our marriage plans came close to being ripped up once and for all. Scott's stag weekend in Amsterdam almost succeeded where cancer had failed.

It's still difficult to work out exactly what happened, as I've never been able to extract much information from the others on the trip. What goes on between stags stays between stags, and all that nonsense. To this day Scott remains a bit reticent about disclosing the details, but it seems my soon-to-be husband, who had never in his life taken drugs, sampled some of the notorious cakes on offer in Amsterdam's cafés. They didn't exactly agree with him. He spent the weekend in semi-blackout, incapable of socialising. Back home in Scotland, I kept calling his mobile to see how things were going and couldn't understand why he never answered.

'Hi, Mandy,' said a voice on the line one night, but it wasn't my gallant groom. It was one of his pals. 'Scott's not feeling very well. He's having a sleep. Can he phone you later?'

But he never did. Instead, Catherine phoned me to pass on some information from her husband, who was among the revellers. 'They were all eating dodgy cakes, but they didn't realise the strength of what was in them,' she said. 'It has hit Scott really hard. He had one too many and he's not compos mentis.'

I was fuming. How could he be so stupid, particularly when my dad was there to witness it all, my dad who is ardently anti-drugs and can't even abide people who smoke cigarettes, never mind anything else?

I'm not sure why Dad agreed to go along in the first place. A weekend in Amsterdam with a group of young stags must have been his idea of hell. Still, he wanted to get into the swing of things in advance of the wedding and it was a good opportunity to spend some quality time with his future son-in-law. Big mistake. After Catherine's call I was bracing myself for the tirade, and it came via Mum. Dad wanted to kill his future son-in-law.

'Your dad has been on the phone and he's furious with Scott,' she told me. 'He hasn't seen him the whole weekend, doesn't know what on earth he's playing at.'

I could have killed Scott myself.

When it was finally time to fly home, Dad refused to address a word to the man who was about to marry his daughter and continued to ignore him all the way to the airport, blanking any of his attempts to apologise. 'I don't have anything to say to you,' was the only acknowledgement he gave.

Then their flight home was cancelled and the less-than-merry gang were stranded. They had a choice: shell out for replacement flights back to Glasgow or accept the airline's offer of a free flight . . . to Newcastle. That was the last straw. Outraged by it all, Dad decided he'd rather endure the hassle of a trip to Newcastle – and a connecting train ride to Glasgow – than board the same flight as his son-in-law-to-be. Shame-faced, Scott paid up for the flight to Glasgow, grateful to be spared Dad's wrath for a while.

'Your dad hates me,' Scott whined, when he finally staggered through the front door and hurled himself on to the couch. 'I don't think he's going to let us get married. I've tried to say I'm sorry, but he won't even listen to me.'

He was a bit pathetic, lying there clearly still suffering the after-effects of something.

I knew our only hope was to get Mum on side. She would know how to handle Dad.

She took up the role of peace-maker. 'Come on, Joe, it was his stag weekend,' she encouraged Dad. 'Give the boy a break. The wedding's in a few days' time. He was probably just nervous.'

Dad snorted at that.

'And I'm really sorry, Joe,' Scott added. 'I won't make that mistake again. Honest. I'm still feeling sick now, if it's any consolation.'

It took a few days, but Dad mellowed a bit.

'We'll put it behind us,' he said grumpily. 'But I won't forget about this in a hurry.'

Oh well, at least he would talk to Scott. I'd been having nightmare images of our top table sitting in sulky silence throughout the reception, hardly the best start to married life.

We weren't about to risk any more bad luck by flouting tradition and staying together the night before our wedding, so Scott was dispatched to the hotel. I spent my last few hours as a single girl at home, with Mum, Dawn and bridesmaid Catherine, drinking champagne and joking about how nervous I was.

'I just hope my fake nipple doesn't fall off when I'm walking down the aisle,' I grimaced. 'How embarrassing would that be? One of you will have to jump up and grab it if that happens.'

Most couples have ring-bearers; I had nipple-snatchers.

Dawn was on top form that night, even though she was going through the most horrendous time. The cancer had spread to her bones and her back ached terribly, despite the powerful painkillers she was taking, yet somehow she found the strength to join in the fun as if nothing was wrong. She was the Dawn of old, the life and soul of the party.

She even insisted on ironing Mum's wedding outfit. 'Please let me do it – I'm great at ironing,' she said, wrestling the iron from Mum's hands. 'You get your feet up, Marie, and have another glass of champagne.'

Then she volunteered to paint my toenails. 'I wouldn't normally agree to touch your feet,' she said, wrinkling her nose in disgust. 'This is a one-off, you remember that. Think of it as my wedding gift to you.'

What a laugh it was, reminiscing about the adventures we'd had. It was just like it had always been, before any of the crap we'd both been through. I realise now that she did it for me. She shared my last night of single life, like she knew I wanted her to, but she made sure I saw not a trace of her illness to remind me of my own. Now I know how poorly she was then, I can see what an Oscar-winning performance she put on, what a selfless act that was.

I opened the curtains on my wedding morning to the most mournful weather a Scottish spring could muster.

'Could it be any wetter?' I groaned to Mum as she joined me at the window. 'The sky is completely grey. It's never going to stop by this afternoon.'

Scotland's weather is far from reliable, but we thought we were playing it reasonably safe with a May wedding. We weren't banking on glorious sunshine – Scotland hardly provides that in July or August. A nice spring day would have done. Even a dull day. In fact, any kind of dry day. Unfortunately, May 2003 was one of the wettest in Scottish history. Typically, April had been glorious. Just our luck.

'You won't be getting the soft-top down in your car in this weather,' said Dad sagely.

By the time the Rolls-Royce convertible finally arrived to take Dad and me to the hotel, a crowd of hardy neighbours had gathered outside the house, sheltering under umbrellas as they cheered and waved and told me I looked great.

Dad was demanding they admire him too. 'Don't you think I look good in my kilt?' he joked. He was trying to soothe my nerves when I knew he was more terrified than me. He'd been up since 6 a.m. preparing the speech I'd been nagging him to write for weeks. 'Calm down now,' he kept saying, though he may have been talking to himself.

The car journey took for ever. The Rolls seemed to have a top speed of about ten miles an hour and I was getting more stressed by the minute.

When I finally arrived at the hotel and saw Scott, ashen-faced with terror and in danger of fainting clean away, all I could do was laugh. I giggled all the way through the service, even though I'd never been more serious about anything in my life. We said our vows on the sweeping staircase of the hotel, with 100 of our dearest friends looking up at us. They all laughed when I fluffed my vows and declared I knew of 'no unlawful impediment' why I couldn't marry Scott, but when we turned round as man and wife and saw everyone smiling and clapping, it was such a fantastic feeling.

My God, I did it, I thought. I made it here. I'm having my dream wedding.

It was such a wonderfully happy experience that the day flew past and suddenly Dad was on his feet, telling the guests about his beautiful daughter.

'Raise your glasses to the bride and groom, Mandy and Scott,' he ordered, and everyone cheered.

Mandy and Scott. Mr and Mrs McMillan. We were officially a team.

Then the best man got up and made a speech that included the production of a giant chocolate-chip muffin. He informed the guests, 'I've brought this all the way back from Amsterdam for Scott 'cause he enjoyed them so much when we were there.'

The room erupted and Scott's face glowed red. Even Dad laughed, a bit.

The dancing went on till the small hours, with Scott and me leading the shindig.

'I am not leaving my own wedding reception,' I told Mum when she suggested that newlyweds traditionally went before the rest of the guests. 'I'm staying till the bitter end.'

Everyone seemed to be having a ball. Sharon, one of my great friends, had a little too much to drink and decided to have a rest in the loos. It took two hours to free her, but she just swaggered back into the ballroom refreshed and ready to carry on. It was exactly what I wanted, the best party ever. Through the action of the dance floor, however, I caught sight of Dawn among the guests, sitting at a table watching the fun. She was smiling, but her face was weak and pale and I saw her pain immediately.

The day has probably been too long for her, I thought, giving her a wave.

Weddings are pretty exhausting even for the fit and healthy and she'd been up late with us the night before. I was so caught up in my own happiness that I didn't want to admit what was clear. Dawn was in a bad way. Her plight was staring me in the face.

By 4 a.m., when all the other guests had gone, Scott and I were sitting in the bar with Joseph and Natalie, tired but elated. I wanted the night to go on for ever.

'We'll have to go and get packed,' Scott said eventually. 'We have to be at the airport in a couple of hours.'

Joseph and Natalie would be leaving for Manchester the next day. They'd moved there a couple of months before to be closer to Natalie's family and I missed seeing them every day. Joseph had always been my protective 'big brother' and I liked having him around, especially since he now had a baby son, Josh, as well as Olivia. I didn't want to say goodbye to all of them.

'We'll be back up in a few weeks' time and I'll see you then,' said Joseph, giving me a hug, which was probably as demonstrative as he could ever be. He was never the touchy-feely type, Joseph. He was a bit like my dad that way. Like Dad, though, I never doubted how much he cared for me.

'You enjoy yourselves,' he told us, and we finally went our separate ways.

Our wedding night was spent throwing our belongings into suitcases and rushing to catch our honeymoon flight. I didn't even have time to take out the 300 kirby grips that were holding my hairstyle in place.

Scott and I changed only one thing in our new wedding plans: the honeymoon. Our first booking for a fortnight in Cyprus would have been lovely, no doubt, but it wasn't exactly a dream holiday.

'Let's push the boat out,' Scott said. 'Let's do something we've always wanted to do. We've got an excuse for blowing a bit of cash, so where would you go if you could go anywhere?'

That was easy. We spent a fortune on a two-centre holiday in the United States: a week in Los Angeles followed by four nights in New York. It was worth every penny. It felt so special, like we really were starting out on something fresh and exciting. We were soppy honeymooners, strolling hand in hand down Hollywood's Walk of Fame, or taking snapshots of each other shaking hands with Mickey Mouse in Disneyland.

'Oh, you're on honeymoon!' trilled the receptionist checking us into our room at the Hilton, Anaheim, Los Angeles. She was very LA, all glamorous and gushing. 'Let me see if I can find you an upgrade in that case.' Scott and I crossed our fingers. 'We have an executive suite with access to the rooftop Jacuzzi,' she said. 'I'm sure you'll like it.'

Like it? We didn't want to leave it. We felt like movie stars lounging in the hot tub sipping cocktails.

Relaxing there one night, I glanced down at my chest and noticed a patch of dry skin on my reconstructed breast was showing.

Oh, this bikini must have shrunk, I thought, adjusting the fabric to cover the patch again. It definitely covered the dry skin when I bought it.

I'd chosen the black halterneck bikini specifically because the top was a pretty generous cut, covering more of my breast and hiding both my surgery scars and the little troublesome area of irritated skin that had been bothering me for months.

It had appeared just as I reached the end of chemotherapy. In fact, I'd first mentioned it to the breast-care staff when I'd arrived at the Beatson for my final chemo session in July 2002 – a full ten months before. It had developed on the sliver of my original breast left behind after the mastectomy, only a couple of millimetres wide and hardly noticeable, sitting unobtrusively beside my cleavage and at the edge of the reconstruction scar.

I'd actually dithered about mentioning it initially. It seemed so insignificant after everything I'd been through, but I decided it was probably wise to point it out, in case it happened to be something very straightforward and obvious I just hadn't heard about. No one I showed it to was overly worried, even when it stubbornly refused to respond to any cream I was prescribed. More confused than concerned, I would raise it at every check-up and each time I was told there was nothing to fret about. It was just a little area of dry skin, that's all.

As I took off my bikini to get showered after our Jacuzzi that night, I could see the irritated skin seemed to have small whiteheads on it and the whole thing covered an area about two centimetres round – bigger than it was before we left Scotland but all still entirely on the skin that remained of my natural left breast.

'I think that patch of eczema is spreading,' I said to Scott. 'I'll have to get some different ointment for it.'

Scott had a look at it. 'I really think you better make an appointment to see about that when we get home,' he said.

I was so annoyed. 'But I'm fed up asking about it,' I groaned. 'I feel like I am being neurotic, like I'm going on about nothing. I've asked everyone about it. They're sick of me rabbiting on about the dry skin on my breast. I'm sure they think I'm nuts.'

After so many reassurances, I wasn't about to let it interfere with our honeymoon, so by the time we flew from Los Angeles to New York a few days later, I'd managed to put it right out of my mind.

New York blew me away. I was mesmerised by the skyscrapers and the neon lights. We were staying on the thirty-fourth floor of a hotel on Times Square and we seemed to be miles above the ground. Remarkably, Scott loves to shop as much as I do, so we hit the big department stores as soon as we arrived, buying jeans and T-shirts and make-up and handbags like they were giving the stuff away.

'This has been the best holiday ever,' I told Scott, as we walked through Grand Central Station together. 'I love you so much. We should have done this years ago.'

The honeymoon had to end, though, and back in Scotland, I made an appointment at the GP's again in the hope that someone could suggest a different treatment for the dry skin. I'd already been given some hydrocortisone cream to try, which didn't do much, but the patch looked a little different since the spots appeared and I thought that might give more of a clue as to the cause. It didn't.

'Mandy, I have to admit I've got no idea what this is,'

the doctor told me honestly. 'I really don't think it's got anything to do with the cancer, but I've never seen anything like it. I'd better refer you to Stobhill just to be on the safe side.'

So back I went to the breast clinic, where a junior doctor was so dismissive of me that I blushed with embarrassment. 'It's just a skin condition,' I was told. 'If the cancer was going to come back, it wouldn't appear like that. It would probably be a lump.' The junior doctor barely spent any time looking at my breast and didn't seem inclined to waste energy on a lengthy conversation about it. I was told I would be referred to a dermatologist who might be able to help by giving me different cream.

I felt like such a malingerer that I almost didn't bother keeping the follow-up appointment.

'What's the point?' I asked Scott, the night before I was due to attend. 'It's not painful or anything, and I'm trying not to take any more time off work if I can possibly avoid it.' I'd had so much sick leave already, with all my previous treatment, that I didn't want to take a sickie needlessly.

'You have to get something for it,' Scott insisted. 'It's been going on too long and it's getting worse. Just go to the appointment and see what they say. If it's nothing, it's nothing. No harm done.'

I returned reluctantly to Stobhill, this time to the dermatology department, feeling a bit stupid for making such a fuss about a patch of eczema. It was the first time

I'd been in the hospital without having to go to the breast clinic and the thought cheered me up a little as I walked in.

The dermatologist had already been through my medical records and she questioned me a little about the dry skin before asking me to remove my shirt and bra and lie on the couch. She pulled an Anglepoise lamp closer to my chest to get a really good look and immediately said, 'Well, that's not a skin condition.'

I felt myself stiffen. What could it be in that case?

'Have you had a biopsy done on it?' she asked.

I was suddenly aware of my heart pounding fast in my chest.

'I don't want to frighten you,' she continued, 'but I think this might be related to the breast cancer.'

Oh God. Oh God, no.

'But they only told me last week that this was nothing to worry about,' I blurted, sweating now and struggling with my own panic.

'I'm sorry,' she said, 'but I know a skin condition when I see one, and this isn't a skin condition. I'll get a biopsy organised right away.'

Chapter 9

I fumbled with my bra, trying to fasten the hooks while shivering with fear and shock. I felt like I was plummeting backwards into the blackest hole, arms and legs flailing as I desperately tried to grab at something that would save me, but every horror of the past year kept flying past my eyes: surgery, chemotherapy, pain, hair loss. I just couldn't go through it all again. I couldn't face it. It couldn't be true. I thought I was here for some ointment, for God's sake!

'Just give me some ointment and I'll go,' a voice inside was screaming.

Within minutes I was ushered into another examination room, where I was asked to strip to the waist, and another doctor performed a needle biopsy on my breast. There was no one to hold my hand, no one to comfort me as the needle went in, and no one had even thought to ask a breast-care nurse to join us. The breast clinic wasn't far away. Why hadn't they brought someone I knew, someone who knew me? All my experience of that hospital in the past year didn't mean anything. I was starting from scratch, surrounded by unfamiliar faces, going through an all-too-familiar routine.

Then it was over and I was sitting in my car, shaking and sobbing and trying to pull myself together at least a bit before I called Scott.

'We'll give you a phone in about ten days, when the results come through,' the doctor told me.

They wouldn't even give me preliminary findings this time. I'd have to wait for the full detailed analysis. The same thing all over again. The same nightmare wait.

'Scott, they think it's the cancer again,' I stammered when he answered the phone and asked how it had gone.

'What do you mean?' he said. 'How can it be cancer all of a sudden?' I could hear his anger. 'You've been asking about that dry skin for months now. Everybody's told you it's fine. How can they be telling you it might be cancer now? These are people who know what cancer looks like. What the hell is going on?' He was furious, like I would be if I could only calm down enough. I couldn't find the strength for anger.

I phoned Mum and she just lost it. 'Don't you dare go into work,' she cried. 'Come straight here.'

At Mum's, we sat together trying to comfort one another and talk ourselves into believing it would probably turn out to be nothing. Here I was, in the honeymoon period of married life, with a full head of freshly grown hair and all the crazy exhilaration of having faced down my own mortality, and the cancer was back.

'It's not fair, Mum,' I was crying. 'This isn't fair.'

When the call finally came from the dermatology department ten days later, I was at work again. I heard all the same words that I'd heard the first time, that tired old script: 'Could you come up to the department so we can talk to you about your results?'

'You don't have to say any more. I know it's bad news,' I said.

'We would rather that you come up to the department,' was the clipped response.

So back we went, Scott, Mum and me, back to Stobhill. This time we were in a room in the dermatology department when they confirmed I had breast cancer again. The change of scenery didn't help much.

'So what happens next?' I asked the doctor.

She didn't have a clue. 'Well, you'll be referred back to the breast clinic and someone from the department will contact you very soon, I expect,' she said.

She was a dermatologist, not a cancer specialist. We'd have to come back another day for a chat with whoever would be handling the cancer treatment. We looked at one another in disbelief. We'd gone all the way up to the hospital and no one was available to talk to me. We left, holding one another, dazed and distraught all over again.

'We're not putting up with this,' Scott said. 'Let's go and find one of the breast-cancer nurses right now.'

And like he'd just spoken the wisest words ever uttered, we straightened up and marched directly to the breast clinic.

A nurse called Aileen came out to see us. I'd never met her before, but she was instantly sympathetic and kind, leading us into a private room and letting us vent our fury at everything that had happened. She promised she would get to the bottom of it.

'Give me the rest of the day to make some phone calls and get something sorted out and I'll give you a call tomorrow,' she said.

'What if it's secondary cancer, Scott?' I asked him as we drove home. 'Secondaries are incurable.'

He swallowed hard. 'Let's just wait and see what they say, Mandy,' he replied. 'We can't jump to conclusions.'

Aileen had said that if the cancer was still in my breast, it was classed as a localised tumour, not as secondary cancer, and I took some mild comfort from that.

Better in my breast than in my bones, I thought. Please, please don't let it be in my bones.

We were only home a couple of hours when Aileen phoned to say she'd arranged an appointment for me to see one of the oncologists the following day. That was when I first met Dr Sarah Hendry, the woman who has guided me through the very worst of my cancer journey. I have so much to thank her for. Through everything that I have thrown at her – pain, desperation and desolation, not to mention brain-taxing problems – she has never faltered and I have come to trust Dr Hendry literally with my life.

I wasn't sure what to make of her that first day, though. A petite woman with light brown hair framing her small face, she gave a businesslike smile as we walked into her office. She had my file on the desk in front of her, and she asked me a few questions about the dry skin.

I've learned, over the years since, that her softly spoken, matter-of-fact approach can seem a bit downbeat. 'Sometimes I wish she sounded more hopeful,' Scott grumbles from time to time. I know she finds it hard to tell me negative stuff, but she's always very controlled. I think it's her way of coping with the toughest part of her job.

Back then, though, unused to her manner, Scott and I were quickly becoming convinced that the outlook was dismal.

She peered at the red patch on my breast, puzzled by what she was inspecting. 'I've never seen anything like this before,' she said finally. 'I want to consult with my colleague on the best course of action.'

She arranged a CT scan, a bone scan and an MRI scan to check for any spread of the cancer. Mercifully, it hadn't travelled anywhere else and seemed to be entirely contained in that tiny piece of flesh just outwith my mastectomy scar.

'It can only have come from that bit of my natural breast they left behind,' I told Scott. 'Why didn't they just take it all away?'

I still don't know why they didn't. No one has ever really explained it fully.

After some discussion amongst the specialists, and much to my relief, chemotherapy was ruled out. I couldn't bear the prospect of losing my hair again. It had just reached a decent length, touching my collar.

'We'll use radiation to try and sterilise the whole area,' Dr Hendry explained. 'It seems the best way to get rid of any cancer cells which remain.'

I'd be given seven weeks of radiotherapy, five days a week, and at the highest possible dose they could give me. They had to plan it very carefully, marking with tiny 'tattoos' the exact spots where the radiation would be directed, then sliding me into a huge space-age machine for the actual 'zapping'. The process took no more than five minutes and I always spent much longer in the waiting room, queuing for the treatment, than I ever spent on the radiation table itself. I'd leave work around 3.30 p.m., drive to Gartnavel Hospital on the opposite side of Glasgow and be back home in the north of the city in time for dinner. At times my skin felt dry and itchy, like I had a bit of sunburn, but it was tolerable. It was only the weariness, the bone-heavy tiredness, that got to me every now and again.

'I think the radiotherapy is working already,' I said to Scott after the first couple of days' treatment. 'It might be my imagination, but I think the patch is shrinking.'

The rough skin was losing its angry red colour, and the spots were flattening out so that every time I looked at the breast, I felt a little flutter of joy that the problem was going away. When I went to see Dr Hendry for my weekly checks, she'd take out her ruler and carefully measure the area, then note the reduction in millimetres. It was four centimetres across when the treatment started, and thankfully, it shrunk a couple of millimetres every time.

'Do you think I'll be able to try for a family after I've finished radiotherapy?' I asked Dr Hendry. It was becoming my war-cry of late, and I would not let one appointment pass without asking for an opinion on my chances of motherhood.

'Let's just get the radiotherapy over with and we'll take it from there,' she'd say.

But I was thinking about my future, Scott's future, and since it had dawned on me that I might lose the chance to have kids, I'd suddenly developed a powerful desire to start a family.

Dr Hendry didn't really discuss this with me. Maybe she suspected it was already too late and was trying to spare me some more devastating news, which I could deal with more rationally once I was strong and healthy again. At that stage in my treatment – without knowing what lay ahead – it was probably the right thing to do. I had to concentrate on the radiotherapy, not be distracted by side issues. I could get over this.

Then Joan died, my chemo companion. Her husband called me out of the blue. I thought for a second he was going to ask if I could give her a lift somewhere. I hadn't seen her for a while, and I hadn't even bumped into her at the shops, but I didn't think much of it because Joan had been doing so well. But her cancer had come back, her husband told me, and she couldn't beat it this time. Her funeral was already past – she'd died a month or so earlier – but he'd just realised I probably didn't know. I wasn't sure what to say to the poor man. I didn't want to burden him with news of my recurrence too. I told him how very sorry I was and thanked him for thinking to let me know, but when I put down the phone, I felt gripped by fear. Joan was at exactly the same stage as me. I really thought she would be fine. I sat down and calculated how long she had got from her treatment. Approximately a year and a half. So what would I get? Another six months, maybe?

It's creeping closer, I thought.

At work the next day, my regular customer came in – the man who liked to tell me about his friend who had breast cancer. He'd avoided me at his last visit, a few weeks before, and Liz had cut his hair instead. He'd even waited till I was out of earshot before telling Liz that his friend had died; the cancer had recurred.

'He didn't want to tell you in case you got upset,' Liz told me later.

'Oh, that's the last thing I need,' I said. 'I don't want customers being too scared to talk to me.' I'd made up my mind to raise the topic with him myself the next time he came in, get it out of the way.

So when I saw him walk through the door that day, I waved him over to my chair. 'I heard about your friend,' I said, tucking a towel round his neck as he settled into the seat. 'Liz told me. That's really sad. I'm sorry to hear that. How are her family?'

He looked relieved I'd broken his tension. 'Aw, it's such a shame,' he said. 'She was a lovely woman, Joan.'

Joan? Not my friend? It couldn't be the same Joan, surely? But it was. I checked the details with him: same address, same surname, same grieving family. I couldn't believe what I was hearing. He'd told Liz weeks ago that she'd died and I hadn't a clue he meant my friend. Why hadn't I asked her name right at the start? I would have found out she was ill again, I could have phoned her, tried to support her. I could at least have gone to her funeral.

'And are you doing all right yourself?' he asked, not noticing my shock.

I was far from all right. Another brutal breast-cancer coincidence. There seemed to be one round every corner for me. I was so fed up with it all.

'I'm doing fine,' I said flatly, and changed the subject.

I finished radiotherapy two weeks before my twenty-ninth birthday, exactly two years since I had found the original lump in my breast. Scott booked a trip to London for us, a romantic break as a joint celebration of the *real* end of treatment and the final year of my twenties. It was such a sweet thought and I couldn't wait to go. Our honeymoon period had come to a kind of abrupt end, after all.

'I'm so looking forward to going away – just the two of us,' Scott said. 'We don't seem to have had a minute to relax since our honeymoon and I want to spend some time with my wife.'

I decided to give the house a really good clean before we set off because I hate coming home from holiday to find a mess waiting for me. I was gaily vacuuming the bedroom when I unconsciously put my hand up to my left shoulder, just where my neck meets my collar bone. I have no idea why I did this. Was I scratching an itch? Was I responding to a pain? I've tried so hard to remember what prompted me to rub it, but all I know is that I immediately felt a lump, a hard, pea-sized lump.

Ooh, that felt a bit strange, I thought.

I touched it again. There was definitely something there.

I called Scott into the room and he gently moved his fingers around my neck as I directed him.

'Mmm . . . it does feel like a lump to me,' he said quietly.

Well, it couldn't be cancer because I'd just finished radiotherapy. That would have killed off any cancer cells in there, wouldn't it? Anyway, why would breast cancer be in my neck? It didn't make sense. It must be something unrelated.

I phoned Mum to see what she thought and she made no attempt to think of other possible explanations.

'Don't bother going to London – go and get it checked out right now,' she said.

I told her not to be ridiculous, that was such an overreaction.

'If you call now, you'll at least get an appointment at the breast clinic for Monday morning,' she insisted.

No, no, no. I didn't want to cancel the trip. Scott had already paid for everything, and he'd put so much effort into it. Anyway, Monday was my birthday. I didn't want another birthday tumour. It would be too cruel.

'We're going to London,' I told her. 'Whatever it is can wait till we get back.'

Scott and I arrived at Glasgow Airport with both baggage and nerves more or less under control. I reasoned it was only three days. Nothing was going to change dramatically in three days, even if there was something sinister.

Scott was relieved, I could tell. I knew his thought process. He figured things couldn't be too bad or I would have cancelled. We wandered along Oxford Street, had a ride on the London Eye and went for a fabulous meal at a little restaurant in Chinatown, but I couldn't quite lose the fear that would churn my stomach every now and then. Dark thoughts were beginning to enter my head. I'd been having a bit of back pain for a few weeks, nothing unbearable but an ache in my lower back that made me groan when I straightened up. I'd assumed that I'd strained it in exercise class because I'd been doing a bit of weight training, so I hadn't worried about it much. Suddenly it leaped back into my mind, armed with a big alarm bell.

What if the back pain is related to the lump in my neck? If the cancer has spread, if it has reached the bones in my spine, it would explain the pain. How would I get through that?

Lying awake in the hotel room, Scott slumbering beside me, I was sweating with sheer terror. The recurrence had been easy to deal with because it was localised – it hadn't travelled; it was all neat and contained – but if the new lump, so far from the first, proved cancerous, there could be tumours anywhere in my body.

The next morning I gave in to my fears and phoned the breast clinic to make an appointment for Thursday, our first full day back home in Glasgow. I knew they'd fit me in. I'd gotten to know the nurses, Aileen and Helen, so well that they always bent over backwards to help me.

'You don't have to bother,' said Aileen. 'Your mum has already called on your behalf, so we've been waiting to hear from you. Come up on Thursday, whenever you get the chance and we'll squeeze you in.'

I went to work on the morning of my appointment, determined to try and function normally, but I have to admit I was struggling.

'Do you want me to come to the hospital with you?' Liz asked, realising I was a woman on the edge. 'We could go right now. Get it over and done with. It might help to have someone to keep you company.'

It was a chance to give Scott and Mum a break, and if everything was fine, at least I'd have spared them an afternoon of needless anguish. I was risking Mum's wrath by going without her. She always insisted she didn't need a break from my hospital appointments and was well able to cope with them all, thank you very much. I knew she'd be furious that I hadn't called with the details as I'd promised I would, but I was doing it for her sake. She would just have to see that. Plus I knew I could confess to Liz I was terrified.

'I'm really not looking forward to this,' I said, as we neared Stobhill Hospital. 'I know the drill now. They'll probably do a biopsy. It'll be painful, and then I'll have to sit around waiting to see what it all means.'

We were shown back into the room they always seem to take me to, the same place where they had diagnosed my first tumour, a treatment room off one of the wards. Just to complete my sense of *déjà vu*, in walked Mr Hansell and he was cheerful as ever as he examined me.

'Ah, yes,' he mused as he felt the neck lump. 'It's quite mobile . . . about the size of a pea.' He pressed gently with his fingertips around the area. 'I don't think this is anything to worry about,' he said, running his fingers along the contours of my neck, clearly checking for more dodgy spots. 'It might just be a wee gland that's become a bit swollen. That's pretty common.'

I'd heard that your glands swell when you've got a sore throat, so I kind of understood what he was trying to say, but I couldn't remember ever experiencing it myself and I was pretty sure I would have noticed a lump like this if it had appeared before. Still, he was the expert and he lifted my spirits with his upbeat conversation.

'We'll do a wee needle biopsy on it to be certain,' he said, pulling over a trolley of equipment.

The results took a week to come through, and once again I was at work when I got the call. I leaped at the sound of my mobile ringing.

'Can you come up and see us, please?' said the nurse.

I couldn't bear it. Not again. Not that phrase again. Jackie didn't hear a word of the conversation, but she must have sensed that I was going to collapse. Before I could fall, she was in front of me, her arms stretched out to catch my limp body.

Dr Hendry said little as she examined me a few days later; she was concentrating on her fingertips as she pressed her way round my breast and into my armpits. She lingered for quite a while on my right side.

Why is she spending so much time there? I wondered. All my surgery has been on my left side. Surely it hasn't spread to the right?

She read my thoughts: 'Yes, there's a small lump in your armpit here too,' she said. 'We'll get it biopsied, but I think we both know what it is.'

I couldn't think straight any more.

'Sit up and get dressed and we'll talk about what to do next,' she said, as if she was still deep in thought.

The cancer had spread to my lymph glands after all, she explained, and because they had found no trace of that at my original mastectomy, it must have travelled to the lymph nodes behind my breastbone, spreading both upwards to my neck and outwards to my opposite under-arm. The recent CT scans must have missed it. They only register potential problem areas if they are over a certain size. It must have been too small to show up at the time. If I hadn't happened to touch that swollen lymph gland in my neck, I might never have known until it was too late.

'We'll have to get a CT and a bone scan done again to make sure there are no other problems,' said Dr Hendry, 'and we'll do an MRI scan to look at your spine, just to check on any possible causes of your back pain. We'll also get you started on chemotherapy. Taxotere is probably the best option.'

My mind had emptied of all thoughts but one: I can't do this again.

Cancer again. Losing my hair again. This was only supposed to be a year out of my life. Where had that idea gone? It was dragging on and on and I didn't seem to be getting anywhere.

'Keep fighting it,' people would tell me, and I was. I was punching and kicking and spitting and scratching against cancer, believing I could knock it out, but it kept getting back up to have another go. Now it was getting the better of me, and for the first time I realised, I'm not going to win.

'Can't you operate to remove the lumps?' I asked Dr Hendry, steadying my voice to try and disguise my terror.

She shook her head. 'The neck is so small, and there are so many veins and arteries – it would be too difficult to take it away,' she said.

'Am I going to die?' I asked.

Her answer revealed the truth without saying it.

'Well, it's about keeping you well and maintaining your quality of life. It's about stabilising the cancer.'

Mum caught the significance at exactly the moment I did and she shattered before my eyes. I had inoperable cancer. They could do little for me. I would never, ever be free of it.

Please just say you can take it away. Please say you can operate. Please give me something. Don't leave this inside me. I thought my head was going to explode.

Undiluted and unsugared, the hard facts of my situation were indigestible. They would try to stabilise the cancer, but they couldn't cure it. It was going to kill me. I'd lost.

At home, Scott was angry. 'Why is this happening to us?' he snapped. 'Can't we just hear something good for once?' He wanted optimism and potential treatments, promises that there would be something else to try, a game plan.

'Dr Hendry's only doing her job, Scott,' I told him. 'It's not her fault. Anyway, I would rather know what I'm facing.'

She didn't know how much time I had left and she was right to prepare me. She was the bearer of bad news. It was as simple as that.

Dad gave me one of his pep talks. 'As long as you're living, you're fighting,' he said. 'Don't give up. You can't let this beat you. There are new treatments coming out all the time. There's always something round the corner and you don't know when it will be the right thing for you.'

Since my original diagnosis he'd taken to buying every daily newspaper, scouring them obsessively for stories on cancer breakthroughs or medical trials. If he spotted the smallest piece of information, he would be straight on the phone. 'Make sure you ask about that next time you're at the hospital,' he'd say. 'I've got the cutting here for you if you want to see it.' He'd become a cancer expert from the comfort of his own HGV cab and every time he found something new to report, it really did give me a bit of a boost.

This time was different, though. Dr Hendry's words kept coming back to me. 'Quality of life', 'keep you well', they echoed around my mind constantly, making it difficult to concentrate on anything and impossible to sleep, even when the GP prescribed some powerful tablets. As soon as my head hit the pillow, I was wide awake and tormenting myself with thoughts of my own funeral. What songs would I like? Where would it be? Who would read the eulogy? I was trying to carry on the only way I knew how, going to work, doing the house-work, going shopping – more than anything I wanted life to be ordinary – but I was down, lower than I'd ever been before, and I was aware of everyone tiptoeing around me, pitying me. 'Poor Mandy,' I imagined them whispering behind their hands. 'There's not much they can do for her now. It's only a matter of time.' I wanted to blot it out, close my eyes and dream myself somewhere beautiful where I was happy and healthy and nothing mattered.

The CT scan showed up three affected lymph glands in all: one in my neck, one under my right arm and an additional one in my left armpit. The inevitable phone call to my work, informing me of the results, was cut short this time.

'Don't tell me to come up to the hospital,' I barked. 'Just tell me the news. I know what to expect. I've been told what it's likely to be, so don't ask me to come up there to hear it again.'

The nurse was stopped in her tracks. 'Oh, oh . . . OK,' she stammered. 'These glands are cancerous, I'm afraid.'

'Fine, thanks,' I said, and went back to cutting tramlines into a schoolboy's hair.

The MRI scan and the bone scan were more worrying, so when they came back showing no spread of the cancer, I was stunned. At last some good news. Friends bombarded me with calls to say how delighted they were, but it didn't really make a blind bit of difference. Even if they had found a tumour somewhere else, the prognosis was unlikely to change and the treatment would be the same. Hold it at bay. Keep me well. Trouble was, by December, with Christmas fast approaching, I hadn't actually started on any treatment at all.

The chemotherapy, which I thought would begin immediately, seemed to have been put on hold.

'I'm getting really worried that I haven't started on chemo yet,' I confessed to Scott one night. 'What if the cancer is getting worse while I'm waiting for treatment to begin?'

Scott was stressed. 'Just keep phoning until you get an answer,' he said. 'You can't let yourself wait for ever with something like this.'

For three arduous weeks I barely heard a word from Dr Hendry, and whenever I called, her secretary told me there was still no news on a start. 'Dr Hendry is looking into something, but she'll be back in touch as soon as she has a date for you,' the secretary said.

Then, on 23 December, I got a phone call from Dr Hendry herself. 'I'm going to start you on a new drug along with the chemotherapy,' she said. 'I had to check that you would be suitable for this treatment and it seems that you are. So next week we'll be starting you on a drug called Herceptin.'

Timing

I felt my belly shudder. 'What was that?' I said cautiously. 'Did you feel anything, Scott?'

It was Valentine's night and we were snuggled up in bed watching TV, which was as romantic as it got five months into my pregnancy.

'No, I didn't feel a thing,' he said, gently pushing my head back on to the pillow and out of his line of vision. He hated it when I disturbed his viewing.

I nestled down again, resting my hand on my tummy this time, just in case. Then it happened again. A definite thud just below my ribs.

'Quick, put your hand here,' I said. 'Come on, baby, give Daddy a kick.'

And she did, a swift and firm kick right against Scott's hand.

'Oh wow, I felt it, I felt it!' he cried. 'It's amazing. She must know it's Valentine's Day.'

Our daughter was already demonstrating a remarkable sense of timing.

'She's going to be all right, Scott,' I said, cuddling into him. 'I just know it.'

Chapter 10

'Get the laptop out,' I said, turning to Scott as soon as I put down the phone on Dr Hendry. 'She's prescribing a new drug and I've never even heard of it. Put "Herceptin" into Google and see what comes up.'

Surely there would be something online about it, new treatment or not. Even in her trademark understated style, Dr Hendry had made it sound quite promising. Scott began setting up the laptop on the dining-room table. We weren't prepared for what we were about to see.

The search threw up thousands of sites. How had we missed this? We were always searching for the latest development in cancer treatments, but we'd never come across Herceptin before.

'Click on some of them, Scott,' I urged, as he scanned down the endless list of tantalising topics. Forums, blogs, medical sites, patients' groups – they were all referring to the new cancer wonder-drug. Every site we opened seemed to tell a more positive story. The more we read, the more elated we felt. Apparently, Herceptin was already widely available in the United States and in many European countries for the treatment of advanced or late-stage breast cancer but had only received a licence for use in the UK the previous year, in 2002.

'This sounds great,' said Scott, reading through a personal account on how Herceptin had turned some American woman's life round.

'I'm scared to get too excited about it,' I said, momentarily distracted by the frank description of my illness as 'late stage'. For some reason, it shocked me to see it spelled out in black and white like that. I was in the late stages.

God, this has really got to work for me, I thought, without drawing Scott's attention to the wording.

Some of the forums carried postings from breast-cancer patients who claimed to have been cured, their tumours wiped out by Herceptin. I almost fell off my chair.

'Am I reading this right?' I said.

Scott was screwing up his eyes as if he couldn't quite believe what he was seeing either. 'I don't get it,' he said. 'I mean, I don't think we can count our chickens here. We need to keep things in perspective. I just can't believe we didn't know about it before now.'

Of course, it didn't mean it would work for me. I couldn't afford to get carried away, but a small voice somewhere deep inside me was secretly screaming, 'I could be cured! I could be cured!'

Dr Hendry must have been beavering away behind the scenes for the past few weeks to try and get me Herceptin. She clearly hadn't wanted to mention it until she knew it was both appropriate and available. It was a hugely expensive treatment – about £20,000 a year for each patient – and though the Scottish Executive had given approval for its use on the NHS, individual health boards had the right to decide whether or not to prescribe it. Thankfully, NHS Greater Glasgow, the board covering my care, had agreed to fund my treatment, but other trusts were arguing that it was just too costly. It was what they call a postcode lottery.

When Scott told his boss that I was to start Herceptin treatment, the man was horrified. 'My sister was refused it,' he said. 'It's too dear, apparently.' Scott found himself apologising for my good fortune. It was a horrible situation.

'Somebody somewhere is making a decision whether it's good value for money to give a sick person new treatment,' I said. 'How can anyone say it's not cost effective to give someone a chance to live?'

Just a few months later the woman passed away.

I'm embarrassed to admit I had no idea what type of breast cancer I had until Herceptin appeared on the scene. Up until then it was enough for me to know I had the disease and it never struck me as important what particular form I'd developed. Turns out I had invasive ductal carcinoma, which was both oestrogen and progesterone negative. That meant my cancer was not related to hormone levels. The tumour was described as HER2 positive, a form of the disease that accounts for about twenty per cent of all breast-cancer cases. On the downside, these tumours seemed to grow more quickly than others, but my one stroke of good fortune was that HER2-positive cancers were responsive to Herceptin.

Apparently my body was producing too much of a protein called HER2, which basically encouraged cancer cells to grow. Herceptin was something called a 'monoclonal antibody', which blocked the HER2 and stopped it doing its damage. At least, that was as much as I was able to work out from some very complicated explanations on various websites.

Right at the start of my cancer treatment, I had wondered why the drug tamoxifen had been ruled out. I'd actually worried about that for quite a while. Dawn had been prescribed tamoxifen and lots of patients I'd come into contact with along the way had received it, but I'd readily accepted the explanation that it wasn't right for me.

Anyway, I thought naïvely, I probably don't need any follow-up medication. The doctors were so confident the mastectomy had got rid of all the cancer. Why should I need anything else?

In reality, tamoxifen was used in cases of hormone-related breast cancer. Not my type.

'Herceptin is a very new drug, but it seems to work well when given along with Taxotere chemotherapy,' Dr Hendry explained, 'so you'll be starting on both. For the initial treatment, you'll get the Herceptin first. Then the following day you'll get the Taxotere.'

I'd have to stay in the Beatson Oncology Centre over-night while they monitored my reaction to the Herceptin, and I'd have to get some heart tracings done to make sure it was strong enough to withstand the treatment. Apparently, Herceptin can put a bit of strain on the heart.

'But I don't expect you to have many side effects from Herceptin,' Dr Hendry went on. 'It targets the cancer cells and doesn't damage the healthy ones, so it shouldn't affect you like chemotherapy.'

I would receive six Taxotere treatments, one every three weeks, but I'd have Herceptin weekly.

'So how many Herceptin treatments will I need?' I asked.

'You will stay on Herceptin indefinitely,' said Dr Hendry. 'We'll just see how you get on with it. As long as it is working, we'll keep you on it. But you shouldn't think of it as a cure, Mandy. It's a way to keep the cancer under control.'

Scott and I were winding ourselves into a state of some excitement. We couldn't stop reading up about it, spending hours trawling the internet for more and more information about Herceptin. It was as if a huge beacon had been lit for us. We were in the black pits of our despair, but suddenly we had something to focus on, something to keep us motivated. It was exactly what we needed. Hope.

Herceptin is a clear liquid administered in exactly the same way as chemotherapy: attached to a shunt in the back of the hand. For my first treatment, I was to be given a 'loading' dose through a drip, which would only take about an hour and a half, and they'd keep an eye on me for a while afterwards. Dr Hendry came round to see how I was coping and found Scott and me chatting happily.

'I'm feeling great,' I beamed. 'No problems at the moment – touch wood.'

She pulled up a chair and started briefing me about the chemotherapy I'd be having the following day. 'Taxotere is a powerful one,' she said. 'Your side effects might be a bit worse than they were the last time.'

That put a bit of a dent in my positive attitude, but chemotherapy held few fears for me. Been there, done that.

'For instance, your periods will probably stop,' Dr Hendry went on.

That wasn't particularly surprising either. They'd vanished for a while when I'd started the last course of chemotherapy, but they'd returned after a few weeks.

'Yes, I know that has happened to you before,' Dr Hendry continued. I suddenly twigged that she was trying to tell me something. 'But I don't think they will come back this time . . . I don't think they'll come back at all,' she said quietly. 'It means you won't be able to have children.'

I gasped. Scott drew back into his chair. Where had that bombshell come from? She'd just lobbed a hand grenade at us.

'Are you OK?' she asked cautiously. 'I'm so sorry to have to give you news like this. It's just that there's so much treatment ahead of you. And you've been through so much already . . .'

We couldn't speak. We were frozen, dumbstruck.

Dr Hendry's eyes explored the floor for a few moments. When she raised them to mine again, I saw real sadness. She was hurting for us.

'I can arrange for you to see a counsellor if you think it would be of any help,' she said. 'Have a think about it.'

I started to cry when she finally walked away. Scott sat on the bed beside me, his hand resting on mine, neither of us quite knowing why this piece of news had blown us off our feet. We were well and truly floored. All our hopes were being stripped from us one by one. We weren't being permitted any trace of a normal future. Just when we'd allowed ourselves to think there was a chance, a slim chance we could go on, carry on with our married life and maybe even start a family at some point, it was all snatched away from us.

'Scott, I really think we should start seeing a counsellor,' I suggested, when he arrived to collect me the next day. 'One of the nurses came round to tell me more about it this morning and I think it sounds like a good idea. We've got so much to deal with. Maybe we could do with a bit of help.'

Scott shrugged. 'I'm not sure,' he said. 'It's not really me, is it?' He carried on packing away my toiletries. Then he added, 'But I'll do it if you really want me to. If you think it will help you.'

It wasn't his style to discuss his emotions with anyone, never mind a stranger, but I desperately wanted Scott to open up. Since the cancer had come back, he'd retreated even further into his own world, grown quiet and distracted, hiding from difficult discussions and awkward situations. I couldn't reach him. I tried to provoke him into reaction. I even cracked a few tasteless jokes in an attempt to force something out of him.

'You never know . . .' I said one night as he got ready to go out with his pals '. . . this time next year you might be able to go out with your mates and not worry about your wife sitting at home waiting for you. You'll only have to worry about the two cats.'

I thought he was going to explode.

'Don't say things like that!' he yelled. 'That's not even funny.'

I protested, 'But we need to talk about things.'

He was having none of it. 'Well, we don't need to talk about things like that,' he shouted, storming upstairs away from me and sending the terrified Coco and Kia diving for cover in the process.

There were things I wanted to say to him, things I wanted to hear him say, things you don't say every day to your partner, but you don't just launch into emotionally charged conversations like that, do you? You plan for them, lead up to them. The counselling was worth a go if only to help with that preparation process. So I made an appointment to go and see a specialist at the Royal Infirmary and Scott reluctantly agreed to go with me.

'Just be honest and it'll be fine,' I whispered to him as we waited to be seen.

He shrugged and turned away.

The counsellor, a thirty-something woman called Lorraine, was friendly and down-to-earth. She welcomed us both and had a brief chat with us before addressing Scott. 'Would you mind waiting outside while I speak to Mandy on her own for a while?' she said.

'Is that OK with you?' he asked me, before seizing the chance to head for the exit.

'Right, Mandy, tell me a bit about how you're feeling,' she said, as Scott closed the door behind him.

And I told it all.

'I actually think I'm coping,' I said. 'I think I've come to terms with my situation. I'm more upset about what my mum and dad are going through, and what Scott is going through.'

I thought Mum and Dad were at least talking to each other about the latest setback. It was such a strain on them that they preferred to avoid discussing it with me and to pretend everything was OK, but the occasional thing one of them said made me think they had been talking privately. I was more concerned about Scott, with his tendency to internalise everything, keeping all his fears to himself. I knew he wasn't sharing his feelings with anyone else. Mum had told me she'd tried to speak to him a couple of times, but he hadn't engaged at all.

If Scott ever confided in anyone about anything, it was me. We'd been together for fifteen years, since I was fifteen and he was seventeen, when I was a daft schoolgirl and he was a dafter shop assistant working in a trendy clothes shop in Glasgow called the Athlete. We were meant to be together; we both knew that because our best attempts at destroying our relationship over the years had always failed. To be fair, I was the reluctant party in the beginning. I didn't even like him much at first and I'd no intention of calling him when he offered me his phone number in a nightclub. I'd sneaked out with my pals that night, telling Mum and Dad I was going for a sleepover at a friend's but heading out dancing instead. My parents would have hit the roof if they'd found out I was an underage clubber. They trusted me to be sensible, and I was, but I liked a bit of excitement too and conning some bouncers into thinking we were over eighteen was a real coup.

That particular night we bumped into Scott and his friends and got chatting. He pursued me relentlessly for weeks and wore me down until I agreed to go out with him. He grew on me quickly and we went out for a while. Then he got fed up with me and broke my heart. We split, got engaged, then split again and still we had somehow ended up as man and wife. He was my only serious boyfriend. My one love. And I was his. We thought we were inseparable. Suddenly we could see that we weren't and Scott had no idea how he was supposed to accept it. He couldn't share that with anyone, he just couldn't open up, so he would shoulder the burden alone, even though he was in deep, deep pain.

I told the counsellor, 'Once, when we were having an argument, he said to me, "You're the one going through this, and it must be terrible for you, but no one ever asks how I'm feeling." ' And it was true. Everyone was concerned for me. Scott could take care of himself. Or that's what people thought.

'Well, Mandy,' said Lorraine, when I got to the end of my spiel, 'you're the first person who has come here and spoken for the full hour about other people. You've only discussed your family. You haven't once said how you feel about your illness.'

I felt a bit foolish. I'd done the wrong thing.

'I'm sorry,' I sighed. 'I just don't think I'm the one having trouble dealing with this.'

She nodded thoughtfully. 'I think we'll see if Scott will come and speak to me on his own,' she said. 'What do you think about that?'

I was so relieved. She understood.

'But while you're thinking about other people,' Lorraine added, standing up as if to bring the conversation to an end, 'don't forget about yourself.'

Scott did go back and see Lorraine for a couple more sessions, although he wasn't particularly happy about it and never once mentioned what he discussed there. Still, at least his defensive wall had been breached; someone was making him open up a little. I felt like I'd achieved something.

'We need to be able to tell each other how we feel,' I said one night, as we lay in bed together.

He was so quiet I thought he may have already drifted off to sleep. Then he spoke: 'I'll try,' he said, and I knew not to ask for any more.

The cancer was threatening to tear us apart, but I would fight it for all I was worth, with any weapon at my disposal. Trouble was, handling the weapons was pretty dangerous in itself. In fact, the treatment looked like it might kill me first.

Guilt

'Everyone probably knows by now that breastfeeding is the best possible start you can give your baby.'

The midwife in the antenatal class was using a little naked dolly to demonstrate the correct way to hold a baby while breastfeeding. She was cupping her fully clothed left boob and turning the doll on to its side to face it. One of its legs had fallen off, which was a bit distracting.

'Your baby will not need anything but breast milk for the first six months of its life,' she continued, 'and the very first few feeds you give your baby – immediately after birth – are absolutely packed with antibodies and nutrition, so it's very important to at least give it a try after delivery.'

Most of the women in the class were nodding in approval, patting their bulging tummies as if to reassure the little one inside they'd be getting the best start possible when they finally appeared in the world. I was squirming and could feel myself getting hotter and hotter. I'd been on a breastfeeding guilt-trip for weeks, ever since I'd started the classes. Posters all around the antenatal rooms praised the merits of breast over bottle. 'There's nothing fitter than a breastfed nipper,' they told me in three-inch letters, so I couldn't possibly ignore the message. But there was absolutely no chance I'd be doing it. Twenty-eight weeks pregnant and I was a bad mum already.

Honestly, if you believed all the literature the midwives crammed into our pregnancy-swollen hands every week, breast milk could practically reverse global warming and bring about world peace. Ear infections, colic, diarrhoea, allergies, even some types of cancer, breastfed babies would avoid them all. They'd grow up smarter too. Surely only a terminally selfish mum or a bone-idle one would deprive her baby of such a wonderful start in life. My poor unborn daughter.

Chapter 11

It was January 2004 when the weekly Herceptin treatments started and I was relieved to find they didn't give me any problems whatsoever. I'd been warned I might develop mild flu-like symptoms – sniffles or sweating – while it was being administered, or very quickly afterwards, but I didn't suffer a single sneeze. The Taxotere, on the other hand, floored me from the off. It was given by drip instead of by syringe and the solitary bag of clear liquid looked as unthreatening as water as it dangled on the drip-stand. It soon revealed its true nature, though.

'I've got a strange metallic taste in my mouth,' I complained to Mum on the way home from hospital after the initial treatment. 'It's quite disgusting.'

Nothing I ate could mask the sensation. I was snacking on strongly flavoured foods like curries or salt and vinegar crisps, but the horrible taste overpowered them all. Heartburn started quickly too, just a few hours after I arrived home. Then the lethargy hit me so badly it was a huge effort to stand up.

Oh great, I thought, making my way slowly upstairs to

bed. This is going to be every bit as bad as the last time. I'm going to get every possible side effect.

Over the next few days I developed mouth ulcers, nausea and an excruciatingly sore throat, so I moped around the house feeling utterly lousy and thoroughly sorry for myself.

'I always feel awful for a few days, then start to get back on my feet again,' I reassured Scott, who was beginning to worry that I didn't seem to be improving. 'Remember what I was like the first time I had chemo? I just need a bit of time.'

Spoken like a true chemo veteran. I knew everything. Except I'd forgotten one crucial point. Around ten days after treatment, levels of infection-fighting white blood cells drop and you feel pretty grotty until they start rising again. That's normal. Sometimes, though, they drop to dangerously low levels – a condition called neutropenia – leaving you at very high risk of catching an infection. In severe reactions, you're susceptible to every bug going and they'll really wipe you out if you catch one. Every chemo patient knows to be alert and watch out for possible symptoms. Except mule-headed me.

'Don't forget to call us right away if your temperature starts to rise,' the nurse had reminded me after the first dose, wise words that went in one ear and out the other.

'You look absolutely terrible,' said Scott, as he brought me a glass of water to try and soothe my raw throat.

I could barely swallow for the pain. Nearly a week after the chemo, I was actually feeling worse than ever.

'It's all right,' I maintained weakly. 'It was probably quite a high dose. That will be why it's taking me longer to get over it. I'll ask if they can reduce it next time.'

I didn't have a scrap of energy and my bones ached with tiredness. I had terrible diarrhoea, so I had to drag myself back and forth from the loo. One minute I was sweating so much that my clothes stuck to my skin, the next wrapping myself in my dressing gown to try and get warm.

On Wednesday morning – exactly seven days after my first Taxotere session – it was time to go back to hospital for my Herceptin treatment, but I just couldn't get myself moving. Mum arrived to collect me and found me still lying on the couch.

'What's wrong with you?' she asked tentatively, watching Coco and Kia step gracefully through the bits and pieces I'd left scattered around the living room, too tired to put them away. 'It's not like you to go without make-up.'

'I don't feel very well, Mum,' I groaned. 'I haven't even had a shower yet. I think I've got a cold.'

She held out her hands to pull me up to my feet. 'Come on,' she said, heaving me upright. 'We've really got to get going. I'll help you dress. You'll feel better once you've got your make-up on.'

With Mum doing most of the work, I was finally ready to go and I clung to her arm as she manoeuvred me out to the car.

'Well, what side effects have you had from the chemo?' The nurse smiled as she busied herself preparing to take some blood samples.

'Erm . . .' I hesitated, slipping down into the treatment chair and pressing my cheek gratefully against the cool sides. It was so comfortable. It made me want to sleep again. I forgot about answering her.

The nurse looked up quizzically, clearly waiting for me to speak. 'Mandy, are you all right?' she asked.

Mum answered for me: 'She's not well at all. She's been saying she's got a cold.'

The nurse snatched a digital thermometer from the trolley and popped it into my ear. 'Right, your temperature is going through the roof,' she said calmly. 'It's nearly forty. I'll get you into a bed and fetch the doctor.'

She indicated to Mum that she'd need a hand to move me and between the pair of them, they lifted me out of the chair and guided me in the direction of a bed further down the ward. At that moment it looked like the most wonderfully welcoming bed in the world. I wriggled deep down into the cold, crisp sheets, pulling them around me to try and find some warmth. I was freezing, my teeth chattering. I just wanted to sleep.

The nurse left to go and find the doctor, while Mum

stroked my brow, softly chiding that she'd told me to come to hospital before now and had known there was something wrong.

'Just leave me alone for a minute or two,' I mumbled, no longer able to open my eyes.

The nurse came back and started fussing around the bed, plumping my pillows and shaking out the sheets, and generally just disturbing me. 'No, Mandy, don't go to sleep now,' she was urging. 'You'll have to stay awake until the doctor gets here.'

I was so comfortable, so drowsy, I must have drifted off.

Suddenly a male doctor was standing over me, gently shaking my shoulder to bring me back to consciousness. 'Come on, Mandy,' he was saying. 'I need to have a look at you. Your mum says you've not been feeling very well.'

I tried to force my eyes to stay open. 'I'm all right,' I told him. 'I've just got a bit of a sore throat and I'm really sleepy.'

He carried on, checking my temperature, feeling around my jawbone. I opened my mouth to let him take a look at my throat – and that's when he blew his top.

'This is ridiculous!' he scolded. 'Don't you realise how sick you are? You could have been dead if you hadn't come in here today.'

Mum gave a little whimper of fright.

'Your body could start shutting down,' he continued.

'You have no immune system. Your organs could start to fail.'

I couldn't be bothered listening to his telling-off. All I wanted to do was sleep. 'Let me rest for a while and I'll be fine,' I tried to tell them, but no one seemed to hear.

The doctor started calling out instructions: 'Let's get her hooked up to antibiotics right now, but we'll have to transfer her to the Beatson. Get an ambulance organised.'

An ambulance? Ooh, it must be serious, I thought hazily. I've never been in an ambulance before.

Mum was traumatised, shaking like a leaf as she continued stroking my head and telling me I was going to be fine. 'They won't let me come in the ambulance with you,' she said in my ear, 'but I'll follow you in the car. I'll see you when we get to the Beatson.'

I often wonder how many motorists she traumatised along the way.

At 1 p.m. I was lying on a trolley-bed in a corridor at the Beatson, a drip-stand at one side feeding antibiotics into me, Mum at the other, sitting on a plastic chair. Scott joined her in the vigil as soon as she managed to get a message through to him. I lay there till 9 p.m.

'Can you please tell me when you'll be moving my daughter to a ward?' Mum begged the nurses who came to check my temperature and top me up with paracetamol.

'We're trying to find her a private room,' she was told. 'Shouldn't be too long now.'

The next thing I remember is coming to in a small room off cancer ward G6, the ward where I would spend most of that year. Just as well I didn't know that then. Cancer units are never particularly cheerful places, but I developed a particular hatred for ward G6, where everyone seemed so much older and so much sicker than I thought I was.

During that first stay it took about five days of intravenous antibiotics before I started feeling a little better, though my throat remained dry and rough, and I was still being held hostage to the loo by diarrhoea. A further five days on and I woke up one morning to find my pillow covered in long, dark hair.

Ah, so I'm not getting to keep my hair either, I thought ruefully. So much for the cold cap, then.

I had tried out the cold-cap technique of preventing hair loss during chemo after hearing about some women who'd managed to get right through treatment without losing their hair. Dr Hendry explained that chemotherapy works by killing off fast-growing cells, like cancer cells. Trouble is, it damages other healthy, fast-growing cells too, like the ones in hair follicles or in the lining of the mouth. That's why your hair falls out and you get mouth ulcers. The theory goes that by wearing an ice-cold close-fitting cap while the drug is being administered, the head stays cool, the blood flow is slowed and less damage is done. That's the theory anyway. I knew well enough that smart ideas don't always work in practice. I still had nasty memories of all those ice lollies I'd sucked during my first chemo. I'd never eaten a single one since.

Still, Dr Hendry knew how desperate I was to hang on to my hair this time. It had grown long enough to disguise the fact that I'd ever lost it, so when she suggested I give the cold cap a go, I thought it was worth a try. It seemed to work quite well with some chemos and not at all with others. Taxotere patients found it reason- ably effective, apparently, but using it meant suffering the indignity of sitting, for the best part of three hours, wearing what looked like the hood of a wetsuit, a dark blue Lycra cap that came right down over my ears and fastened under my chin with Velcro.

The nurse took it straight from the freezer and plonked it on my head and the icy cold instantly took my breath away. She tucked cotton wool around my ears and forehead, but my head still felt like it had frostbite for a few minutes, then strangely seemed to be burning before it went completely numb.

I do not care if I look like a prat, I thought, clenching my teeth. If this works, I'll take it every time.

The nurse changed the cap for a fresh one several times each session to make sure the temperature of my head didn't rise. 'It seems to work best if you manage to keep it on for an hour after the treatment is over,' she told me, so I'd doggedly kept the thing on.

And here I was, two weeks later, gathering up the first small pile of hair.

'I'm sure they'll reduce the dose for my next chemo,' I told Scott, as he finally packed my belongings to take me home. 'It won't be as bad next time.'

I was discharged from hospital four days before I was due to have my second Taxotere treatment and Scott was worried that I wasn't well enough for another one. The doctor agreed with me, though, that I would probably be OK with a lower dose, so the appointment went ahead as planned.

'I won't bother with the cold cap this time,' I said, as I sat in the chemo chair, pulling my fingers through the remaining hair and watching it fall to the ground.

'Stop doing that,' said the nurse, who was hanging the bag of Taxotere on a drip-stand. 'You're making it worse. Your hair might be thinning, but that doesn't mean it's all going to fall out. I think you should give the cold cap another try.'

So I did, but a few days later I was on the phone to Liz giving her the news I knew she was dreading.

'You're going to have to shave my head again,' I said. 'It's coming out in clumps now and the cold cap is just prolonging the agony.'

Poor Liz. She didn't even put up a fight. She knew it was pointless. Scott drove me to Clippers under cover of darkness on a cold, dank Saturday evening that was as miserable as my mood. Liz and Jackie had shut up shop by the time we arrived. The metal shutter was pulled down over the windows, but the lights were on inside and I was terrified one of my customers would pass by and see what was going on.

'There are gaps in those shutters,' I said to Scott. 'If someone looks in, they'll see me.'

Scott sighed. 'Mandy, who's going to be peering through shutters on a night like this? They've got better things to do, I'm sure.'

So in we went.

'Look how bad it is this time,' I told the girls, tugging gently on sections of hair till they came away in my grasp. 'It's all coming out at the same time, so it looks even worse than it did last time.'

In my stressed and paranoid state, I could have sat there and pulled out every single hair. Liz stopped me and quickly began cutting the bulk of the hair away with scissors.

'I don't have any choice,' I told them. 'I can't go on like this.' The long auburn wig I'd bought during another uncomfortable visit to Judy Plum's hadn't filled me with confidence when I chose it. It was artificial hair, nylon probably, and even though the texture was quite convincing, it just didn't move like real hair. It didn't swing freely – it wasn't light and loose like the real thing – so if I turned my head, all the hair seemed to move as one. I'd looked into genuine-hair wigs, but they were extortionately expensive – around £500 each – and my NHS voucher didn't stretch to that. The wig selection it covered only went up to about £130, so I'd resigned myself to another artificial one, another 'best fit' option.

Sitting in the salon, surrounded by mirrors, I could see from every angle that it was a disaster. I gathered it at the nape with a clasp and put on my trusty baseball cap, then went to the back of the shop, collected the brush and pan, and began sweeping up my own hair.

'What do you think you're doing?' cried Jackie, jumping up to block my way. 'We'll do that. You get off home.'

'Let's go to the cinema,' Scott suggested, as we hurried back to the car. 'Maybe that will cheer you up a bit. We could go for something to eat first, if you like.'

I didn't really feel like a night out, but perhaps it would lighten my mood. I called Mum and Dad and invited them along.

'Your dad says he'll drive us all,' Mum added helpfully. 'That way, you and Scott can have a drink.'

I can't bear Dad's driving. He's used to steering ten-ton lorries down some of the most dangerous roads in Europe, but put him behind the wheel of an ordinary car and ask him to drive across Glasgow and you'll leave your fingernails embedded in the seat in terror. He behaves exactly as if he's in a lorry cab and other road users had better get out of his way. I was in no emotional state to cope with a *Wacky Races*-style trip through the city, but I didn't feel up to objecting too strenuously.

'Mum, please have a word with him and make sure he goes slowly,' was as much as I said before we headed out, me pulling anxiously at the wig.

Scott and I sat in the back seat, eyes firmly on the road ahead as we seemed to race close behind other cars and take corners too tightly.

'Will you please slow down!' I pleaded, as we veered to overtake yet again and a van seemed to miss us by inches.

'I'm not going too fast, Mandy,' Dad protested.

As I saw it, though, every turn we made took us into fresh danger.

'Stop – just stop – that car nearly hit us!' By this time I was screaming, crying, distraught. 'Just take me home, Scott,' I sobbed. 'I want to go home.'

Mum was yelling at Dad, 'Look what you've done now! Why couldn't you just slow down?'

'What have I done?' he asked, confused and upset. 'Tell me what I've done.'

Scott started shouting at him too: 'You know what kind of day she's had, Joe! She doesn't need this. Why can't you just take it easy?' Scott had never had a go at my parents before, but he was furious. The car was in chaos.

'Right, I think we should all calm down,' Mum

interrupted. 'Mandy, do you want to carry on or should we just go home?'

I knew I'd overreacted and I didn't want to make things worse. 'Let's go on to the restaurant,' I said.

Dad drove the rest of the way under my watchful gaze, checking every few minutes that I approved of his technique.

I regretted my decision to carry on as soon as we walked into the pizza place. At the bar stood a group of girls in their early twenties, all glammed up in tight-fitting trendy outfits. Each of them had long, glossy hair, which they tossed around their shoulders as they posed and postured. We had to stand beside them to wait for a table and I knew they were staring at my wig.

'Don't touch,' Mum mouthed at me, as I patted it nervously to make sure it hadn't moved.

Every time I turned round I seemed to catch the eye of one of the girls and they'd look away too quickly, caught in the act of ogling the sick woman's hairpiece. I'd made an effort to look good before we left home, changing into smart jeans and heels, doing my make-up, styling the wig as best I could, but the reaction of the girls made it clear. I didn't look like them. There was something wrong with me.

It was such a relief to shrink into the darkness of the cinema, where I could be completely inconspicuous and the film – a rom-com called *Stuck On You* – was lightweight enough to make me smile. Even so, I knew it had been a mistake to go out at all. I had underestimated the impact of losing my hair for a second time. The cancer was back, everyone could see that, and there was still another six months of treatment to get through before I'd even know if I would live. What did I have to look forward to? My third chemo? Dad had taken the brunt of my rage against the cancer, which wasn't exactly fair, but when you're busy fighting for your life, you don't want to pop your clogs in a car crash, do you?

I bought a digital thermometer from Boots to keep a check of my temperature in case I developed another chemo infection, though I was quite sure that the first had merely been an unfortunate blip. Apart from the loss of my hair, the second one had been more or less event-free, so when I arrived for my third, I wasn't too concerned about side effects. Three days afterwards, as I lay on the couch shivering, I knew it was happening all over again. My temperature was borderline – about thirty-eight – and I was beginning to feel truly awful.

It was Saturday night and Scott was working late at the Chinese restaurant, so I knew I should call the emergency number the hospital had given me, the one that took me straight through to ward G6, but I couldn't face it. They would tell me to pack a bag and come straight in, ready for yet another ten-day stay in that terrible place.

Best wait and see if I pick up, I thought to myself, but by the time Scott came home, just before midnight, I was lurching between shivers and sweats, my throat as dry as sandpaper, my temperature nudging thirty-nine.

'You really need to get to hospital,' Scott said softly. 'You know you need antibiotics.'

So I was back in again, and in I stayed, hooked up to a drip, bald and helpless, and totally crushed.

The old woman in the bed opposite must have been in her late eighties, small and wizened. I would watch her and wonder how she was hanging on when she looked so fragile, like if you blew on her too hard you might snuff her out completely. She never seemed to have any visitors, so once I started feeling stronger, I would drag my drip-stand over to her bed and ask if there was anything I could do, but her voice was barely audible.

What a way for a long life to end, I thought. All alone in this godforsaken place, staring at the ceiling.

My bed always seemed to be surrounded by visitors, and when I was feeling well enough to get up and dressed, I was regularly mistaken for a visitor myself.

'See – I'm not ill enough to be in here,' I would tell the nurses. 'There's no need to keep me in any longer.'

I wasn't like the other patients, pensioners most of them, who'd shuffle past on their way to the toilets, oxygen masks partially obscuring the pain on their shrunken faces. At night, as I tried to blot out the noisy toing and froing of the nurses, I could hear the hissing of the oxygen cylinders from nearby beds.

Dr Hendry came to see me just before I was discharged. 'This chemo definitely isn't agreeing with you,' she said. 'Let's see how you get on with the fourth session.'

She was altering my Herceptin treatment, from a weekly regime to once every three weeks. I'd missed a couple of sessions already while I'd been ill, so she thought we may as well relax things a little and stick to a formalised three-weekly routine.

'Hopefully you'll find the chemotherapy a bit easier next time,' she added. 'That way, you'll be well enough for the Herceptin as planned and things should settle down into a pattern.'

I was confident that would work. Surely the same thing wouldn't happen again after the fourth treatment? But it did.

It was a sunny spring morning and I had managed to go to work. I wasn't exactly feeling great, but I was stubbornly trying my best to ignore the familiar symptoms in the hope they'd go away. I suppose I knew I shouldn't have gone to the salon, but I was determined not to give in, convincing myself there was always a chance things wouldn't be so bad this time. Clippers was busy with kids as the schools were on holiday, but I couldn't summon up the energy to speak to any of my customers. Anne, the boss, was in the shop and I could tell she was concerned.

'You really don't look well,' she kept saying. 'You should go home to your bed for a while. Why don't you take the rest of the day off?'

I brushed her away with a curt 'I'm fine', but everywhere I turned the mirrors told a different story. I watched my face grow paler as the shadows around my eyes darkened, but I hadn't taken my thermometer to work, so I couldn't confirm I was running a fever, and as long as I couldn't confirm it, I wouldn't believe it. Jackie kept opening the door to let fresh air into the packed shop, but I could tolerate only a few minutes before I was shivering.

'Do you mind if I put the heating on for a while?' I asked her, and she looked at me like I was crazy.

Every haircut seemed to take an hour and taxed my strength to the limit, but I made it through to closing time, much to everyone else's amazement.

I can't be too bad if I managed my whole shift, I thought to myself, driving home in the sunshine with my jacket fastened right up to my neck and the car heating on at full blast. Even so, maybe I should pop in to see the GP on the way home, I thought.

The receptionist looked up at me and immediately rushed through to get Dr Barrie. My favourite GP, Dr Barrie has always been sympathetic and I knew she wouldn't overreact. At the same time, she doesn't pull any punches.

'Mandy, I could fry eggs on your head,' she said, as she took the thermometer from my mouth. It read forty-two degrees. 'You're seriously ill. We need to get you an ambulance.'

'No, I don't want one,' I moaned, railing against the inevitable stay on ward G6, but she was already on the phone to the Beatson, priming them for my arrival.

'OK, I'll let you make your own way,' she said. 'It will probably be quicker anyway. Get Scott to drive you and promise me you'll go straight there.'

I hesitated, wondering how long I could put it off without her knowing.

'Promise me, Mandy,' she insisted. 'This is serious. I can't believe you've been at work in this state. Your immune system is shot. You could be picking up all sorts of germs from your customers, especially the children.'

I hadn't thought of that before, though it was blindingly obvious now she'd mentioned it. Kids are walking germ factories.

Scott was at home by the time I arrived. 'Jesus, you look terrible,' he said.

'I'm being sent back in,' was as far as my explanation went before I slumped beside him, longing to sleep.

So there I was, back in ward G6. It felt like purgatory. The nurses were lovely, but whatever wonders they were performing to try and repair my body, it was all but undone by the psychological damage of just being there.

Three days into my antibiotics treatment I was feeling well enough to sit up in bed, and at around one o'clock in the morning I was flicking through a magazine, looking for something remotely interesting to read. When I wasn't drugged into oblivion, I could never sleep soundly in ward G6, so I liked to skim through celebrity magazines well into the early hours, hoping they'd finally bore me into slumber. The ward was always noisy at night. Nurses on the night shift behave like it's midday, chatting to each other as they bustle around taking readings or dispensing drugs, but on this particular night a commotion further down the ward distracted me from an article on the slimming secrets of the Spice Girls. A woman was shouting and crying while nurses fussed around her. I found myself listening in, trying to interpret what was going on without being able to see it. I couldn't make out what she was saying at first, but she seemed to be thrashing around and several nurses were trying to pacify her.

'You're OK, you're fine – just calm down,' a nurse was saying in a raised voice, as if to try and shout through the patient's brainstorm.

Her cries were getting louder and more frantic, like she was fighting off the nurses, and I suddenly understood what she was saying: 'Help me! I'm choking! I'm choking!' My blood ran cold. I strained to see who it was, but in the dimly lit ward I couldn't make out exactly which bed the noise was coming from. Her terror and pain were reaching me in waves, though, making me cover my ears. 'Help me. Please help me,' she was shouting, really shouting, scared and desperate.

Oh, someone do something, I thought. She's panicking.

The nurses moving back and forward between her bed and the nursing station were talking urgently about transferring her to a private ward and calling her family. I felt my heart tighten as I realised what was happening. She was dying.

I could only guess they were probably trying to sedate her, calm her down a little, but she seemed to know exactly what was going on. She knew her life was ebbing away and she was petrified, clinging to nurses like they could keep her in the world if only she held on to them tightly enough, begging them with her last breaths to save her. I looked around the beds nearest me, but all the other patients were still asleep, spared the waking nightmare. Soon I heard visitors arrive who must have been her relatives because the nurses were in the family room with them, a little closer to me, and talking in hushed tones. Lots of voices, lots of discussion that I still couldn't quite hear, but the woman's wails continued to penetrate the twilight gloominess. Then it went quiet and all I could hear were muffled voices talking quietly and calmly. Someone was crying, but a soft, sad cry devoid of panic or fear. I knew what that meant. It was over for her. She was gone.

The ward clock said 4.30 a.m. and I was the one crying. I was the one more scared than ever. All I could think was, Is that what's ahead for me? Not a peaceful, dreamlike passing. No gentle slide into a better place.

Over and over again the nurses had told her, 'You're all right, you're going to be OK,' but they'd known she was dying and so had she. That shocked me more than anything. She seemed so aware of her own final moments and she didn't want to go. I didn't know what she was suffering from. She could have had any form of cancer – ward G6 catered for the whole sorry range – but it was unbearable to contemplate. Lying in the dark too afraid to move, I would have given anything to jump up and run away into the night.

The air fizzed with distress, even as the drama subsided and the nurses began to pull themselves back together. My drip ran out and the alarm sounded to alert a member of staff, so a nurse called Rosemary, with whom I was quite friendly, came to connect up a new supply of antibiotics. She noticed immediately that I was upset.

'Did you hear that?' she asked, tilting her head in the direction of the woman's bed.

'All of it,' I said, and she started crying too.

She held my hand as I told her how terrified I felt, how

I was too young to be going through this, how I didn't think I could cope. I knew I wasn't going to get better, but was I going to die like that woman had? Rosemary listened to me for ages, weeping along with me as I let it all go. Then she gave me a sleeping pill and stayed at my bedside until I finally fell asleep, still holding her hand.

First thing in the morning I dragged my drip-stand to the public telephone and called home. 'Scott, get me out of here,' I said. 'I'm not staying a minute longer.'

'What do you mean? You can't leave right now,' he said. 'You're in the middle of your treatment.' We knew I'd need at least a week of intravenous antibiotics to get over the infection caused by the chemotherapy.

'I don't care,' I said. 'Being in here is making me worse. I feel like I'm here to die.' I told him a bit about the trauma of the night. 'Honestly, the longer I'm here, the more it feels like a hospice,' I wept. 'I can't stand it any more.' I'd made another decision too. I wasn't going to have any more Taxotere. I couldn't finish the course. I had to stop.

I'd had four of the proposed six doses and ended up in ward G6 after all but one session, fighting off infections that came very close to finishing me off. It was in danger of becoming ironic. I could be killed by the treatment, not the disease. I was so weary of being ill and of being stuck in hospital, listening to poor souls breathing their last. I was prepared to take my chances with the cancer.

For the first time since the whole business had begun, I felt I really couldn't take any more treatment. I was forced to admit that I just didn't have the strength – mental or physical – to keep going through the same grief over and over again. I didn't want to spend the remainder of my days that way. On the phone that morning Scott persuaded me to stay and complete the antibiotics treatment at least, but I was determined to stick to my guns and have no more chemo. Scott dismissed my attempts to discuss it further, hopeful that I'd calm down and carry on as before. Not a chance.

When I finally got out, I went straight round to Mum and Dad's and asked them to sit down. I had to speak to them.

'I know this is going to upset you,' I said, 'but I've made a decision. It's not what you'll want to hear. I'm not going to have any more chemo.'

Two mouths dropped in unison.

Dad spoke first. 'No, Mandy,' he said. 'Don't stop. Keep going. You need to keep fighting.'

Scott was agreeing. 'That's what I've been saying,' he said. 'She's not listening to me.'

I tried to explain: 'Dad, I am fighting, but it's such a struggle and it's dragging me down. I can't go on like this.'

It was true. Every session knocked me back a bit

further, and every time it took more effort to get back up. One day I might not get back up at all.

Mum was listening, watching me. 'I totally understand,' she said eventually. 'I know how ill you've been and how it's affected you, but shouldn't you speak to Dr Hendry first, before you make a decision like this?'

Dad leaped on the idea. 'Yes, you can't do anything without speaking to Dr Hendry,' he said, clearly hoping someone else might be able to make me see sense.

I knew, though, that Dr Hendry had told me from the outset that if the treatment ever got too difficult for me, I need only say the word and they'd stop it. At the time I thought it strange guidance. Why on earth would I ever want to stop fighting? That would be giving up and I was never going to give up. And there I was, giving up.

'I'm sorry,' I said, 'but I'm due to go for my fifth session tomorrow and I'm going to refuse it.'

We went to the movies again that night, Scott and me, probably to avoid any difficult discussions at home. At the cinema, there was no opportunity to talk to each other, and I'd had enough debate about my decision. I was glad of the excuse to sit in silence. While we waited for the film to start, the auditorium's PA system was playing gentle background music, although I wasn't even aware of it until a track came on, a song by the Verve called 'The Drugs Don't Work', and as it filtered through to my consciousness, I felt the tears begin. The drugs don't work. Well, wasn't that the truth? Maybe it was a sign. Maybe I was doing the right thing.

The next day Scott and I arrived at Gartnavel Hospital, but instead of escorting me to my treatment chair, the oncologist showed us through to his office, ready to fight the case for chemo.

'I'll be honest with you, Mandy,' he said. 'We really want you to have all six sessions. I know you've had a hard time, but I think it's important to give you as good a chance as possible.'

Scott was looking at me, pleading with me to agree.

'But how much difference could it possibly make anyway?' I said. 'Will it dramatically affect my outcome if I don't have any more? I've had four already.'

Of course he couldn't predict how my chances would be altered. He had no more idea than I did. If I was to halt the chemo and things went wrong, who's to say they wouldn't have gone wrong even after all six sessions? There are no guarantees with cancer treatment. If I'd learned anything, I'd learned that.

The doctor rested his chin on one hand. He'd realised I meant business. 'Try just one more, then,' he said. 'I have spoken to Dr Hendry and she agrees. If you have a fifth one and your reaction is just as bad, then we will stop.' I looked at Scott. 'I'll bring down the dosage this time, but if you still fall ill, then we'll say enough's enough.'

Scott interrupted: 'Mandy, please do it.' He looked so scared. 'I'm really proud of you and I know it's been such a hard struggle, but we've got to listen to the doctor.'

All my bravado left me. I'd managed to cast out so many doubts over the past few days, but they hurtled back into my head the moment the doctor mentioned giving me 'as good a chance as possible'. So I would be denying myself the best chance of survival if I didn't continue – that was the long and short of it. I was condemning myself. I wanted to be strong enough to ignore what the medics were saying and trust my instincts, but I was terrified. I'd always gone along with whatever the doctors advised. Did I dare put myself out on a limb?

'OK,' I said slowly. 'I'll have a fifth one, but this will be my last. No more after that.'

Scott hugged me. 'You'll be all right,' he said. 'You'll get through this.'

I did get through it, but only just. Five days later I was back in ward G6, an infection running rampant through my body while nurses desperately tried to get a line into my rapidly collapsing veins. Scott watched in horror, blaming himself. Sixteen times they tried to connect me to the IV line, inserting needles into my hands, my wrists, my legs, my feet, winding tourniquets round my limbs, holding heat-pads on their targeted zone, but every time the vein would vanish, my body too weakened to stand up to the assault. They started trying at around 8 p.m., when I'd staggered into the Beatson. They were still trying six hours later.

By 2 a.m. I couldn't stop crying. 'Please leave me alone,' I was saying. 'Leave me till the morning.'

But the nurses were agitated.

'We can't leave you till morning,' one told me. 'Don't you realise what happens if this infection goes right through your body? We've got to do this now.'

Scott kept disappearing to pace the corridor for a while and try to regain his composure. I was in such pain, such distress that he could hardly look at me. Finally it was in, slotted precariously into a vein in my left foot. At last they could let me sleep.

'Scott, please don't try to talk me into another chemo,' I said, as he sat by my bed, relieved and exhausted. 'There is no one on earth who could talk me into having one. It is not going to happen.'

When Dr Hendry came to see me the next day and told me she couldn't possibly give me any more chemo because my body was so worn out, I was grateful. The decision wasn't all mine, then. There was good medical reason to stop. Would it make any difference in the long run? That was a chance I was prepared to take. The way I saw it, if I'd had a sixth treatment, it would have wiped me out anyway.

'Yes, Scott,' I imagined Dr Hendry saying, 'the

treatment was very successful, but I'm afraid we still lost the patient.'

Anyway, Dr Hendry was pleased with the way the cancer had been reacting. CT scans showed both the tumour in my chest and the affected lymph glands in my neck and underarms had shrunk. Now it was up to the Herceptin to keep it under control, and it was up to me to try and get myself healthy again. I never asked Dr Hendry how long I might have and she always pointedly avoided saying anything too specific. I was holding on to the fact that Herceptin was something of an unknown quantity as it was so new. I would be on it till it stopped working, which could be in a few months' time or it could be in five years. I couldn't dwell on it, one way or another. I had to concentrate on being well and top of my agenda was enjoying myself as much as humanly possible.

Chapter 12

I was still recovering in ward G6 after the fifth – and final – chemo when Mum arrived for a visit, all excited about an article she'd spotted in the newspaper.

'They're looking for people who've had breast cancer to take part in a fashion show,' she gushed, brandishing a newspaper cutting at me and demanding I have a read of it.

Bald, bloated and barely able to move, I couldn't have felt less like model material.

'Don't be ridiculous, Mum,' I said without even taking the paper. 'Look at the state of me.' I was trying to be as positive as possible about my prospects, but I wasn't going to fool myself that I could suddenly give Claudia Schiffer a run for her money. I didn't even want to look at myself, for God's sake, so why would anyone else?

'But the show's not till September,' Mum continued. 'Five months away. You'll be feeling much better by then.'

Reluctantly I read the article. The fashion show was being organised by the charity Breast Cancer Care Scotland, which I'd heard a bit about through patients at the Beatson. They offered peer support services, advice on wigs, information about treatment options, that kind of thing, but I'd never actually called upon them myself. They'd had the fabulous idea of setting up a fashion show to raise funds – with breast-cancer patients as models. It had been such a runaway success the previous year they were about to do it for a second time, so they were looking for applicants, twenty people who'd been through breast cancer and lived to tell the tale.

Wow, I'd love to do that, I thought. If only I could be sure of being well enough.

The article was about a forty-year-old woman who'd taken part in the first show and loved it so much she'd applied again. She'd found a lump in her breast when she was breastfeeding her baby son a few years before but had developed secondaries and was on some type of experimental drug in a last-ditch attempt to find something that worked. I looked at the photo of her, smiling and beautiful with her arms round her two young children. 'In my heart I don't believe I'll be taken from my kids,' the headline read. She was so full of life, talking about how she focused on having a good time with her family and friends and how that helped her get through the hard times. She was right.

'That woman's really got her hands full,' I said to Mum. 'She's in the same boat as me and she's got kids to worry about, but she's doing the right thing. She's staying positive.' Then I added, 'OK, I'll fill in the entry form, but don't expect me to get picked. They're not looking for people in my state. They'll want women who're a few years past their treatment, not baldies like me.'

Secretly, I was desperate to take part. It sounded like the most amazing experience, getting pampered for the day, wearing some gorgeous clothes and strutting your stuff on the catwalk. What a way to show that I wasn't down and out just yet.

I phoned Dawn. 'Do you fancy being a model, Dawn?' And once she stopped laughing, I told her all about it too.

'That's it . . . I'm going to enter,' she said. 'We can both do it together.'

A week later I was waiting to be discharged when Scott appeared. He was a bit twitchy. 'I've got a letter for you,' he said. 'It's from Breast Cancer Care.'

'Oh, that was quick,' I said, suddenly nervous.

I opened it. The first word said it all. 'Congratulations!' I'd been selected!

The letter said they wanted me to be a model in the Fashion Show 2004 and were inviting me along to a special welcome day at the Radisson SAS Hotel in Glasgow the following week.

'I've been picked! I've been picked!' I was jumping up and down while Scott shook his head in disbelief. The other patients must have thought we'd won the lottery.

I phoned Mum. 'I'm going to be a model! We need to go shopping!'

I didn't have a thing that I could possibly wear to something this important. I'd spent most of the last few months in my pyjamas. It was bad enough that I'd have to turn up with an unconvincing wig and a swollen face; I couldn't risk a fashion failure too. They'd show me the door before I got anywhere near the catwalk. Then I remembered: I wonder if Dawn's had a letter?

I phoned her right away, but I could tell by her voice that she wasn't feeling like me.

'No, I didn't get in,' she said. 'But that's all right. You'll be great.'

I knew she was disappointed. I felt awful that I hadn't even considered what would happen if one of us got in and the other didn't, especially when Dawn could really have used a confidence boost. Since the spread of the cancer to her spine, her mood had been quite low. I found out later that the charity had received hundreds of entries, which they'd had to whittle down to the final twenty. It was just good luck they'd chosen me.

'Oh, Dawn, that's rotten . . . I want you to do it too,' I whined.

She wouldn't allow me to feel down on her behalf, though. 'You go and do it for both of us,' she said, with her knack of making things easy for me. 'I'm just glad one of us got in.'

I took a couple of days to find enough strength, then Mum and I headed off to Braehead Shopping Centre, just outside Glasgow, to find an outfit that was effortlessly stylish. Nothing too elaborate or expensive.

'I don't want them to think I'm trying too hard,' I coached Mum, 'but I need to look like I've made an effort.'

After much deliberation, and a good couple of hours' legwork, I settled on a pair of tight bootcut trousers and a blue-and-white polka-dot top teamed with some very on-trend wedges. I was having a final nosy around the rails in H&M when I overheard Mum at the cash desk, telling the assistant details of my treatment.

'Yes, she's just finished chemo,' she was saying, as the young girl behind the counter pretended to be fascinated and suitably impressed. 'I know – she looks great, doesn't she?' Mum was going on. 'But she's had so much surgery, you wouldn't believe. She's absolutely brilliant. And she's going to be a model now . . .'

I fell over my own feet rushing to her side. 'For goodness' sake, Mum,' I said, steering her away from the counter. 'The girl's not interested in my life. Come on.' I was trying to usher her out of the door before I died of humiliation.

'What?' she objected. 'She's amazed at how good you look after everything you've been through, that's all. I'm just proud of you.'

I directed a little forced laugh at the cashier. 'OK, Mum,' I grimaced, 'but you really don't have to tell everyone.'

Come welcome day I didn't look too bad in my new outfit, but I felt like a neurotic disaster area.

When will I ever learn to ignore Mum's ideas? I was thinking as I walked through the very posh hotel in search of the meeting room. The nineteen other models, including two men (I didn't even know men could get breast cancer!), were milling around, eating healthy crudités from a buffet table and striking up stilted conversations with one another. A quick scan of the room showed some had lost their hair and didn't bother trying to disguise it, a couple – like me – were wearing wigs, and the rest must have been further along in their treatment and looked perfectly normal.

I bet I'm the youngest, I thought, as I sidled up to the buffet and tried to look entirely relaxed, but there were quite a few women in their thirties and forties. I spotted the woman from the newspaper article. So she'd been chosen again after all.

'Hi,' said one of the other women, reaching to shake my hand. 'I'm from Breast Cancer Care. Are you one of our models? Let me introduce you . . .'

Suddenly it was all underway and I was caught up in a growing sense of excitement. The more I listened to some of the others, chatting freely about everything they'd been through, the more inadequate I felt. A few of them seemed so much worse off than I was. At least Herceptin had given me some hope to hang on to, and I was young and strong too. A couple of the women weren't so lucky. Then someone from the charity started reading out the itinerary for the fashion show and my anxieties really began to get the better of me.

I can't do this, I thought, scanning through the information. Rehearsals, costume fittings, umpteen changes and a bit of publicity stuff, if required. I wasn't strong enough for all that. I'd just finished chemo. What was I thinking?

Suddenly all the other models seemed super-healthy and self-assured. I looked like I might keel over of my own accord the minute the going got tough, and it was nothing to do with my new wedge sandals.

Oh, no, what have I done? I thought. I'm going to be a disaster.

'Let's book a holiday,' I said to Scott that night, after bending his ear for ages with my confidence crisis. 'We could both do with the break, and I really want to get a tan for the fashion show. It'll make me look better, and if I look better, I'll feel better.'

Scott seemed to recoil, probably doing some speedy mental arithmetic that wasn't giving palatable answers. We were already booked to go to Cyprus immediately after the show, so the addition of an extra break was the last thing our bank account needed.

'If we book one of those Freestyle holidays, it will probably save us a bit of money,' I pleaded. Freestyle holidays were Club 18–30-style breaks, but we'd found they were often a bit cheaper than ordinary package deals and had booked them in the past to save a bit of cash. 'I really think it will help me,' I added, a little sneakily.

Scott gave a moan of resignation. 'If you can find a good deal, then we'll go,' he said, and even though the best deal I could find happened also to be to Cyprus, he didn't complain too much.

Mum and Dad decided to come too, along with my aunt and uncle, though clearly they wouldn't be booking a Freestyle 'under 30s' package. Scott and I would be in Cyprus party capital Ayia Napa, of course, while the others would be staying in a neighbouring resort called Protaras. Scott and I would simply body-swerve the organised disco foam nights or underwear-swapping competitions and head into the pubs in the centre of town, where we could steer well clear of the other Freestylers. I wanted to be incognito, blend into a crowd of people we didn't know and who wouldn't ask any questions about my GI Jane-style cropped hair. We wouldn't find out what hotel we had been allocated until we arrived at the local airport, Larnaca, but fingers crossed we'd get somewhere reasonably large where we could go unnoticed among the families and the pensioners and the usual mix of Brits abroad.

'Often you don't even see the other people on the same Freestyle package unless you go to the organised events,' I'd reassured Mum, who was a bit concerned we'd have to take part in wild parties. 'You can do your own thing if you want to. The accommodation tends to be a bit cheaper, that's all.'

When we arrived at the check-in desk at Glasgow Airport, we feared it might not be quite so easy to avoid the Freestylers. The queue was throbbing with about thirty hormonal teenagers, pretty things with long hair and hardly any clothes. I slunk into line, uneasy and self-conscious, with my baseball cap pulled down so tightly over my shaved hairdo that I could hardly see where I was going. We ended up with seats in the middle of the trendy crowd and spent the whole flight feeling like disapproving old dears. It wasn't that long since we might have been happy there among them. Now Scott was too old, I was too bald, and we were both too tired.

When we were directed to our transit coach at Larnaca Airport, they filed on after us, singing and shouting, their vocal chords oiled by the litres of booze they'd downed on the flight.

'Scott, please tell me they're not getting off at this stop,' I whispered, as we finally approached our hotel.

Unfortunately, as if on cue, one of them noticed the sign outside. 'Right, troops – we're here.' Off they all staggered, several of them falling down the steps from the bus.

'You realise this is going to be a nightmare?' I said to Scott, as we stepped over the human tangle on the pavement.

I was right. All day they hung around the pool, the girls parading in tiny wee bikinis that hardly covered their bits, while the boys ogled and whistled and cat-called. All night they partied, the girls in teeny dresses or strappy tops, while I tried to stay out of sight, too embarrassed to let anyone see me wearing my wig. I'd hoped to give them a wide berth, but there was no chance, no quiet corner out of the way where Scott and I could relax.

'Why didn't we just pay the extra to go to a family hotel?' I'd grumble every day, as I watched them cavorting in the water.

'Mandy, no one is even looking at you,' Scott told me, but I knew they'd already noticed my newly sprouting hair. I'd seen them looking.

'If they see me with long hair all of a sudden, they'll know I'm wearing a wig,' I replied. 'Either that or they'll think you've got two women in tow.' Either way we would end up as hot gossip among the lilos and I just wasn't up to it. I quickly decided there was no way I would be sunbathing beside the pool; in fact, I wouldn't even walk past it if the group of party pals was there to see me in my cover-up vest-style bikini and baseball cap.

'I'm going for a walk,' a decidedly grumpy Scott declared. He was getting annoyed with my paranoia.

I knew I was being a pain, but I just couldn't stop myself. Scott was grinning when he came back, which wasn't what I expected.

'I've found a back gate to the complex,' he said triumphantly. 'It leads to a road into Ayia Napa town centre.'

What he meant was, 'If you leave our apartment block by the back gate, walk down a flight of stairs, along a dirt track, climb over a fence, go down an embankment, climb another fence, then walk for ten minutes along a secluded road, you'll reach Ayia Napa town centre.' Of course, if you simply walked out of the front of the hotel, you'd reach the same place after a pleasant ten-minute stroll past shops and restaurants, but everyone saw you if you went that way.

'Scott, you're a genius,' I said. 'Let's do it.'

So every night I'd get dressed up in my best gear, slap on my make-up and pull on my wig, then set off on our ramble into town, where we'd meet Mum, Dad and the others. Scott would have to lift me over the fences when my skirts were too tight or too short to let me climb.

'I feel like a burglar,' he'd complain. 'We're going to end up arrested for breaking and entering if we keep on behaving like this.'

'Oh, don't be daft,' I'd tell him. 'Who's going to put a breast-cancer patient in jail?'

Back home and bronzed, the fashion show became the

centre of my attention. Even though I was surrounded by other breast-cancer patients, they helped keep my mind off my own predicament. The three-weekly Herceptin regime seemed to be working, however. Dr Hendry had found little change in the tumours and she was as good as her word and didn't try to talk me into more chemo.

My hair had grown back enough to have it styled into a funky crop, which I would paint with flashes of hair mascara to make it ultra stylish. I was examining it in the reflection of the lift doors at Gartnavel Hospital one afternoon when a small, grey-haired woman in her sixties approached me.

'Excuse me, dear,' she said. I thought she was going to ask for directions to some ward or other. 'I just wanted to tell you, there's an angel sitting on your shoulder.'

Instinctively I checked my shoulders, like she'd just told me I had dandruff. Then I caught myself. I was looking for an angel. Accosted by a nutter, just what I needed.

'Oh, right, thanks,' I said, wishing the lift would hurry up.

She didn't say anything else. She just smiled and turned away. The lift doors finally slid open and I scuttled inside.

Who was that? I wondered, peeking out to see if I could make out where she'd gone, but there was no sign of her.

I thought about the strange encounter all afternoon. In a weird way, I found it quite comforting to imagine a wee angel following me around. I knew it was a bit crazy. It wasn't like I was the religious sort. I never went to church. I'd put my faith firmly in medical science. Still, I couldn't help but feel a little, well, relieved. The more I thought about it, the more I loved the idea someone was looking after me, someone other than the doctors. I told Scott about the old lady when I got home that night.

'Why would someone come up to me and say such a thing?' I pondered. 'I mean, she couldn't have known I was a patient going to get Herceptin. I was on the ground floor, waiting for a lift. I could have been going anywhere. I could have been visiting someone.'

Scott just laughed. 'She probably hangs about there waiting to say nice things to sick people,' he scoffed. 'It's her good deed for the day.' It would take more than a granny in a woolly coat to convince Scott that angels were taking care of us.

A couple of weeks later, at the end of September, it was showtime. Predictably, I was a bag of nerves. I sat at a table in the Radisson SAS Hotel with Scott, both sets of parents and the rest of my 'supporters' as we waited for the fun to start, sipping champagne and trying to stay calm. A slideshow of photos was being beamed on to big screens around the room showing pictures taken at the welcome day four months before. When the sequence reached my picture, our group gasped a collective intake of breath.

'My God,' said a stunned Liz, 'you look so . . . ill.'

There I was in glorious Technicolor, my face puffy, tired and drawn, my eyes sunken deep into dark holes, my long ginger wig utterly laughable.

'I didn't think you looked particularly sick back then,' said Mum, 'but now that I see it, you looked terrible.'

Not a great ego-boost before my modelling debut. Still, I must have come further than I'd realised in the past few months. From ward G6 to the catwalk. Who'd have thought it?

Backstage was chaos but a really exciting, happy chaos. Twenty nervous novice models were careering around between dressers and stylists and stagehands, trying their best to be in the right place at the right time, while not entirely sure where or when that was. Every time I bumped into another model we would burst into fits of giggles, like we couldn't believe what we were about to do. Everyone was getting stripped and changed in front of one another without a second thought. No one cared about scars or modesty. We were all in the same boat, and all so busy getting ready that it didn't matter if the woman beside you only had one breast or someone else was busy trying to make their 'falsie' secure inside a bra. It was the perfect communal changing room for breast-cancer survivors. No one was at all interested in what my boobs looked like because they'd seen it all before anyway.

I was actually more concerned that I was carrying a few extra pounds and felt a bit embarrassed by my bulging tummy, but I'd just finished a course of steroids, so there wasn't much I could do about my swollen appearance. I wasn't happy with my hair either. I just about got away with it for the 'scenes' where I was casually dressed, in jeans and sweaters with chunky accessories, but in the gorgeous silky evening dresses that should have been the highlight of the show, I looked a mess.

'I look like a boy in a frock,' I'd grumbled to Scott. 'I'll kill you if I see you laughing, though.'

Yet in the swing of the last-minute preparations backstage, none of us really gave a damn what we were wearing. We just wanted to get out there and do our thing.

The ballroom began to fill up, 350 people nudging their way to their seats. While I waited for my turn in the make-up chair, I sneaked off to watch the audience file in, all done up in their finery ready to be entertained. How terrifying. I was shaking with stage fright as the first bars of music struck up and the crowd started cheering.

I wish I was watching this from out there, I thought. This would be great if I didn't have to be in it.

Even so, I knew this was my chance to say all the things I wanted to say: 'Look at me, the lot of you. I'm twenty-nine and I've got breast cancer. But I'm not on my last legs yet. Look at me.'

We were all poised behind the curtain, mentally going through our steps for the first scene, when the MC – TV sports presenter Dougie Donnelly – announced that the husband of one of the previous year's models wanted to say a few words. The man's wife had died just a few weeks before, but he wanted to acknowledge how much it meant to her to have been part of the show.

'She was so positive,' he told the audience. 'She didn't see stumbling blocks, only stepping stones.'

I'd felt frazzled enough before he started speaking. By the time he'd finished, I didn't think I could go out. I was a wreck.

Then music blasted out like a fanfare and the crowd started roaring. Before I knew it, I was walking out in front of them, dazzled by flashing lights and cameras, and laughing with excitement. To the right side of the catwalk, a table full of people leaped to their feet, shouting and waving and screaming my name. I could see glimpses of Scott, Mum and Dad, and waved in their direction. The whole room was alive, a blur of faces and music and tickertape and cheering. I felt like a superstar. It was incredible. Two costume changes, three, four…we seemed to go through them all in a blink, but none of us wanted it to end. We felt so special. We were winners. We were fantastic.

Even when it was truly over, the finale had played out, and the hotel staff had moved in to start tidying the room, I didn't want to leave.

'Let's get another bottle of champagne,' Dad said, and we sat together on sofas in the bar, going over every last morsel of the show and toasting a truly unforgettable day.

'I want to do it all over again,' I said. 'I could get used to all this attention.'

Scott laughed. 'This must be a first – Mandy McMillan enjoyed people looking at her.'

Three days later Scott and I flew out for another week-long break in Ayia Napa, this time for some post-fashion-show relaxation and staying in a quiet family hotel where we wouldn't have to mount nightly raids over walls and waste ground just to get to the nightlife. Anyway, this time I was brimming full of confidence. I was a catwalk star. I even felt reasonably comfortable with my short-but-sassy hairstyle.

'We can really chill out this time,' I told Scott on our blissfully peaceful flight. 'I'm so looking forward to lying in the sun doing nothing for a while.'

We arrived on Sunday afternoon. The following night, as we were having a drink at the hotel bar, my mobile rang. It was Catherine. Dawn had passed away.

Chapter 13

The bar was teeming with holidaymakers, all having a laugh and a drink on a balmy night, not a care in the world between them. I was among them, head in hands, crying like I thought I would never stop.

I'd known Dawn was very ill before I got on the plane for Cyprus, but I'd carried on, flying out to lie on a beach with my husband when she was lying in a hospice. Somehow, in my heart, I knew she would die while I was away. Everyone had convinced me she'd be all right at least till I got back and that she wouldn't want me to cancel my holiday.

'Just go,' Mum had said. 'You need a break. We'll keep in touch with Dawn and Catherine and keep you posted.'

I'd allowed myself to be persuaded there was no immediate need for concern. Still, something told me time was running out fast. Dawn's health had gone downhill so rapidly.

'I think it's probably a good thing that she didn't get chosen for the fashion show,' I'd remarked to Scott as the event had drawn closer. 'She's so poorly at the moment I don't think she would be able to do it, and she'd be devastated if she'd been selected then had to pull out.'

In a matter of weeks she had gone from being independent and feisty to wheelchair-bound and fragile. The cancer had spread to Dawn's spine; her vertebrae were weakened so much that she could no longer use her legs. Yet the very last time I saw her, she was positive and cheerful, even as she told me that she was going into a hospice for a few days.

'I'm only going in until the council fit a stair-lift in my house,' she insisted. 'They're going to refit the bathroom too, so I can get my wheelchair in. Don't worry – I'll only be in for a couple of weeks. I won't be staying there.'

She was extremely convincing, though in my darker moments I did find myself wondering if she was just doing what she had done since the day I was diagnosed: shielding me from the worst.

I'd seen her quite a bit in the months after my wedding and I'd felt her terror when she first discovered the cancer had spread to her backbone. She confided in me that it had shown up in other sites too. The Tuesday girls' nights that used to alternate between each of our houses were latterly held at Dawn's place so she could be as comfortable as possible. Some nights it was obvious she couldn't be bothered with our company. She was distant, distracted by her pain, while the rest of us chatted. That's actually why she eventually went to the doctor to have herself checked out again. She was complaining so much about her sore back we all nagged her to make an appointment.

'You've probably just strained it,' I told her. 'You must be overdoing things. You really should give yourself more rest.'

Her daughter, Stephanie, was only twelve at the time and Dawn was the type to want to do all the work on her own. She didn't like too much help, so she was always tired.

'You should still get the doctor to have a look at it, though,' I added. 'There might be something they can give you.'

When she finally did go for an examination, the news was the worst possible. The cancer was inoperable and spreading quickly. There was little they could do but make her comfortable, and they couldn't even do that very successfully. Dawn couldn't sleep at night because it was excruciating to lie flat, so she would try to rest as best she could while sitting upright. Her mum and dad were her constant support, and I knew Catherine had taken to staying over some nights, trying to help out however she could, but it was young Stephanie who was Dawn's inspiration.

'Stephanie runs my bath for me and gives my shoulders a massage,' Dawn would tell us proudly.

It broke my heart to think of what that little girl was

going through trying to help her mum, and what her mum was going through trying to protect her from it. Dawn didn't talk much about the effect of her illness on Stephanie. It was too painful for her to discuss, even with me, perhaps especially with me.

The year had started badly for Dawn. I knew that because she'd called me in the early hours of New Year's Day. My mobile rang as Scott and I were walking home from the local pub where we'd joined the Hogmanay celebrations and toasted the bells. I used to love a Scottish New Year, going to parties with our friends, singing and dancing till we fell over, full of optimism and plans for the months ahead. All that changed when cancer came into my life. I found myself looking round at the faces of the people I loved and wondering how long I'd get to see them. I envied them, all healthy and happy with so much to look forward to. I scanned the room, wishing I had someone else's life, wondering whose would be best.

That New Year heralded the start of my Herceptin treatment and yet more chemotherapy, all beginning in a few days' time. The only resolution I could think of was to get through it. Survive it. Just once I'd have liked to get to the end of a bad year and look forward to a better year, instead of an even worse one. I wish I could go to bed and ignore the significance of the event, but there's something important about facing up to your future, whatever it may hold. That particular New Year Dawn was having difficulty facing her own.

'Happy New Year, Mandy.'

I knew it was her voice, but it was stilted and breaking. She started to cry. It was about 5 a.m. She was at home. Stephanie was asleep in bed upstairs.

'Dawn, what's wrong?' I asked.

'I can't take this any more,' she sobbed, really hard and deep sobs. 'I've had enough of it, Mandy. The cancer's in my bones. It's so painful. I don't want this.'

I'd never heard Dawn talk like that before. I'd never even heard her particularly down. 'Come on, Dawn,' I said. 'Calm down. You can't think like that. I know it's hard, but you're still fighting it.' There was no use telling her everything was going to be fine. I knew things wouldn't be fine and so did she. 'I'll get a taxi and come over right away,' I said. 'We'll have a talk, eh?' But she wouldn't hear of it.

Scott had walked on ahead of me when he realised I was caught up in conversation, so I wandered down the road on my own, hardly concentrating on where I was going because I was so immersed in Dawn's trauma, a crisis I knew could easily be my own. It took a while to talk her round, she was in such a state, and I was having a hard time staying calm myself. Eventually her breathing became more even and the sobs started to peter out.

'I'm so sorry, Mandy,' she said. 'I'm just not coping

with it very well right now. You know what it's like.'

Of course I did. As much as I didn't want to hear a lot of what Dawn had to say that night, I couldn't hide from it either. We had cancer in common. If Dawn had chosen to tell me these things at 5 a.m. on New Year's Day, it was because she thought I would understand and she needed to speak to someone who understood.

'I'll give you a phone tomorrow,' I said, when I thought she'd calmed down enough to risk hanging up. 'You try and get some sleep now.'

She said she was all right. She was sorry. She'd go to bed. When I pressed the button to end the call, I was alone with my own fears. It felt like I had glimpsed the year ahead already and it was clear 2004 did not have good things in store for Dawn or for me.

A few weeks later I bumped into her at hospital, me going for Herceptin, Dawn for some more chemotherapy for cancer 'hot spots' they'd found on her liver: random active areas that could progress if untreated. Her face seemed swollen, probably the effects of steroid treatment, and it had a yellow tinge, a sure sign her liver wasn't working properly. Nevertheless she was resolutely upbeat: 'The treatment's going quite well,' she said. 'We must get together for a catch-up when we're both feeling a bit better.'

Between her treatment and my own extended stays in ward G6, I didn't see Dawn for a while after that, though we kept in touch by phone or text, so we each knew how the other was progressing. Well, I thought I knew how Dawn was keeping. I was shopping in town one day, not long after the end of my chemo, when I looked up from a rail of skirts to a sight that chilled me. Dawn was ten feet away, her eyes half closed, her feet shuffling.

'Dawn, are you OK?' I said, taking her arm.

'Oh, Mandy,' she whispered, 'I'm in a lot of pain.'

I was certain she was about to slump to the floor.

'Come on, I'm taking you home,' I said.

She seemed to be moving in a trance. 'No, no, I'm all right,' she said, her weak voice faltering.

Her sister-in-law, Joy, appeared, looking flustered. She explained they were out to buy Stephanie's new school uniform and Dawn had insisted on choosing it herself, even though she was doped up on the strongest painkillers around and could only walk in baby steps. They'd all tried to convince her to stay home, but Dawn was determined. Stephanie needed a uniform and her mum was going to get it for her.

The next month Dawn lost power in her legs. Her mum had taken her to hospital for some treatment to stem the pain in her back, but when they arrived at the Royal Infirmary, Dawn collapsed. She never walked again. While she was being rushed inside for emergency treatment, in the street outside a parking warden arranged the clamping of her mum's car. Abandoning your car in blind panic while your daughter's spine crumbles is no excuse for bad parking in Glasgow.

Strangely, I still didn't believe that Dawn might not pull through until she was admitted to ward G6. In the weeks leading up to her death she was taken in three times before she was ultimately moved to the hospice. Sometimes I'd visit and she'd seem fairly well and we'd talk away the hour without pausing; others she'd be lying in bed, partially awake and trying to force herself to listen to the conversation going on around her. Catherine was in close contact with Dawn's family and occasionally she'd call to say that they'd asked us not to drop by that night because she really wasn't up to it. Every time they did, I felt a pang of fear, but she always seemed to rally and the next time I saw her, she was just Dawn again. That's why I let myself be convinced to go on holiday. The old Dawn was still there, wounded but fighting. Then it got the better of her. She was lost. The last words she spoke were to Stephanie. 'I love you,' she said.

I'd always thought my illness mirrored hers. She was my breast-cancer mentor. Yet I was sunning myself on a foreign holiday when she was dying. How come I was fit enough to swan off abroad when Dawn had already been robbed of her life? She was only thirty-seven. She'd been diagnosed just seven months before me. She'd fought it from March 2001 to October 2004, three and a half years, and she'd fought as hard as I had. If all I had on my side was luck, how much longer could that last?

'Do you want to try and go home?' Scott said tentatively.

I did. I wanted to go back right away. The funeral would be in a few days' time.

'I'll ask the rep if we can get an early flight so you can go to the funeral,' he added.

Unfortunately, we couldn't transfer our tickets – we'd have to buy new ones and it was going to cost a fortune.

'Why don't you just stay till the end of your trip?' Mum said when we phoned home. 'Your dad and I will go to Dawn's funeral as your representatives. We'll make sure her family know why you're not there.' Then she added, cautiously, 'You know, Mandy, it might not be a bad thing if you stay where you are. It's not going to help you to go to Dawn's funeral.'

That was true. I really wasn't certain I could cope with it. I wanted to treasure the last time I saw her, smiling and friendly even in the most dismal of circumstances.

'I think you're right,' I told Mum.

Mum and Dad went along, gave a donation to the hospice on my behalf and tried to make sure her family knew I was thinking about them. Stephanie allowed a personal letter from her mum to be read at the funeral. Mum and Dad said it was beautiful. Dawn would have been so proud. Her daughter had inherited her courage.

Aghast

How many of you are planning to breastfeed?' the midwife asked.

It seemed every woman in the room put up a hand except me. I felt their eyes bore into me as they realised they had a traitor in their midst. I thrust my own hand in the air and blurted out, 'I would love to breastfeed, but I'm not allowed to because I've got breast cancer and I'm on a special drug for it at the moment – a new drug that no one knows much about – so they don't think it would be a good idea for me to breastfeed – even though I've got one healthy breast – because the drug might cross over into the breast milk.'

The midwife was open-mouthed. I turned round hesitantly in my chair and saw that every other mum-to-be in the class was staring at me, utterly aghast. I knew some of them fairly well by this stage. A few of us had started going for coffee after class, sharing pregnancy stories and swapping ideas on where to buy the latest baby must-haves, but I'd kind of neglected to tell them I had advanced breast cancer. I'd also failed to mention that when I left them most weeks, I went downstairs for my check-up in oncology, a very different part of the hospital. Every third week I was hooked up to an intravenous line and drip-fed the new breast-cancer wonder-drug, Herceptin. It all seemed a bit much to offer up for discussion over an empire biscuit and a cappuccino with people I'd only just met.

Now they were looking at me like they couldn't believe their ears. My face flushed bright crimson and I wished I'd never opened my mouth. The midwife had gone red too, I noticed, when I dared look back at her. She was dangling her wee dolly by its remaining leg – probably not best practice.

She cleared her throat and said, 'OK, fine. Yes, er, if that's what you've been told, er, that's absolutely fine.'

Then she obviously decided there was no chance of resuming the class as all her students were in a state of shock the like of which they may not experience again until labour. 'I think we'll leave it there for this week and pick it up again next time,' she said. 'See you then, ladies.' She gave an uncertain smile and set about putting her baby away in a box with some other plastic objects that looked frighteningly like body parts.

The other girls practically rugby-tackled me into the coffee shop and plonked me in a chair to begin interrogation. Lorna and Nic, who'd become my two closest pals in the class, were reeling.

'Jesus, you kept that one quiet,' said Lorna.

'Why didn't you say anything before?' Nic added.

I tried to explain it wasn't really the type of thing I wanted to throw into a conversation about three-wheeler prams or the best nappy-wrapping device.

'Anyway, I didn't want anyone to think any differently of me,' I said. 'I'm all right. I get checks every week to make sure the baby's OK, but I feel great, better than I have in the four years since I was diagnosed, in fact. I think this baby may be saving my life.'

Chapter 14

Dawn's death was such a blow that I floundered for a while. I couldn't understand why she had gone and I was still around. All the traumas of the previous months were taking their toll. I seemed constantly exhausted and would fall asleep anywhere if I sat down for too long. It was actually becoming embarrassing. When Joseph and Natalie travelled up from Manchester to see us, I was struggling to keep my eyes open whenever we spent time together and it was beginning to appear rude.

'Are we keeping you up,' Joseph joked, as I yawned through dinner, 'or is our conversation really that bad?'

One night I was lying on the floor listening to the others chat when I was overwhelmed by weariness. I fell into a deep sleep, face-down in a cushion while they watched me in amusement.

'I think I need a tonic or something to perk me up a bit,' I told Scott, but deep down I suspected it was my body's reaction to having too much to deal with. It seemed to want to close down.

I also had a new worry to add. By November 2004, a

month after Dawn died, I could no longer ignore the pain that had been growing in my natural breast. It was sensitive all the time and sore to the touch, and of course my thirtieth birthday was approaching, so I was bracing myself for my regular birthday gift of some bad cancer news.

Then stomach pains started, a strange tightness right across my tummy that felt like my reconstruction scar was about to burst open. If I had to sneeze or cough, I would hold the scar first for fear of it splitting apart.

Don't tell me the cancer's in my stomach now, I thought to myself, too scared to mention my fears to Scott.

Dr Hendry was worried as well. She'd always said there was no reason to think the cancer would develop in my remaining healthy breast, and whenever it was examined, no lumps were found but it had never been painful before. Dr Hendry sent me for a mammogram on my natural breast, which was incredibly sore because my boob was so tender. The results came back clear.

Right, that's it, I thought. If things are going wrong, I'm really going to enjoy the time I've got. From now on I'm in party mode.

Scott was plotting my thirtieth-birthday celebrations in secret, organising a surprise party in the Muirhead Inn, the pub I used to work in. I knew he was up to something. He'd been making furtive calls for weeks, demanding I leave the room in case I overheard anything he was saying, so when a stretch limo appeared at our door and Scott produced a blindfold, I was at least mentally prepared. A bit. We cruised around, sipping drinks and waving at nosy pedestrians, until I realised we were pulling up outside a pub near Clippers. Liz and Jackie were waiting, with their partners and a bunch of our other friends, all of them singing 'Happy Birthday' and cheering like mad things. Then they climbed into the limo with us.

'Right, blindfold on,' said Scott.

'Oh, no,' I objected, suddenly more than a bit self-conscious. 'I'm enjoying myself with my eyes open!'

He wouldn't have it, though. His plan wasn't quite complete.

By the time the mask was removed, I was standing in the Muirhead Inn surrounded by all my family and pals, who greeted me like a returning hero. I didn't buy a single drink all night, but there was an endless line of vodka-and-orange drinks on the bar, just for me. I ended up more than a bit tipsy.

'This has been absolutely brilliant,' I slurred to Scott, as he helped me to bed. 'Thank you so much.'

'Aye, aye, birthday girl,' he said, struggling to manoeuvre me under the duvet. 'I think you'd better have a glass of water before you fall asleep.'

Christmas was approaching fast and the obligatory

festive nights out were rolling in too. I went to as many as possible, determined to live it up, but my party lifestyle was telling on my figure. Going out for late meals and drinking into the small hours isn't the best recipe for staying in shape.

'I'll really have to stop eating so much,' I told Scott, as he made dinner one night.

He turned round from the cooker to have a look at me, standing there in the velour tracksuit I put on when I came home after work. 'Whoa,' he cried. 'You look about four months pregnant!'

My stomach was sticking out a mile. We both burst out laughing.

'I know,' I said. 'It's ridiculous. I'll have to get my act in order or I'll be huge after Christmas.' My clothes had all become a bit snug round my waist, bum and tum. 'I've got a million nights out over the next few weeks,' I moaned. 'I'd better lose a bit of weight or I'll have nothing to wear.'

Meanwhile lots of minor complaints were beginning to worry me. I was suffering terrible heartburn. I felt pretty nauseous most days and all I wanted to eat were crusty white rolls – preferably with sausage or bacon. Out shopping with my friend Esther, I thought I'd gauge her opinion. I ran through all the symptoms with her, adding, 'If I didn't know better, I'd think I was pregnant,' fully expecting her to dismiss such a mad suggestion.

'Sounds like you could be,' she said thoughtfully. 'Maybe you should buy a testing kit.'

That caught me off guard. Esther already had a nine-year-old daughter, so she had some pregnancy experience of her own.

'I'm sure there's a chance it might still be possible,' she said.

Esther thought I might be pregnant. Should I buy a test, then? Really?

I sighed, suddenly remembering the reality of my situation.

I'd just been through the most horrendous treatment I could imagine and it had nearly killed me. I was relying on Herceptin to keep me alive. Dr Hendry had told us I wouldn't be able to have any children back when I was about to start on the Taxotere. I'd had one short, stray period since that chemo ended and that was eight months ago. Nothing since. Just as Dr Hendry had predicted. I was obviously getting carried away in a dreamy notion that I was a normal young woman.

'No, there's no way I'm pregnant,' I told Esther, shaking the idea out of my head. 'I know it can't happen to me. There's not even any point in doing a test. I'll just have to get myself on a diet and start going to the gym again.'

It was the first weekend in January when Mum phoned to see if I fancied a night out with her girlfriends.

I dithered. I was really trying to take it easy since the festivities were officially over. Scott was working that weekend, though, and I would only end up sitting watching TV on my own. Anyway, I always had fun with Mum's mad pals.

'Yeah, why not?' I said, and went straight upstairs to get changed. Standing in front of the full-length mirror in my bedroom, I gazed at myself in disgust. I could barely get my size 10 jeans on and had to lie on the bed, straining at the zip to get them fastened.

These fitted me perfectly on Christmas Day, I thought. There is no way I've put on this much weight in two weeks. I must have put them in the tumble-dryer by mistake and shrunk them.

They were brutally uncomfortable, and as I sat on a bar stool trying to have a conversation and hold in my stomach at the same time, I was wishing I'd worn something stretchy. I was annoyed at myself. My hair was finally approaching a reasonable style – complete with chunky blond highlights – the constant nausea of the past few months was finally relenting, yet I still looked awful because I'd put on so much weight.

To top it all, other people were noticing that I was spilling out of my clothes.

Mum's friend Ann-Marie leaned right across the table to ask, 'Is Mandy pregnant?'

Mum was taken aback. 'No, no,' she said. 'She's just

put on a bit of weight recently and she's finding it hard to shift.'

Undeterred, Ann-Marie went on, 'It's not just her weight. She's got a pregnancy glow, don't you think?'

That lit the touch-paper all right. Mum exploded into full-blown panic. 'Oh my God, oh my God, you'd better not be pregnant,' she was saying, clasping her hands to her temples. 'You can't be pregnant now, can you? Not with everything that's been going on. Oh my God, that would be a disaster.'

Her friends were laughing and I joined in, but I was already turning the idea over in my mind. Could I actually be pregnant? It would explain a lot of the strange symptoms I'd been experiencing. Then again, cancer is quite good at giving strange symptoms too.

Let's face it, I argued with myself, with my record, there's more likely to be a new tumour growing inside my body than a baby.

Still, it was a lovely thought, so by the time I'd said goodnight to Mum, I'd made up my mind to buy a pregnancy testing kit the next morning when Scott and I went to Asda for our regular Sunday grocery shop. It would give me an answer one way or the other.

I announced this to Scott as he was making a beeline for the DVD shelves, his favourite part of the store.

'I'm going to the medicine aisle to get a pregnancy test,' I declared.

'You're doing what?' he asked, suddenly less interested in the promise of new releases and some £3.99 special offers.

'I don't think I am pregnant,' I reassured him, 'but I've put on so much weight and I've been feeling a bit strange. I just want to rule pregnancy out so I can start trying to find out what could be wrong.'

Scott was appeased. There was a justifiable medical reason.

'OK, that's a good idea,' he said. 'Then you can go and tell Dr Hendry that you've ruled out everything else. That's sensible.'

I couldn't get out of the car fast enough when we arrived home, and while Scott was lugging heavy shopping bags into the kitchen, I abandoned him and ran upstairs clutching the kit.

'Now just tell me the truth,' Scott shouted up, staggering through the hallway with arms full of groceries. 'Don't wind me up,' he added.

As if I could joke about this. It was taking a concerted effort to pee accurately on the little plastic stick because I was so excited. I'd never had any reason to test myself for pregnancy before and I was enjoying the whole situation. Even if the result was negative, it was a nice feeling to behave like an ordinary woman. Ordinary women have unexpected pregnancies all the time. Women who've been fighting breast cancer for three years generally don't. For once the waiting time was thrilling.

Don't look at it until the two minutes are up, I was telling myself, forcing my eyes in the opposite direction.

The plastic stick had a pink dot in the 'control' window, and according to the instruction leaflet, a matching dot would appear in the 'result' window if I was pregnant. My watch told me to look.

That looks a bit pink, I thought, then glanced back at the instructions to check I was doing the right thing. By the time I looked at the stick again, there was a bright pink dot in the result window. No doubt about it. I checked the instructions again, feeling a little shaky now. The words were unequivocal: 'A pink dot in the result window means that you are pregnant. It doesn't matter if that dot is pale. You have still tested positive for pregnancy.'

Pale? My dot was proud cerise! My hormones must be surging. I was giggling. This was incredible. It was amazing. Could I really be pregnant? What should I do now?

Calm down. Take it easy now, I thought, pacing back and forth in front of the bath. It might just be that the Herceptin is interfering with the chemicals in the testing kit. It's probably giving a false positive. I need to get some advice from Dr Hendry.

But what if it was correct? I couldn't stop smiling.

Gingerly I walked down the stairs still looking at the plastic stick. Scott was waiting at the bottom.

'Well, what does it say?' he asked.

'Er, well, it says I'm pregnant.' I couldn't even believe I was uttering the words. I started to giggle.

Scott just looked at me, the colour draining from his face. If I'd nudged him with one finger, he'd have fallen like a ton of bricks. He started hyperventilating.

'Are you sure? Right, right. What does this mean? Right. We'll need to phone Dr Hendry. Right, right. Should we go and buy another test?'

I took his hand. 'Don't panic, Scott,' I said, already behaving like some serene pregnant woman. 'There's another test in the box. I'll wait half an hour and I'll go and do that one.'

'Right, right. That's a good idea.' He nodded frantically. 'It's probably just a blip because of your drugs.'

I knew I should feel like him. I knew I should be panicking, but I was loving every minute and trying to hide my grin from his anxious eyes. If I could feel pregnant for just half an hour before facing childlessness again, that was a treat I was going to enjoy.

I made us both some lunch and stuffed my face with sandwiches as a way to suppress my smile. Scott couldn't eat a thing and sat watching me, looking so pale that he might throw up. After exactly thirty minutes I got up.

'OK, let's give it another go,' I said, and went off upstairs to try the second test in the box.

I piddled quickly and sat on the loo holding the plastic

stick so I could see any change the instant it happened. And there it was. Within a few seconds the bright pink blob had appeared, as bold as it had been the first time.

Scott was waiting outside the bathroom door this time, panic all over his face. 'Mandy, what are we going to do?' he said.

'I don't know,' I replied. 'This is as new to me as it is to you. It might still be my treatment giving a false result. There's no point panicking right now.'

He was not reassured in the slightest. 'You've got to phone the GP first thing in the morning and get the first appointment you can.' He was freaking out. 'Somebody is going to have to tell us what this means.'

For the rest of the afternoon we chewed our finger-nails and walked the floors, trying to watch the telly but shooting furtive looks at one another, each half expecting the other to jump up at any moment and declare it had all been an elaborate practical joke. Every time I caught Scott's eye, I started laughing. It was so cruel, because he was deathly white and wearing his most grim expression, clearly worrying himself sick, but I couldn't help it. It was all I could do to refrain from running around the living room crying, 'I'm pregnant! Yes! Yes!' but I didn't think he'd take that very well. Suddenly I didn't have a care in the world and all my ridiculous health problems had vanished as quickly as the pink dot had appeared.

I was pregnant. I didn't know how long I would be

pregnant; I didn't know if I'd need a termination; I didn't know whether my body would reject it; I didn't know whether the drugs would cause me to miscarry. At that moment, though, I was having a taste of what our lives could be like, and it was sweet. My damaged body had somehow managed to generate a new life. For the first time in years I had some good news and I was going to savour every second of it, relish it, hang on to it, cherish it until it was taken from me by cold, heartless reality.

Scott was getting ready to go out to work that evening when Liz phoned to ask if I'd like to join her and Jackie at the pub.

'No, I can't,' I said, considering whether to tell her. 'I'm not really feeling up to it.'

Pause. Liz knew I seldom turned down the opportunity of a night out.

'What's wrong with you?' she asked. 'Is everything all right?' I'd only succeeded in making her think I was poorly again.

Without covering the receiver, I shouted to Scott, 'It's Liz on the phone. Do you think I should tell her?'

'Oh God,' I heard her say quietly, convinced I had more bad news. 'What is it, Mandy?'

I was desperate to tell her anyway.

'You'll never believe it,' I said. 'I'm pregnant,' and all I heard was screaming.

'I don't know what to say to you,' she said finally. 'Are

you happy? Should I be congratulating you? What happens now?' I couldn't tell her because I had absolutely no idea.

'Will you phone Jackie and let her know?' I said. 'Don't tell anyone else yet. I don't know what's going to happen, so I don't want a lot of people knowing.' I was already forfeiting a night out to stay at home, abstain from alcohol and get some rest. Yup, I was convinced I was pregnant.

'Oh, wait till I tell Jackie,' said Liz. 'She'll just faint.'

Telling Mum was going to be an altogether different story. She'd almost had apoplexy in the pub when someone suggested I might be pregnant. How would she react when I confirmed it?

'Mum, are you sitting down?' I said when she answered the phone with a bright 'Hel-lo'. I was about to take the wind out of her sails. 'I've done a pregnancy test . . . and it's positive. I think I'm pregnant.'

You could have heard a pin drop.

'How do you feel?' she said after a few moments, and I knew she was already many steps ahead of me, weighing up my treatment options as a heavily pregnant woman, and worrying about how pregnancy would affect the cancer. Mum was less concerned about my baby than she was about her own . . . me.

I knew she was thinking that way because I'd had the same thought processes myself over the previous few hours, but I'd managed to cut them short. Negatives were not about to destroy my positive mood. Yes, I knew I had fresh scarring on large parts of my body that wouldn't respond very well to stretching. Yes, of course I was aware that it's in no way advisable to take a drug like Herceptin while you're pregnant and I'd been taking it for a year already. Plus, I'd had a few bucketfuls of booze over the festive period. Oh, yeah, and there was the small matter that I had incurable cancer. But what the hell. I was pregnant!

Chapter 15

Mum and Dad must have broken the land speed record in their rush to get to our house. They arrived within a minute, barging in to find me standing at the fireplace, my hand resting on my stomach, which seemed to have ballooned since the pregnancy test.

'Look at you!' Mum cried. 'You've only just discovered you're pregnant and you're standing there looking five months gone.'

My swollen tummy was so evident that I couldn't believe I'd been trying to hold it in for so long. When I unclenched my stomach muscles, I had an undeniable baby bump. How could we have failed to notice?

Dad was in deep shock and sat quietly contemplating the latest twist in his daughter's life. I told Mum to keep the news to herself for a while, at least until we knew what would have to happen next. She swore she'd keep it quiet, but it proved an impossible promise to keep. She was just overwhelmed. I found out later that she'd immediately started calling her closest pals to tell them what Mandy had gone and done now. Everyone, except me, was flying into a panic, sighing their sympathies and offering their support – presumably in preparation for it all going completely and hideously wrong. I didn't entertain that notion for a single second. My baby (because that's what it had already become in my mind) was going to be absolutely fine and I was going to be a great mum and we were all going to live happily ever after. Everyone around me was trying to get a handle on the situation and think sensibly about what we should do. I wanted to dance around cheering, though I realised if Scott and Mum knew that I was utterly ecstatic, they'd think I'd had some kind of breakdown and they'd have me in a straitjacket long before I got anywhere near the labour suite.

Excitement kept me awake most of the night, and next morning I went straight round to see Dr Barrie at the surgery.

'I've done a couple of home pregnancy testing kits and they've both come back positive,' I told her. 'I'm not convinced it's a genuine result because I'm having Herceptin every three weeks and was wondering if that might be affecting the test.'

Dr Barrie went into meltdown. I'd bamboozled her often enough over the years with my ever-changing health problems, but she must have thought pregnancy was the one thing I wouldn't be able to pester her with. She looked at me in horror.

'Get up on to the table and I'll examine you,' she said, after a few minutes of head-scratching. 'Mmm . . . don't really feel anything,' she said, pressing her fingers on my abdomen. It was uncomfortable and made me squirm, but that seemed to be normal. 'I can't find anything that says "Pregnancy", to me,' she added, and I began to fear that maybe I had got it completely wrong after all. 'We'll do a urine test and see what that says. Call me back this afternoon and I'll have the results.'

It may have been my imagination, but I'd actually begun to *feel* pregnant, so when I called back in the afternoon and a flustered Dr Barrie confirmed the news, I was simply relaxed and happy.

'You've got to phone your oncologist first thing in the morning,' Dr Barrie was telling me. 'She'll know what happens from here. I'm afraid I haven't got the foggiest. This needs expert opinion.'

My next appointment with Dr Hendry was scheduled for Wednesday, just two days later, so I decided I would wait and tell her about it face to face. She was going through all the usual rigmarole, taking notes on how I'd been feeling, asking me if I'd had any particular problems.

'Well, I think I'm pregnant,' I said, and I swear she almost dropped her pen.

'What makes you say that?' she asked, pen still hovering above the form she was completing like she'd forgotten it was there.

'I've done three pregnancy tests and they've all come back positive,' I told her. 'I don't know whether it's because of the treatment that I'm having. I don't know whether the Herceptin can interfere with pregnancy tests,' I was gabbling. 'We didn't actually think this could happen, so Scott and I haven't really been taking precautions. I'm still not a hundred per cent sure, so I won't get my hopes up until I've had some kind of scan. Though I have to say, the results of the home pregnancy tests were pretty definite. The dots were supposed to be pink if you're newly pregnant, but mine were bright fuchsia pink.'

Dr Hendry sat staring at me throughout my minor outburst. She was shell-shocked. 'Uh-huh,' she said, when I paused for breath. 'Sounds like you're pregnant.'

Oh, brilliant!

'Couldn't the Herceptin be interfering with the results?' I asked.

'No, there's no reason why the drug should give a false positive,' she said, her face as sober as Scott's had been for the past couple of days. 'We're going to need a bit of help now. Let's think about what we're going to do.'

I'd taken Mum with me as moral support and she'd remained quiet during these initial discussions, nervously twisting a handkerchief, but as soon as Dr Hendry agreed that I was undoubtedly pregnant, she could hold back no longer.

'Is everything going to be OK?' she said. 'I mean, I thought she couldn't get pregnant. Isn't that what you told her? I can't believe she's pr—'

'Mum, will you please be quiet,' I interrupted. I wanted to concentrate on what was going on and I needed some peace to focus. This was serious. Dr Hendry was in no doubt whatsoever.

So where exactly was I supposed to go from here? Dr Hendry was concentrating, tapping her fingers gently on the desk. She'd never heard of anyone who'd had a baby while on long-term Herceptin treatment. She didn't even know of a pregnancy. She'd never discussed it with her colleagues; she'd never even thought about it. Trust me to present her with another challenge.

'I'm going to go and speak to an obstetrician I know at Princess Royal Maternity Hospital in Glasgow,' she said finally. 'Can you wait here while I make a few phone calls?'

So Mum and I sat in her office together. I was beginning to realise this whole thing could turn out to be a terrible mistake.

Within half an hour Dr Hendry was back, clutching a piece of paper with some notes written on it. 'I want you to go and meet with a great obstetrician called Dr Mathers. I've told him all about you and he'd like us to sit down together and talk about this. We want to do that as soon as possible, but in the meantime we'll try and find out more about how Herceptin may affect the unborn child. We'll need to ascertain if you can continue taking it, if it would affect the baby's development or if it may interfere with your ability to carry the baby to full term. Clearly you will need to consider your options of what happens next carefully.'

Medical terms, intervention, negativity . . . she was ruining my happy dream. I could tell she was studiously avoiding using the word 'termination'. The way she looked at me when she spoke about having 'options of what happens next' said it all. I understood abortion would be an obvious course of action. I hadn't completely ruled it out; I just didn't want to think about it because I was so happy. Plus I wanted to be armed with all the facts and potential scenarios before I made a decision like that.

'I'm not really sure what to say to Scott,' I told Mum after we left. 'I'm getting worried about how he's handling this.'

Things had become very tense between us. We couldn't even discuss the pregnancy without rowing. Fundamentally, we had come to opposing views on what we should do if it turned out I really was expecting. I wanted the baby so much I was determined to continue, even if all we had was a remote chance that everything would be OK. I was prepared to take a risk with my treatment if it meant having this child. Scott would accept no risk to my health whatsoever. He wanted me, the wife he had dedicated his life to, the partner he'd nursed through cancer, the woman he helped keep alive.

If the choice was between me and an unborn baby that may not survive, he wanted me. He had someone to love already. Why gamble her on something that may never happen, on someone who may never come to be?

'We didn't think we could have children anyway,' he'd argued. 'We got our heads round that. We don't need to change our minds now, not if it's dangerous for you.'

Certainly, we had never planned or prepared for having a baby, and I'd never been the type of woman who really longs for children. Nevertheless the mothering instinct had taken hold of me. I thought of Joseph and his two kids; I thought of Dawn and Stephanie, my mum and me, all of them really special relationships. I could have that too, with a child of my own. It was amazing. I was excited and exhilarated. Scott was dejected and morose. I told the people closest to me and revelled in their reaction. Scott told no one. I ached to shout it from the rooftops and go out shopping for baby clothes. Scott wanted it to go away. The friction was making life difficult at home.

A week later we were walking through the doors of the Princess Royal Maternity Hospital for our summit meeting with Dr Hendry and Dr Mathers. Not a cancer unit this time, but a maternity unit, where new lives came into the world every day. Not like ward G6, where lives vanished on a regular basis.

'I can't believe this is happening,' I said to Scott.

He ignored me.

Dr Hendry was waiting for us and led us into a private room to wait for Dr Mathers. I tried to question her about what she'd heard from the Herceptin manufacturers – a pharmaceutical company called Roche – but she insisted she wanted to wait until Dr Mathers arrived before we spoke in detail.

'Dr Hendry, there is something that I need to know,' I said. 'How long do you think I've got left?'

The question took her by surprise. She'd become so used to steering me away from the issue with a few lines about Herceptin being a new drug and no one really knowing how long it could keep me well. I'd never pushed it before, but she knew the information was crucial to me. If there was any chance to have this baby, I had to know how long I might be around to raise it.

'This isn't just about me now,' I continued. 'I need to know what I might reasonably expect.'

Scott would always get by without me, even if he didn't think so, but leaving a child behind was totally different.

'I know you can't be precise, but if I go through with this pregnancy, how long do you think I might last,' I pressed further.

She tried to avoid answering again. 'Well, it's so hard to say . . .' she said. 'It varies so much . . .'

'OK,' I broke in. 'If we just think about someone in my position, diagnosed with the type of cancer I have, would you give them five years?'

She raised her shoulders slightly, trying to shrug me off. But I wasn't deterred. 'What might Herceptin give me? Maybe another year and a half.'

I was doing the mental arithmetic: I was already on my fourth year since diagnosis. Did that mean I might only have a year or so left if I had to stop the Herceptin?

'I don't know, Mandy,' she sighed. 'It could be more or it could be less. Anyway, we are not talking about you, just someone in your position.'

She was spared more interrogation by the arrival of Dr Mathers, a tall, friendly-looking man with thinning sandy hair who swept into the room, looked directly at me and said, 'Well, we don't need to do a pregnancy test on you. You're wearing the pregnancy mask.'

I was slightly taken aback.

'Pregnancy can cause pigmentation changes in the facial skin, making it darken,' he went on, peering at my face as he shook my hand. 'We call it the "pregnancy mask" and you've definitely got it.'

I hadn't noticed it at all, but he was the top man, so if Dr Mathers said I was pregnant, I was most certainly pregnant. An absolute confirmation from an expert – so much more reliable than a few disposable testing kits.

Dr Hendry started speaking first. She'd been searching for information on previous patients and consulting with many of her colleagues but she hadn't found any other

British women in my situation. 'And the Herceptin manufacturers do not recommend Herceptin in pregnancy at all,' she added.

I'd worked out that I'd already had at least twenty Herceptin treatments since I started on the drug the previous January. It was a bit late to start thinking about damage control.

'I've only found twelve documented cases worldwide of women becoming pregnant while on the drug long-term and none of their cases have been published so it is extremely difficult to advise you,' she went on.

It was mind-boggling.

Oh, yes, Mandy, I thought to myself, when you do something, you do it big time.

Scott wanted a definitive answer: did she think we should continue with this pregnancy or not?

'I don't think Mandy should stop the Herceptin,' he added. 'It has worked for her up till now. I don't want to mess about with that.'

Dr Hendry concurred, 'You're right. If Mandy continues with the pregnancy, Dr Mathers and I think she should keep having Herceptin. It's a balancing act between the risks of Mandy stopping treatment and the risks to the baby of continuing treatment. We think Mandy would be in greater danger than the baby, but we can't be certain.'

So the decision really had to be ours. We had to weigh

up the risks. What meant more, life or motherhood? Why couldn't I have both?

'I'm sorry that I can't tell you more,' she said, leaning back in her chair, 'but there is so little information available because Herceptin is such a new drug.'

She didn't complete her explanation, but I knew what she meant. Women with secondary breast cancer weren't really expected to get pregnant. They weren't expected to be well enough. They certainly weren't expected to be crazy enough to go through with it – especially if they were taking a new drug.

Dr Mathers took over the discussion. 'Mandy, Dr Hendry and I will support you all the way if you decide to go along with this pregnancy.'

I gave a sigh of relief. There was still a slim chance I could do this.

'We'll monitor both you and your baby very closely, probably giving you an ultrasound every couple of weeks. We'll keep a very close eye on the baby and a very close eye on you. You'll get your usual blood tests and you'll have your heart checked frequently, but we won't be able to do any of the regular CT scans you've been having to keep track of the cancer.'

Apparently CT scans are a no-no for pregnant women because the radiation they emit could damage the baby.

Regardless of our decision, I would need to have an ultrasound scan to date the pregnancy. It was scheduled for Friday, two days' time. I was mortified to admit it, but we had no idea when I might have conceived, and without periods to help the calculations, they could only work it out by the size of the baby.

'I'd guess at about three months,' said Dr Mathers, 'but I'll know better once I can do some measurements.'

He explained that we wouldn't have to watch the images of the baby if we didn't feel we could: 'The screen will be turned away from you, so you won't have to see anything,' he said. 'Some people find that easier in case they decide not to proceed with the pregnancy.'

So we had an urgent decision to make, Scott and me. By the time we arrived for the scan on Friday, we would have to know whether we wanted to keep the baby. I couldn't possibly look at pictures of a child inside my tummy if there was any prospect of a termination. We had to make up our minds over the next two days. There was nothing else for it.

I felt compelled to state my case as soon as we got home: 'I don't know what you've decided, Scott, but I want to keep this baby.'

I was prepared for a battle. We'd had some spectacular arguments over the past few days, but I'd found it quite easy to reassure Scott because we'd always been able to walk away thinking, Oh well, it might never come to a big decision. It could all be taken out of our hands.

'If we listen to everything the doctors have to say and

if you still want me to terminate, then I will definitely think about it,' I'd told him only the day before.

Now I realised, though, that the choice had been placed in our hands. There seemed to be a faint hope that I might actually be able to have the baby. I wasn't about to give it up for anything. All bets were off. I was having it.

'We'll have to think about it,' he said, refusing to meet my gaze. 'I just don't know if it's the right thing.'

The row built with every comment we traded. He loved me more than the thought of having a child and he didn't want to lose me. But he was losing me. If he pushed me to have a termination, deprived me of my one chance of motherhood, I couldn't have forgiven him. I wouldn't have forgiven him. We'd drifted through the past few days not believing any of it could be real.

'Whatever we decide, it won't break us up,' we'd agreed with each other, like the deluded fools we were, but there was already a huge gulf between us and suddenly I could see it. Scott had a future, if not with me, then with someone else he might meet after I was gone. Whatever happened to me, whatever happened to the baby, his life would go on.

'I'm prepared to take my chances,' I said, as he got ready to go to work for the remainder of the day. 'I don't know what's ahead for me, but I'll face things as they come up. I'll play it by ear.'

Scott didn't reply. He slammed the door behind him.

It was late evening when he came back, but I was still on edge, readying myself for the next bout. He was ready too.

He followed me into the living room, threw his jacket down and said, 'I think you should have the baby.'

I was stunned. Was he serious? I could tell from his smile of resignation I'd won.

'Oh, I'm so glad. I'm so glad, Scott,' I said, wrapping him in the tightest hug, pulling him as close as I could. 'There's no way I could terminate. I just couldn't do it.'

We were both crying. I hadn't been fair on him. He was facing the prospect of losing both of us, me and the baby, and while I was being carried along merrily by hormones and euphoria, he was weighing it all up logically, trying to come to the right decision, not just a knee-jerk one.

We talked for ages about how to handle the situation, what we would do if things went wrong. We had to be brutally honest with one another.

'I know there's a chance I could be leaving you to look after a baby on your own,' I said. 'Whether it's sooner or later, at some point you'll be a single parent. That's a terrible pressure to put on you.'

The very thought of leaving my baby behind was agonising, the idea that my child may grow up without memories of me, without my influence or my support, was so painful. I had to be certain Scott could cope; it was the only way I could tolerate the guilt. If he was willing and ready to go it alone with our child, I would at least be leaving him with part of me. Would that make things better or worse? Easier or more difficult? Neither of us knew.

I was asking Scott to prepare himself for being a single parent at some point, but how was he supposed to do that? We didn't even know what it was like to be joint parents.

'This is going to be a lot of pressure on you too,' Scott was saying. 'What if you need more chemo in the future? You'll have a baby to look after when you're feeling awful. What if you need more surgery?'

Of course it wouldn't be easy, but we had a support structure that hadn't failed us once: our parents. We called Mum and Dad, and launched into one of the most difficult conversations we'd ever had, and that's saying something.

They knew I would make up my own mind about the pregnancy, so they weren't too surprised to hear that we'd decided to carry on with it and they didn't try to dissuade us. I know they had some really deep conversations between themselves about what we were doing, but they never shared them with me. For as much as they were terrified, they respected my decision. Our decision.

'We will do anything to help,' said Mum, her voice faltering. She rallied. 'We will always be around, no matter what,' she went on. 'Anything you want us to do, anything Scott wants us to do, we will do it. Anything the baby needs, we'll get it. We'll always be here. For ever.'

Scott's mum and dad lived about thirty miles away, a lot further than my parents, but they would be involved in any future child-rearing too. We had to ask their views, so we called them next. It was a dreadful thing to do to them, disturb their telly viewing of a Wednesday night to inquire if they'd be available to babysit or take over the school run if Scott suddenly found himself a single parent. They had probably been quite happily having a cup of tea before bedtime when we phoned with our scary queries. We probably ruined a perfectly good night's sleep for them.

'It's just that we've decided to go ahead with the pregnancy,' I could hear Scott tell his dad, 'and we need to know if you'll be able to help with the baby if anything were to happen to Mandy.'

Once he got over the shock of our requests, Scott's dad gave us the reassurance we needed. Of course they would do anything to help.

We went back to see Dr Mathers on Friday, feeling like newlyweds again, all jittery and excited, like the whole world should know about the incredible thing happening to us. I couldn't wait to get started, and we listened anxiously to Dr Mathers tell us exactly what would happen during the scan. Then he said, 'OK. Do you want me to turn the screen away?'

We looked at each other and grinned. 'No. We want to see it,' I said, rubbing Scott's hand. 'We're going on with the pregnancy.'

Dr Mathers smiled: he'd already sussed us. He started smearing gel all over my tummy with a device that looked a bit like an electric shaver and immediately the outline of a baby appeared on screen. It was the most incredible thing I'd ever seen. I could see the silhouette of its head, its little mouth and a tiny up-turned nose. It had one hand over its eye. It was squirming like it was annoyed at the intrusion on its peace and quiet, and it was big, much, much bigger than I'd expected.

Scott was squeezing my hand, and when I looked at him, he had tears in his eyes.

'That's our baby,' I whispered.

Dr Mathers was busy checking measurements and counting organs, clicking over the fuzzy white shape of our baby and typing figures into boxes. 'Well, this wee one seems absolutely fine,' he said eventually. 'A tiny bit small for its age, but then it is eighteen weeks, a lot older than we thought.'

Eighteen weeks! I almost fell off the table. I was four and a half months pregnant. I was halfway through. No wonder I was showing.

'The heart is fine,' Dr Mathers went on. 'Ten fingers, ten toes. If I didn't know any better, I'd think you were a normal pregnant woman with a healthy baby growing inside you.'

We were floating on air; the nerves were gone, replaced by sheer unadulterated joy.

'I am so unbelievably happy,' I declared. 'Let's go buy baby clothes.' And off we went touring every baby shop in Glasgow city centre and spending a small fortune on babygros and vests and little jackets.

Dr Mathers wouldn't tell us the sex of the baby, despite my persistent requests, but a couple of appointments after our first scan he caved in.

'What sex do you think your baby is?' he asked, rubbing the sonic device over my stomach.

Scott was convinced it was a boy.

'I'm afraid you're wrong, Scott,' he said, wiping the remains of the gel off the wand with a paper towel.

'Aha, it's a girl!' I shouted, frantically trying to straighten up my clothing so I could run out and phone my parents.

'Mum, you're having a granddaughter,' I bawled, when she finally answered. 'Do you want to come shopping for pink things?'

Dad was so excited he grabbed the phone from her to shout a message to Scott. 'Tell him not to worry,' he said. 'There's nothing like a daddy's girl.'

Chubby

I lowered myself carefully into a seat in the waiting room of the oncology department and puffed with relief to finally rest my weary bones. A nurse at the reception desk looked up and smiled at me kindly, probably under the impression that I'd hauled my pregnant self a very long way to visit a poor cancer-stricken relative.

'Mandy McMillan, please,' called out another nurse, who'd emerged from a treatment room nearby.

I lifted myself up again and started to waddle down the corridor. 'Hi there,' I smiled as I walked into the room in front of her.

Cancer nurses are not easily surprised, so I was always quite amused to come across one I'd never met before and watch her jaw drop as I heaved my enormous baby belly into the chair, ready to be hooked up for my Herceptin treatment.

'Are you definitely here for Herceptin?' she asked, checking the details on my file.

'Yup, that's right,' I replied.

'And you're pregnant?' She had to check I wasn't just chubby.

'Yup, right again, and before you ask, yes, I do know what I'm doing.'

The last bit wasn't strictly true.

Chapter 16

My pregnancy was destined to be remarkably short. The entire first trimester and nearly half of the second had passed before I'd even found out I was expecting. Dr Mathers had informed me that if I developed any problems, he'd be happy to deliver from thirty-two weeks.

'Anything over thirty-two weeks will be a bonus,' he said, 'but if we get you to at least thirty-two weeks, I'll feel comfortable. From my calculations, I think your baby would be due on 25 June, if she were to go full term, so you can expect to be having her anytime from May onwards.'

That meant I could have as little as fourteen weeks of pregnancy left, which would have been a doddle for anyone less impatient than me.

'I'm so fed up waiting,' I moaned at Dr Mathers at my mid-April appointment. I was about twenty-nine weeks gone and felt around twenty-nine stone. 'Time is dragging by and I'm so uncomfortable. My feet are really swollen. Can't we deliver the baby a bit earlier?'

He leaned back in his chair chortling, his hands behind his head. 'So, let's get this straight,' he said, 'you want me to deliver this baby as soon as possible because the only shoes you can wear at the moment are flip-flops.'

We had these spats every week, because every week I tried to give him a different reason to deliver earlier, and every week he almost bust a gut laughing at my arguments. I'd already attempted to convince him that he really should have me induced soon if only to cure my awful carpal tunnel syndrome.

'My wrists are so sore that I can't cut hair properly,' I protested. 'You should see the state of some of my customers.'

Cue another eruption of hysterics from the good doctor.

'I'll give you some splints for your wrists,' he said eventually, once he'd stopped laughing. 'Wear them to bed every night and see if that helps. If not, I might bring you in for some steroid injections to ease the pain. What I won't be doing is delivering your baby right now, I'm afraid.'

I thought it worth mentioning that I was too fat for my favourite maternity clothes and didn't want to waste money on more.

'Argh! Stop it,' he cried, waving his hands in protest. 'No, no, no. Off you go. Back to your poor customers. And don't drag your flip-flops on the way out.'

I've noticed that people – particularly doctors – expect

me to be extremely tolerant of what they consider minor ailments because I'm so used to dealing with major ones, but human nature doesn't work like that. I might know I'm not going to die of a cold or a tummy bug, and definitely not from pregnancy-related carpal tunnel syndrome, but that doesn't stop it being miserable. Anyway, I quite liked having normal things to moan about for a change. I enjoyed bumping into people I hadn't seen for a while and discussing my pregnancy ailments instead of my cancer.

Truth be told, I was the healthiest I'd been since the cancer was first diagnosed. Irritating pregnancy symptoms notwithstanding, I seemed to be free of any major health problems. Of course, I couldn't have my regular CT scans, so I did fret over every unexplained twinge or ache anywhere in my body.

'You have to accept that every pregnant woman experiences pains like that,' Dr Mathers explained. 'Your organs are getting squashed by a growing baby and you'll undoubtedly be getting some discomfort. That doesn't necessarily mean your cancer is progressing. I know we're working in the dark, but we have to go along with that for a while.' He could be really quite tender at times, but he'd have to throw in a barb too. 'Right now you seem like any other pregnant woman to me,' he'd add. 'A bit more annoying than most pregnant women, but normal nonetheless.'

My antenatal classes were fun for exactly that reason: I was just an ordinary mum-to-be like all the others there. Dr Hendry transferred my Herceptin treatment from Gartnavel to Glasgow's Royal Infirmary, which was attached to the Princess Royal Maternity Hospital, so I could have my cancer treatment and maternity care in the same place, coordinating appointments whenever I could. I went to antenatal class in the maternity wing every week before going along the corridor for a chat with Dr Mathers. Every third week I'd waddle down to the oncology department in the adjoining hospital and have my Herceptin check-up and treatment. I got to know those hospital corridors like the back of my hand.

The girls in my antenatal class had no idea about any of that until I announced my predicament to the whole group during the infamous discussion on breastfeeding. The girls I'd become most friendly with wanted to know the detail of everything that had happened to me, not realising it was such a long tale. By the time I brought them up to speed with a potted version, their coffees were freezing cold and their expressions priceless.

'How on earth are you managing?' said Lorna eventually. 'I'm finding it hard enough just being pregnant and you've got so many other things going on.'

I didn't really know how to explain.

'I don't think about cancer all the time,' I said. 'It's probably quite hard to believe, but I don't go to bed worrying about it every night and it's not in my mind all day.'

The girls were bamboozled.

'I can't believe there's anything wrong with you,' said Nic. 'You look perfectly healthy to me.'

I was quietly enjoying the fact that I'd been able to shock them, fool them into thinking I was just like them.

'I've lived with this for such a long time,' I went on. 'I've learned to get on with things and take each day as it comes. Having a baby is such a surprise. I'm loving every minute.'

Surprisingly, I wasn't particularly worried about the condition of the baby. The ultrasound scans I was having every week showed she was developing normally.

'She's still maybe a little small,' said Dr Mathers, 'but she seems healthy enough.'

From the dates the doctor had worked out, we figured I must have conceived Holly at around the end of August, probably when we were on that embarrassing holiday in Cyprus. Who would have thought it? All that clambering around over fences and sneaking along back streets must have been good for me. That meant I was about five weeks pregnant during the Breast Cancer Care fashion show, which would go some way to explaining why I was so bloated. When we'd watched a video recording of the show, Dad had commented, 'My God, you're looking a bit tubby there, Mandy.'

I'd tutted while everyone else sniggered. 'Thanks a lot, Dad,' I said. 'I was recovering from chemo, you know.'

If he'd only known at the time the real reason I was fat: his granddaughter was taking up a lot of space in that round tum!

The dates also meant I was pregnant when Dawn died. How unpredictable this illness is. One of us was generating new life, while the other was losing her own. It was beyond belief.

My friend Esther, the one who had originally encouraged me to take my pregnancy symptoms seriously, was chuffed to bits when I told her she'd been proved right. She came round to visit, bringing the most touching gift. 'It's a pregnancy angel,' she said. 'It's supposed to look after you while you're expecting.'

In my hormonal condition I could have wept. Esther had always been so thoughtful, often sending cards and little presents to let me know she was thinking about me, but the angel was particularly beautiful. It was the winged figure of a mother gently cradling her swollen tummy. Esther knew I loved to keep my angel trinkets close so they could look after my health. Now I had one especially to look after my pregnancy, my most precious gift. I still treasure that angel.

The *Sunday Mail*, which sponsored the fashion show, heard about my pregnancy through Breast Cancer Care and called to ask if we'd like to tell our story.

Oh, that would be great, I thought right away. I can keep the cutting to show to my little girl as she gets older and then she'll have a record of everything that has happened to us.

Scott agreed, and before we knew it we were posing for photos in our living room, Scott standing behind me, his hands on my seven-and-a-half-months-gone bump. They even worked a bit of computer magic on the photos to get rid of the outline of the hideous maternity bra that was showing through my stretchy top. So that's how the stars get to look great all the time. You can't beat a bit of airbrushing.

When the piece appeared on Sunday, it called me 'Scotland's bravest mum' and I was taken aback. Not for a second had I thought of my decision to continue with the pregnancy as 'brave'. It was risky, and probably selfish, but it wasn't brave. They listed what I'd been through – a mastectomy, two courses of chemo, radiotherapy, a recurrence of the cancer, then secondaries – and even I had to admit it seemed pretty dramatic. Add to that the fourteen doses of Herceptin I'd had before conceiving in August – plus the six I'd received while unaware I was pregnant – and suddenly I could see what a gamble I was taking. The article said my baby would be the UK's first known Herceptin baby – conceived, carried and born to a woman on long-term Herceptin treatment for advanced breast cancer. 'Mandy's million-to-one baby' they called her. She would be utterly unique.

'We're actually doing something quite special,' I said, as Scott and I read the piece for the twentieth time. 'When you see it written out in black and white, it does sound pretty incredible.'

From the moment the piece appeared, our phone rang off the hook with magazines looking to tell our tale.

'Oh, let's do it,' I'd persuade a reluctant Scott. 'If we make any money out of it, we can put it in a trust fund for the baby.'

We became mini-celebrities for a while, thanks to our little Herceptin girl, and she hadn't yet made her appearance.

Everything was ready and in place for my wee bundle's arrival, though. We had already decorated the nursery and ordered her pram. The baby's room had been finished for weeks because I'd known exactly how I wanted it to look. I chose a cream-coloured border with bunnies and teddies all over it and picked out pale beech furniture and a squashy armchair where I could nurse the baby to sleep. I might not be able to breastfeed, but I could certainly give my baby plenty of cuddles. Once Dr Mathers told us we were having a girl, I started adding pink accessories – picture frames and cushions and little toys – until it became the perfect little haven for our daughter. Some nights I'd sit in there, absorbing the place and trying to imagine what it would be like once our baby had taken up residence. Within days of being completed the wardrobe was full of clothes. I just couldn't stop buying things, my favourites being little shoes made of the softest leather. I had half a dozen pairs.

Near the end of April, just after my seventh antenatal class, I was sitting in Dr Mathers's room waiting for the results of some urine tests.

I wish he'd hurry up, I was thinking. I'm supposed to be meeting Scott in an hour.

Dr Mathers had other ideas. 'You're not going anywhere,' he declared. 'There's some protein in your urine, so I want to keep an eye on you for a while, it seems you're developing pre-eclampsia.' He glanced at my feet, bulging against the flip-flops I was wearing. 'Your feet are pretty swollen too,' he said. 'That's another sign.'

I was beginning to realise what he meant. 'Is the baby coming soon, then?' I asked nervously.

'Well, we'll see how you are over the next couple of days,' said Dr Mathers. 'We'll keep an eye on you over the weekend and see where we are on Monday.'

I knew it! I knew it! By Sunday I would be thirty-two weeks gone and would have reached his milestone. I'd worked out the dates that morning and I had a funny feeling it would be happening soon. Not that I had been so presumptuous as to bring my hospital bag with me or to tell the girls at antenatal class that I might not be back, or even to warn Scott of my hunch.

I phoned him: 'Scott, you're going to have to bring up my bag. They're keeping me in over the weekend. It's going to be soon. Maybe Monday.'

What was I saying? We were finally going to get to meet our little girl. It was too exciting.

'I'm coming right up,' he said, and hung up before I got the chance to ask him for anything else.

He arrived with Mum and Dad, who fussed around me in a mild panic, looking for something helpful to do but only succeeding in getting in each other's way. I sat on the bed in the little private room I had been given, gratefully watching the comings and goings of a maternity ward. Pregnant women tottered past my door; new mums paced the corridors with crying babies in their arms; nurses wheeled little plastic cots containing tiny newborns wrapped in cotton blankets. It was so happy. I'd spent so much of the past few years in hospital, but for the first time I was glad to be a patient. It felt wonderful.

Dr Mathers had advised against a natural birth and suggested that a Caesarean section would be a safer option. 'The baby is going to be considerably premature,' he said. 'We don't want her – or you for that matter – becoming stressed during delivery.'

I was happy to take his advice. He had a look at the reconstruction scar on my tummy and said he'd just open it up again for the C-section, which Scott thought sounded horrific, but which troubled me not at all. I'd suffered far worse for far longer.

'Don't worry about it,' the doctor said. 'It's quite straightforward.'

I wasn't worried in the slightest. A twenty-minute procedure under a spinal anaesthetic...that was nothing.

On Saturday night Mum was visiting with her friend Heather when Dr Mathers came in to run a few checks on me. Mum and Heather went to wait in the corridor.

'I don't have anything to do tomorrow,' said the doctor, as he washed his hands, 'so I might as well come in and deliver your baby ... That is, as long as it's not good weather. If it's a nice day, I'll really have to go and play golf.'

'Tomorrow, Mum!' I called out to her in the corridor. 'The baby's coming tomorrow!' I could hear her whooping with excitement.

'That's it – we're going nowhere,' she said, dashing in to hug me. 'Heather and I will wait here and keep you company. You'll be too nervous to be left on your own.'

They took a lot of persuading to leave, but I convinced Mum, finally, to head off home and try to preserve her energy for the following morning.

'I'll be fine till you see me then,' I shouted after her as she left, waving frantically. They didn't hear me add, 'Then I'll be terrified.'

I called Scott at work at the Chinese takeaway. He'd

already accepted a couple of shifts that weekend, knowing the extra cash would come in handy for the baby, so he was a bit annoyed when I told him he'd have to take Sunday off.

'Oh, come on, Mandy,' he groaned. 'You know I can't ask for that. I've already said I'll work. I'll be up to keep you company for a while during the day, but it's a bit short notice to take the night off.' He had missed the point. The baby was coming on Sunday.

'OK, you work, then, but you might miss your baby's birth if you do,' I said. 'Dr Mathers is going to deliver tomorrow.'

Then I heard him bellow across to his boss that he wouldn't be in the next day. He would be busy becoming a dad.

I knew I should rest as much as I could, but sleep evaded me. My head was crammed with fantasies of what my baby would look like. I was turning over thoughts of how my life was about to change, and shaking off the black fears every time they threatened to invade. They'd been tormenting me more and more as the weeks passed and they always managed to disturb me at bedtime, when my guard was down and I had time to brood. I often found myself wondering what Dawn would make of it all. This night was different, though; it was too precious to sully with sadness. I could feel my baby's little limbs bumping their way around my insides, searching for an exit. By morning I would get to meet her and hold her. The prospect of going under the knife again meant nothing. I wasn't even worried about the baby's health. The button-nosed beauty I had seen on the ultrasound scans was going to be perfect – I knew that deep in my heart.

I'm not scared at all, I realised. I've never felt so alive.

Scott arrived at 8 a.m. sharp. 'How you feeling, Mummy?' he said. 'Are you ready to have our baby?'

We couldn't stop talking about what was about to happen.

'I wish Dr Mathers would hurry up and get here,' Scott said. 'I really want to get started.'

Dr Mathers hadn't given me an estimated time of arrival, and none of the nurses seemed to know when he was expected.

'I hope he hasn't changed his mind,' I said. 'There's no way he's golfing in this weather.'

The rain thudded down just as it had on our wedding day, exactly two years before. Scotland in May, wet and wonderful.

Scott's dad arrived mid-morning. It wasn't like him to turn up unannounced. 'Thought I'd pop in and wish you all the best,' he said.

He'd been at work and decided to come and see how we were doing, but once with us, he didn't really know what to do with himself. He wasn't alone in that.

Everyone was on edge. Mum and Dad were buzzing around me, and Scott couldn't sit still. There was no sign of the doctor. They all ate sandwiches and drank tea for lunch, while I sat watching them enviously. I wasn't allowed any food until after the op.

'Great – I'm uncomfortable, nervous and starving, but you lot get to have your lunch,' I stropped. 'Can we please find someone who knows when I'll be having this baby?'

Every time someone wandered past the door to my room, we'd leap up in anticipation. We ambushed umpteen nurses, thinking they may know when Dr Mathers would be arriving. At 2.30 p.m. he finally swept in and we all practically pounced on him.

'Och, it's such a miserable day that I decided to come in and deliver your baby,' he laughed. 'Golfing in this rain is not fun.'

Scott was squeezing my hand. Mum and Dad were on their feet. This was it.

Then everything happened so quickly. The porters arrived to take me to theatre and Scott went off to wash and change into some scrubs.

'We'll wait in the corridor for you,' Mum said, kissing my forehead. 'I can't wait to see your wee baby.'

By the time Scott appeared at my side, decked out in blue scrubs with what looked like a J-cloth tied round his head, I'd already been given the spinal block and was numb from the waist down.

'What do you look like?' I chuckled, but he was too busy concentrating on the screen the theatre nurses were erecting, which would shield his sensitive eyes from any of the gory action.

'I'm just going to keep looking at you,' he said. 'I don't want to see any of the stuff going on down there.'

I didn't blame him.

'I hope he cleans her before he passes her to me,' I replied. 'I don't really fancy seeing too much blood myself.'

'Right, we'll get started,' Dr Mathers said, and a moment later I felt tugging and pushing and pulling at the bottom half of my body.

Another few moments on he was holding a bloody little creature high above the screen.

'There's your baby girl,' he said, bringing her down towards my face, just close enough for me to manage the merest brush of a kiss on her cheek. Then he whisked her away out of my sight.

Everyone was speaking at once.

'Is she all right? Is she all right?' I was saying. I couldn't hear her cry.

'My God,' Scott was saying, 'you've done it.'

'She's absolutely fine,' a woman's voice was saying from somewhere in the room. 'We're just going to weigh her.'

Then a sudden newborn cry. Thank God. Thank God. Her parents were in floods of tears too.

'She's got dark hair,' Scott said.

'No, I think that's just blood on her head,' I replied.

'Three pounds fourteen,' the nurse called to us. 'She's fine, but we're taking her to an incubator to help her breathing get started properly.'

And she was away, my baby already in another room minutes after leaving my body. I'd only caught the most fleeting glimpse of her, just a brief touch.

'We've got a wee girl,' Scott said. 'We've got a daughter.'

It was 3.04 p.m. on Sunday, 1 May 2005 and our May Day girl was in the world at last.

'Congratulations, Mum and Dad,' said Dr Mathers, who was still hidden from view behind the screen. 'I'm just going to stitch you back up, Mandy. Won't be long.'

I was desperate to get out of there to see my baby. 'Do you think they'll let me hold her?' I asked Scott. 'I know she's small, but I hope I get to hold her.'

I became aware that the pushing and pulling sensation of the delivery had started again. What was Dr Mathers doing? Don't tell me there was another one in there.

'Don't mind me,' he said eventually. 'I'm just having a wee feel around your liver to see how everything is. It all looks fine.'

Cancer stormed back into my world, my Caesarean scar still open, my baby still blood-stained, my post-birth delirium still raging.

'I thought I may as well have a look around while we had you opened up,' Dr Mathers went on, finally starting to stitch. 'You'll be glad to hear that I can't see any problems.'

I was kind of glad, though maybe I would have liked to savour the moment a little longer.

I was wheeled towards a recovery room, Scott still by my side, holding my hand as the nurses guided the operating trolley along a short corridor and congratulated me for being so brave.

'I can't wait for my toast,' I said, suddenly overwhelmed with hunger. 'I've had nothing to eat all day. Will you tell them I don't like tea?'

Scott laughed. 'Trust you to think about food,' he said. 'I'll ask them to bring you something in a minute. Is it OK if I head up to intensive care to see the baby? Should I take your mum and dad with me?'

I'd almost forgotten about them, waiting anxiously further down the hall.

'Yes, of course,' I said. 'Bring me photos of her. Tell her mummy loves her.'

I'm still waiting for that toast. No one ever appeared with it. In fact, I think the midwives must have forgotten I was lying in the recovery room because it was a good four hours before someone arrived to take me back to the ward. Scott had returned clutching Polaroids of our daughter, a scrap of a thing lying stretched out in an incubator wearing only a nappy and a little cloth hat. She had tubes coming out of her nose. She was mine. I was desperate to hold her. Scott was euphoric. He seemed to glow with love for his child.

'She's so beautiful,' he said, 'and she's so small. She's in an incubator, and they've got her attached to a machine to regulate her breathing, but they're saying it's just a precaution because she's so premature. They're really happy with how she's coming along. Honestly, though, she's so teeny.'

Mum and Dad appeared, fresh from making four million phone calls to tell the whole country they had just become grandparents again.

'I think she's got red hair,' Mum said, as she poured forth on the baby's inherited good looks. 'I'm not sure where she would get that from, mind you.'

I felt my eyes fill up. Listening to them was hard. They were talking about my little girl and I hadn't even seen her properly. I stared at the Polaroids, trying to get to know every inch of her.

'I don't think she's a Lauren,' I told Scott. 'She looks more like a Holly, don't you think?'

We'd been alternating between both names in the days before.

'I think you're right,' he said. 'She's definitely Holly McMillan.'

Holly McMillan, my daughter.

Mum and Dad had been wrung dry by it all. 'Right, we'll leave you in peace for a while – we're off to celebrate,' Dad said. 'Congratulations, Mandy. I'm proud of you.'

Scott was itching to spread the news too, so they kissed me goodbye and headed off to the Muirhead Inn to announce Holly's safe arrival and toast her health. And mine, of course.

'Please, please take me up to see my baby,' I begged every nurse who came into my room to check on me.

'You're still too weak,' they would say. 'You'll have to wait till the anaesthetic has worn off a bit,' or, 'We'll wait till your bleeding has stopped, then we'll take you.'

I thought I might erupt with sheer frustration. 'Don't tell me I'm not strong enough to see my own baby,' I snapped. 'I know what I'm strong enough to cope with.'

Still, it was about 11 p.m. by the time they manoeuvred me into a wheelchair and took me to the intensive-care unit.

'I won't even recognise my own baby,' I worried aloud, as we arrived at a ward full of incubators. 'They all look the same.'

The nurse wheeled me straight across the room to a clear plastic incubator that had a name sticker on the end: Baby McMillan.

She was lying on her side, her face turned towards me, her eyes closed tightly but her bare chest fluttering like a bird's. The midwives had curved a rolled-up blanket round her feet and another round her head to make her feel cosy and secure. She was wearing a pale green cotton hat and what looked like a doll's nappy, and she had little identification bands round one foot and one wrist. She was only about twelve inches long and seemed so delicate I was scared to touch her. There were arm holes in the sides of the incubator and I nervously reached through till my hand met hers for the first time. She was safe. She had survived. I had survived. My tears fell like the rain outside. Alone with my daughter at last, I was engulfed. Instant unconditional love.

'You're a little miracle, Holly,' I told her, cautiously stroking her tiny body. 'I'm so glad that you're here. I'm going to do my very best to take care of you. I'm going to be here for you as long as I can be. You're so beautiful. I love you more than anything else in the world, and I'm going to try to be a really good mummy.'

I don't know how long I sat there. It was the most magical time. I was hanging on her every movement, startled every time she gave a little wink, hoping she might open both eyes and look at me. She'd purse her lips or open her mouth or screw up her nose and it was the most amazing thing. How could something so wonderful have come from me after everything else? It was like my body had a dual personality.

'I think you should go and get some sleep now,

Mandy,' said the midwife. 'You'll be too tired to look after her in the morning if you don't rest.'

I kissed my fingertip and touched Holly's cheek. Then the midwife wheeled me back to my room, where I cried myself into the deepest sleep I'd had for a very long time, induced by a powerful mixture of exhaustion and happiness.

I awoke abruptly, momentarily confused by my surroundings. 'Nurse, nurse, can you take me to see my baby, please?' I shouted to a passing midwife.

'Well, you should have a shower and a bit of breakfast first,' she said. 'You want to be sure that the anaesthetic has worn off.'

I was uneasy, suddenly fearful that something was wrong with Holly. Maybe I'd just been dreaming that my baby was all right. Anything could have been happening to her while I was lying there fast asleep. When I finally got taken back to intensive care, though, there she was, dozing peacefully in her semi-naked state. She was real. I hadn't imagined her. The sight of her nearly stopped my heart. Holly was still in a little nappy-and-hat combo, flat on her back in the incubator.

'Baby's doing really well,' the midwife smiled. 'She's holding her own, so I think we'll be taking her off the breathing monitor once the doctor has had a look at her.'

Oh, the relief. She was strong.

Then the midwife started to change Holly's nappy. I

watched intently as she deftly removed a nasty one, cleaned Holly's sticky bottom and put on a nice clean nappy, all at arm's length, working through the two access holes in the side of the incubator. It was clearly an acquired skill.

'Would you like to do this?' the midwife asked, conscious of me staring at her.

'No, thanks, I'll just watch for the first few times,' I said. 'I'm too nervous at the moment. She's so tiny.'

The midwife was keen to encourage me, demonstrating how easy it was to lift the baby's legs and slide an open nappy under her bottom. I thought she was being a bit rough with my little girl.

'These babies are more resilient than you think,' she said. 'When you come up after dinner, you'll probably be able to hold her for a while, and don't panic when you do. She's not going to snap.'

I could hardly wait. I'd read so much about the value of skin-to-skin contact between mum and newborn – it was supposed to help forge a special bond between us – and I was yearning to hold her body to my chest.

Scott arrived, beaming from ear to ear and clutching a little pink elephant. 'How is my daughter today?' he said, giving me a cuddle. 'Isn't she just gorgeous?' he continued, peering into Holly's crib. 'Is she OK, though? I mean, why has she still got a tube up her nose?'

The midwife explained that Holly was being fed

through the tube because she was too small to suck from a bottle. 'Right now she's getting a millilitre of milk at every feed,' she said. 'That's less than a teaspoonful. It's a tiny amount because her stomach is still so small. We'll increase it gradually as she starts getting bigger, and once she can take about sixty millilitres from a bottle, she'll be well enough to go home with her mum and dad.' It seemed such a distant hope. 'You'll be surprised at how quickly she progresses,' the midwife reassured us.

By lunchtime I was swamped with overexcited visitors, all taking turns to file up to intensive care and gaze through the windows at my daughter. Mum and Dad were bursting with pride. They'd arrived with an enormous pink-and-white bouquet for their new granddaughter.

'She's so dinky,' Mum kept saying. 'None of the stuff you've bought is going to fit her.'

The wardrobe full of clothes at home would be of no use, at least not for another few months. Everything was newborn size, but that meant for infants weighing around seven pounds, twice the weight of Holly. They would drown her.

'I'm going to have to find premature baby clothes,' I told Mum. 'I'm desperate to dress her.'

Later that night, when all the visitors had gone, the midwife pulled a large armchair to the side of Holly's incubator and drew a screen round it. 'Take off your pyjama top and make yourself comfortable,' she told me. 'When you're ready, I'll place Holly on your chest.'

My heart was racing. At last I would hold my own child. I watched as she removed Holly's nappy and lifted her clear of the incubator.

'There you go,' she said, resting the feather-light bundle on my healthy breast. 'Meet your little girl.'

I'll remember that moment for ever, nothing between me and my daughter, as close as we could ever be. She was fast asleep, utterly beautiful.

'I-I don't know if I'm holding her right,' I stammered.

'You're doing just fine,' said the midwife, wrapping a blanket round us to keep Holly warm.

Scott sat beside us, gently stroking the baby's back. We were a family. After all that had happened to us, we'd become a family.

'I'm terrified of getting things wrong, Scott,' I said. 'We don't have a clue how to look after her, do we?'

Scott gave a little laugh. 'We're no different to any other new parents,' he said. 'We'll pick it up as we go along.'

I spent every night in that nursing chair, holding my little naked baby. After my last visitors left, I'd go straight back to intensive care and nurse Holly till midnight. I'd talk to her, tell her all about her parents and her grandparents, about how her mum had been sick and needed special medicine to help her get better, about how

I was going to take her out in her pram very soon and we'd see lots of new things. Holly slept through it all, occasionally opening one eye to have a look at the woman who was prattling away so much nonsense.

The girls from the antenatal class arrived for their weekly meeting to be informed that I'd had my baby and that I was waiting upstairs to see them. They hurried in like a flock of mother hens, flapping around and clucking that they couldn't believe I'd beaten them all to it.

'Leave me your phone numbers so we can meet up after you've all had your babies,' I said. 'The little ones can play and we can have a gab.'

'We've got a while to go yet,' said Lorna. 'We'll come and see you before we pop.'

We didn't have long to wait for the next arrival, however, because Alison went into premature labour and delivered baby Grace the following week. Three weeks early, she weighed just five pounds, but she still looked huge next to Holly.

Dr Hendry sneaked in to see her. She appeared completely unannounced and I actually slept through her visit, but I suppose she just had to see the baby that had caused her so much anxiety and made her most challenging patient even more difficult. She told me later that my case had been discussed all over the country. She'd had lots of behind-the-scenes debates with fellow consultants, even contacting one of the most senior breast-cancer specialists in the UK on how I could most safely proceed with the pregnancy. 'Well, I knew from the start how much this baby meant to you,' she confided.

A week after her birth Holly was moved from intensive care into special care, an important step down the care spectrum. She was getting bigger and stronger all the time, which was great, but it meant that I didn't have to be on hand all the time.

'We think it would be best if you went home now,' one of the doctors told me. 'You need proper rest and you have to prepare for Holly coming home.'

So Holly wouldn't be leaving hospital with me: I'd have to leave her behind.

'It's your choice, Mandy,' he went on. 'We're not forcing you to go, but Holly will have to stay here for a few more weeks. You have to go home at some point.'

I knew it made sense, and I knew Scott would like me back home, but the thought of walking out of hospital without my baby was agony.

'I'll go,' I said. 'As long as I can come back every day and spend the whole day with her.' The deal was done. I could come and go as I pleased.

At home, Scott opened the front door ahead of me and I stepped into a house transformed into a pink paradise. Everywhere I looked there were flowers, balloons, cards and presents. Upstairs, there were clothes hanging all round Holly's nursery with piles of toys and yet more balloons.

'I told you we had loads of gifts, didn't I?' Scott said, shrugging his shoulders like he'd surrendered to this girls' world. 'People have been bringing them to the door all the time. I didn't know where to put anything.'

We spent some time going through things, holding up sweet little dresses for one another to admire, but I was itching to get back to the hospital.

'Let's have our dinner and we'll go back and see her,' I said. 'We'll look at all this stuff when we come home tonight.'

We only live about seven miles from the hospital, but the distance seemed enormous when it meant being separated from Holly. Any time away from her was spent wishing we were back by her side, so being at home wasn't particularly restful. Scott had to continue going to work, but he'd drop me off at the hospital first, then pick me up again on the way home. I even started taking packed lunches so I wouldn't have to leave Holly to go to the cafeteria. At home, we'd snatch a quick dinner, then head straight back to stay with her until about 11 p.m.

Three weeks into the visiting regime, we were absolutely shattered. Mum and I were leaving hospital one night, feeling completely worn out.

'Let's go for a drink before we go home,' Mum said. 'You need a break.'

That sounded like a good idea.

In the pub, everyone was asking after Holly, looking at her photos, toasting her health, and everything seemed so blissful and normal, but as we were walking to the house afterwards, I felt that familiar churning in my stomach.

Mum was making herself a cup of tea in the kitchen while I sat on the worktop watching her.

'Mum, what's going to happen to us?' I asked. Mum put down her cup and looked at me. 'I love her so much and I don't know how long I'm going to have with her.' I was biting my bottom lip, trying to hold back. 'I can't bear the thought of leaving her behind. I don't even want to leave her in the hospital. If anything happens to me now, she won't even remember me.'

Mum was crying too. She gathered me into her arms and I put my head on her shoulder and wept and wept.

'It's OK, Mandy,' Mum was saying gently. 'You're going to be around for your baby, and she will always remember you, don't you worry about that. She'll always know who her mummy is.'

I'd been so focused on Holly that I'd managed to avoid thinking about my situation too deeply. All my energy was being used up on my baby. As soon as I got a minute to raise my head, I took the full blast of reality. Dr Hendry had arranged for my CT scans to restart, with the first one scheduled for nearly six weeks after Holly's birth. There would be no hiding from what my cancer had been up to over the past few months. I'd get my first post-birth Herceptin treatment at the same time. Dr Hendry had allowed me to skip one session while I recovered from the C-section, so the cancer had been totally unleashed for nearly two months. I had to prepare myself for the possibility of bad news. But how could I think like that when all I wanted to think about was Holly?

Meanwhile my daughter was making incredible progress all by herself.

'Bring in your car seat and we'll see if Holly's strong enough to sit in it,' the special-care midwife told us one day. 'If she can hold her head up and breathe properly, then you can take her home.'

Scott and I were ecstatic. Holly was nearly a month old and was managing to feed well, but she still had to pass the car seat test before they would consider discharging her. We arrived the next morning clutching the brand-new seat. Little Holly looked smaller than ever when the midwife placed her in it, but we fastened her straps and hoped for the best.

She stopped breathing twice. Her head lolled forwards, blocking her airway, and she wasn't strong enough to lift it back up. Panic stations.

'Sorry,' said the midwife, sweeping my baby out of the seat. 'It's still too early for Holly.'

We were too scared to be dejected.

'I'd be worried sick if that were to happen when we were driving home,' I sighed. 'I'd rather she was in hospital until we are absolutely sure she can cope.'

She passed the test a week later and finally we got to dress our wee girl in her 'leaving hospital' outfit.

Dr Mathers came to discharge her glad to be rid of me, I'm sure. I tried to thank him for all that he'd done, but it was hard to find words to express just how grateful I felt. He seemed slightly embarrassed too, but as he stood to go, he hugged me, then pulled away and gave me a pat on the back. 'Keep well, Mandy,' he said, 'and don't put us through that again.'

The midwives waved us off and we started on our way home, our first journey together. It should have been a ten-minute trip, but it took about an hour because I insisted we stop every few minutes so that I could check Holly's breathing. I was sitting in the back seat beside her, gently holding her chin up to make sure her airway didn't fold.

'I'll just take her out and reposition her,' I said every time we pulled over.

Scott watched patiently as I moved her a fraction of an inch. 'That's the way she was sitting a minute ago,' he protested.

'Just drive,' I said. 'And be careful . . .'

★

Two weeks later, I was waiting to see Dr Hendry to discuss the results of my CT scan; the sense of impending doom was overwhelming. What if the cancer had spread to my organs? I might only have a few months left. Scott sat with me, grey and quiet, his typical nervous state.

'Please just give me a chance,' I offered a silent prayer, while staring hopelessly at an out-of-date magazine. 'Please don't let them find anything bad. I need to be here for Holly.'

Physically, I didn't feel any different to my pre-pregnancy self. There were no particularly worrying signs. In fact, the more time I spent with my baby, the more positive and happy I felt. We'd had her home for just over a fortnight and I was relishing every minute. I felt strong and healthy, well, as strong and healthy as any sleep-deprived new mum. I had no reason to suspect anything had changed for the worse. But what if it had?

'Hello, Mandy and Scott. Come through,' Dr Hendry said, her face giving no clue as to what she was about to reveal. 'I have your scan results here,' she said, her expression still inscrutable, 'and I have to say they're surprisingly good.'

I drew in my breath, waiting for the 'but'.

'Nothing has changed at all,' she continued. 'If anything, the tumours are a bit smaller. Not by much, but they're certainly smaller.'

Was she serious? The tumours had shrunk?

'Are you sure?' Scott asked. 'You were worried about the effect of the pregnancy hormones.'

Dr Hendry nodded. 'Yes, it's surprising news, but there appears to have been no negative effect.'

I started laughing, bursts of stunned, slightly hysterical laughter. 'I should get pregnant more often if this is the effect it's going to have on me,' I chuckled.

Dr Hendry fixed me with one of her famous serious looks. 'No, Mandy, don't do that,' she said. 'I don't think any of us could cope. Once was definitely enough.'

Chapter 17

Looking after baby Holly at home wasn't proving particularly easy. She may have been four weeks old by the time she left hospital but we'd never actually had to care for her on our own and we didn't know any of her little ways.

'I wish there was a midwife here,' I would moan. 'I don't know what I'm supposed to be doing.'

We got off to a bad start. I overfed Holly on her first night at home and she vomited everywhere. Mess and mayhem before bedtime, not a gentle introduction to parenthood. Neither Scott nor I slept a wink because we jumped out of our skins at every sound she made.

'She's so noisy,' Scott said blearily. 'Is it normal to make all those wee grunts and groans?'

I had absolutely no idea.

It would have been wise of us to have tested some of the baby equipment before Holly arrived home from hospital, but we never quite got round to it, so with a screaming newborn in my arms, I tried to read instructions for the electric steriliser and swot up on how to make feeds correctly. Just as Scott and I were fighting over the right way to clean a bottle, our parents – the proud grandparents – arrived en masse and each chipped in with their own view on the procedure. Frayed nerves and weariness combined to produce a major row between Scott and me, which sent the grannies and grandpas scurrying for cover.

'You don't have to sterilise her dummy every five minutes anyway,' Scott yelled.

'Yes, I do, Scott,' I bellowed back. 'Don't tell me what to do. You know nothing about it.'

He snapped, 'Well, I don't need you hovering over me all the time, telling me I'm getting everything wrong.'

That was an easy one: 'Don't get things wrong, then,' I scowled.

Thankfully little Holly snoozed through her mum and dad's shouting match, but her first pram outing provoked a fresh scrap: 'I want to push her first,' I said, laying my beautiful baby in her new pram, ready to face her public.

'No, I want to do it,' Scott objected, attempting to nudge me out of the way.

In the end we put on a show of unity: Scott pushed for the first half of the walk; I took over for the second half. On a warm, dry evening in June 2005 we made our triumphant debut as the McMillan family. Though bystanders may not have thought so just a few minutes before, we were the happiest couple in the world.

'We did the right thing, didn't we,' I said, taking Scott's arm as we strolled proudly.

'Yes, we did.' He smiled, giving me a kiss. 'We definitely did.'

We'd got away with it. It had been a monumental gamble, but it had paid off. I wasn't any healthier, but I wasn't any sicker either, and I was a mother.

'OK, you were right,' Scott said, 'but let's not put your theory to the test again. We'll start using contraception.'

Not that any would be necessary for quite some time. Caring for a new baby was contraception enough.

I knew I was becoming a paranoid mum. As the weeks passed, my neuroses over safety and germs grew to amazing proportions. There were baby monitors in every room in the house, but we hardly used them as Holly was never anywhere but by my side. I couldn't let her out of my sight.

'It's OK to let her sleep in the nursery while you're downstairs,' Mum tried to persuade me. 'She'll be fine in her own cot while you're hanging up the washing or making dinner.'

I didn't need that kind of advice. 'I'd rather she was close to me, thanks,' I said. 'I like being able to keep an eye on her.'

I found it impossible to sleep and spent most of the night perched on the edge of the bed making sure she was still breathing, or adjusting her bedding to keep her warm enough or cool enough, whichever was my concern of choice on any given night. I couldn't leave her to cry if she woke during the night, not even for a few minutes. I'd sit on the floor outside her nursery after I put her to sleep, just to be sure she didn't wake and wonder where I'd gone. If she so much as sneezed, I'd rush back in to comfort her. Once, Scott found me sleeping in the hallway because I'd waited so long for her to settle.

Long past the new-baby stage I would still swaddle her up in her blanket like the nurses used to in the hospital. She was wrapped up so tightly she could barely move.

'You should really stop doing that now,' Scott scolded one night when Holly was about three months old. 'I mean, it's OK to let her move about on her own now.'

What did he know? Holly loved being snuggled up like that. She slept so soundly in her swaddle I thought it made her feel secure and cosy. I loved holding her like that too. She was like a little baby parcel, fast asleep with a contented smile on her tiny face.

She was six months old, and thriving on my diet of homemade vegetable purées, when I left her with Mum and Dad for a couple of hours while I went for my Herceptin treatment. I arrived back to find Dad holding her.

'I gave Holly some of my homemade soup today and

she scoffed it,' he beamed. 'She loves her granddad's soup, don't you, Holly?'

I nearly hit the roof. 'You did not, did you?' I said. 'She can't have things like that, Dad. I mean, how much salt did you put in it? She can't have any salt, you know. You shouldn't have given her it without asking me first.'

Dad was flabbergasted. 'Sorry,' he said. 'I just thought she might like a wee bit of soup.'

Holly looked perfectly satisfied with her bowlful of Scotch broth. She was probably delighted to have some flavoursome food instead of Mummy's bland mush.

'You can't keep wrapping Holly in cotton wool,' Scott tried to tell me. 'There's nothing wrong with her. You don't have to do everything on your own, and you don't have to make yourself sick worrying about her.'

I just wanted to do as much as humanly possible for my daughter while I could.

'Let me spoil her, Scott,' I said. 'I need to do these things for her for as long as I'm well enough.'

I arranged activities for us every day, sometimes going to baby massage classes, others to music-and-movement groups, and the older she got, the more we became friends. When we went walking through the park, she'd gaze at the trees and the flowers and any passing dog, taking in every sight and sound, fascinated by her surroundings.

'She's started holding her arms out to me when people

talk to her,' I told Scott one night. 'She's becoming a bit wary of strangers, and she definitely knows her mummy. I love it.'

Holly turned my dad to mush too. Whenever he wasn't working, he'd take her out for the day. He'd pack her into her pram and whisk her away at any opportunity, desperate to show her off. A quick trip to the local shops would take for ever because Dad had to stop and talk to anyone he met, just so he could introduce them to his granddaughter. It made my heart melt to watch the interaction between the two of them. Holly gurgled and giggled at every funny face he pulled, and he just about exploded with joy whenever she grinned or waved or learned a new skill. She was eight months when she astounded us all with two incredible achievements in one week: first, she suddenly managed to sit up unaided; then she sprouted her first tooth, a tiny wee pearl in the middle of her lower jaw that made her look cuter than ever when she smiled.

The girls in the antenatal class were as good as their word and we kept in touch faithfully as all the babies were born. We started meeting every week for a coffee and catch-up in one of our houses while the little ones played on the carpet together. The mums – Lorna, Nic, Alison and Nicola – were scattered all over Glasgow, but we were all first-time mothers with a bit of time on our hands and an overpowering craving for some sensible adult conversation. Well, it didn't even matter if the conversation wasn't that sensible. Baby talk might be cute, but you still need a break from it.

I enjoyed seeing Holly with the other babies; it gave me a chance to keep a check on her progress. I fretted that her development might be slowed after such a dramatic start in life. Physically, she had a lot of catching up to do, and even though she was the eldest of the five babies in the group, alongside Callum, Sophie, Grace and Eve, my daughter was by far the teeniest. Eve was the last to be born, arriving two whole months after Holly and weighing about seven pounds. At the time Holly weighed only six pounds, poor wee thing. Still, she seemed to be holding her own in terms of baby progress, and she adored the company of the others. When one of the little ones rolled over to grab at a toy, the rest of them would look on in amazement, clearly wondering how they too could do such a thing. It was hilarious, like a mini training camp for ambitious babies.

We were due to meet one Wednesday when Holly was eight months, but I was scheduled for a CT scan. I had them once every three months. So I called Lorna, who had son Callum four weeks after Holly's birth, and told her I'd have to pull out.

'I'll leave Holly with my mum and dad,' I said. 'I can't take her to hospital with me.'

Lorna had a better idea: 'Why don't you leave Holly

here and let her play for a while?' she said. 'You go off and have your scan and we can have a coffee when you get back. If she gets sleepy, I'll put her down in Callum's cot for a nap.'

I'd never left her with anyone but Mum and Dad before, but she was familiar with Lorna and the other girls, and her baby pals would all be there.

'OK,' I said. 'If you're sure you don't mind, that's great. I'll bring her round. I'll only be away about an hour or so.'

I left Holly sitting happily on the floor of Lorna's lounge, gurgling merrily with the four other babies as I headed off to the Royal Infirmary for my scan. But while I was away she took a little tumble. One minute she was sitting sturdily, proudly demonstrating her new 'sitting up' skill on Lorna's carpet, the next she had fallen over. Lorna thought she must have hurt her head because Holly was inconsolable for a while and eventually cried herself to sleep. Lorna put her down in Callum's cot to stretch out, but by the time I got back, she was awake again and playing on the carpet with the others.

'She's been fine,' Lorna smiled reassuringly, 'but she did fall over and bump her head and she cried for a while.'

Holly reached out for me and I fussed over her, commiserating with her that she'd had a little accident but not in the least worried.

'It was a bit strange,' Lorna went on. 'She didn't hit

against anything hard – she just toppled over on the carpet – but I think she's got a wee bump. I thought I'd better let you know.'

I had a look at Holly's head. There might have been a small egg on her forehead, but I couldn't be sure I wasn't just imagining it. When I turned her to face me, I couldn't see anything at all and she was certainly alert and cheerful enough. Even neurotic Mandy wasn't too concerned, and I didn't want to make Lorna feel bad.

'She's fine,' I said to Lorna. 'She must have grazed it on the carpet.'

Holly was lying on the couch at home a few hours later when Mum came round. 'How's my little angel today?' she said, bending to give her a kiss, but she stopped in mid-stoop. 'What's wrong with her head?' she said. 'It's swollen.'

I was stunned. 'What do you mean?' I said. 'I can't see anything wrong with her.'

Mum was adamant that her head seemed misshapen around her forehead. 'Look at her from the side,' she said. 'It's definitely sticking out.'

I told her what had happened at Lorna's and Mum was immediately anxious.

'You'll have to keep an eye on her,' she said. 'If she seems sick at all, get her straight to the GP's out-of-hours service.' It's clear where I get my alarmist tendencies.

'I will, Mum,' I said, 'but she seems all right to me.'

Try as I might, I couldn't get Holly to settle down to bed that night. She refused her bottle, which was a first, and she'd sleep for only an hour or so before crying herself awake.

'She's probably just overtired,' Scott said, as he tried to soothe her. 'I imagine she didn't sleep much at Lorna's.'

But she seemed to have a bit of a temperature too.

'I'm not happy with this,' I said. 'If she wakes again, I'm going to phone the doctor.' I'd crept downstairs for a drink, thinking she'd finally nodded off, when I heard an ear-splitting cry, an eerie high-pitched sound that was almost a scream. I'd never heard anything like it.

'Scott, call NHS-24,' I shouted as I sprinted upstairs. 'There's something wrong.'

She was burning up, and as I tried to pacify her, her little body seemed jerky.

The NHS-24 nurse told us to take her straight to the out-of-hours GP service and the doctor who met us there didn't hesitate. Holly was crying weakly as he ran a few checks. He lifted her arm and let go. It flopped on to the bed beside her. She was like a ragdoll.

'I think we better get her to Yorkhill right away,' he said. 'Shall I call you an ambulance, or can you take her yourself? It might be quicker if you can take her.'

At 11 p.m. we were racing along the motorway to Yorkhill Children's Hospital in Glasgow's west end, the opposite side of the city. Holly was lying in my arms, limp, pale and unresponsive. I wouldn't even put her in her baby seat and had simply fastened the adult seat belt round both of us. Her condition was worsening.

'Come on, Holly-Pops,' I was whispering to her. 'It's OK. We're going to the hospital and they'll help you there.'

Something awful was happening to her. She was so ill she seemed to be fading before my eyes.

'She's all right, Mandy,' Scott was saying. 'She's going to be all right.'

I clung to her, my precious child, still in her pyjamas and wrapped in a pink baby blanket. I couldn't lose her. I just couldn't lose her.

We burst through the doors at A&E to find nurses and doctors waiting for us. They whisked us into an examination room, asking questions as we went, then laid Holly out on a bed.

'Has she got a rash?' someone asked me.

I hadn't noticed one, but she had a couple of spots on her tummy and high on her back when the GP had examined her. They lifted her pyjama top and there was a rash right across her chest. I began to wail. No, no, no, this could not be happening. A doctor began pressing on the spots, lifting his fingertip away quickly to see if they blanched. They didn't.

'What are you looking for?' I was crying. 'What is it?'

From somewhere in the back of my mind I could

remember that a rash was a symptom of something really serious, but I couldn't remember what. Panic was blocking my mind. I couldn't think . . . Meningitis. That was it. Meningitis.

'Is it meningitis?' I begged. 'Do you think it's meningitis?'

A nurse clasped my arms. 'We don't know what it is at the moment,' she said firmly. 'Let's just get some tests done.'

Over her shoulder I could see a doctor about to insert a needle into the back of Holly's hand. Her cry pierced the air. I ran out of the room.

I dropped like a stone, fell on to a chair, crying hysterically. 'My baby, my baby. Please help her. Please help my baby.'

A nurse came to comfort me. 'She's getting the best of treatment,' she was saying, 'and you've done the right thing. You've brought her here as soon as you thought something was wrong.'

I had to get it together. I had to be stronger, but I just couldn't. 'You've got to help her,' I wept. 'You don't know what we've been through to have this baby. I've got breast cancer. I've been on Herceptin. Oh God, Herceptin . . . Could the Herceptin have caused this?'

Scott and the doctor emerged. Scott's eyes were pools of terror. He couldn't speak. He just held me.

'We have to do a procedure called a lumbar puncture,' the doctor was explaining. 'We need to draw off some fluid from Holly's spine so we can test it for infection,' he went on. 'I think it's best if you both wait here while we do it. It's quite straightforward, but it can be a little distressing to watch.'

All I knew about lumbar punctures was that they are extremely painful. Scott and I were hugging one another when she started screaming.

'Stop it,' I was bawling. 'Leave her alone.' I wanted to kick open the doors and grab her. I wanted to switch off the lights and sing her back to sleep. 'Tell them to leave her alone, Scott,' I sobbed. 'Please stop hurting her.'

We had never known fear before that moment. Through all the worst of my treatment and my illness, nothing compared. It was the most searing, painful, all-consuming agony. Every part of me, every organ, every cell, my whole being ached for Holly and I suddenly understood what my mum meant when she told me, 'I wish I could take your illness for you. Why can't it be me instead?' I no longer cared what happened to me. It was nothing. I'd die happy if it meant Holly could live.

'We won't know the results of the lumbar puncture for forty-eight hours,' the doctor said, 'but we're going to proceed with treatment for meningitis. We'll get Holly started on antibiotics right away.'

So we sat with her, holding her hand and stroking her face, as the antibiotic drip was hooked up. She was still crying, still white and weak.

'Sshh, Holly,' I soothed. 'It's OK, baby,' but I was shaking so badly my voice was tremulous.

It was 3 a.m. when I tried to phone Dad. I knew he would be wide awake and alert – he was driving somewhere in the south of England. In my hysteria, I didn't think for a second how he was going to deal with the news, all alone in the middle of the night. I just had to tell someone. I had to hear a voice outside that hospital. I'd leave Mum till morning: her sleep was disturbed enough at the best of times. As soon as I started to speak to Dad, I lost it.

'Mandy, is that you?' I could hear him saying, but I was incoherent with grief. 'Holly's really ill, Dad,' I forced out. 'She's got meningitis . . .' I couldn't manage any more.

Mum phoned within seconds, already distraught.

'Don't come here, Mum,' I told her. 'I'll phone when there's news.'

She sat by the phone all night.

For hours we sat by Holly's bedside, crying and talking, holding each other and comforting her. Eventually she began to settle down. Her sleep became more peaceful. She was resting.

The doctor appeared again.

'Please tell me,' I said, 'could this be anything to do with the Herceptin treatment I had during pregnancy? I really think someone should speak to my oncologist about this.'

He was doubtful. If Holly had meningitis, she'd simply

picked up the bug. 'I don't see how there would be any connection with your breast-cancer treatment,' he said. 'Holly has been fine up till now, hasn't she?'

He said he would have to contact Dr Hendry anyway because Scott and I would have to start on antibiotics too and he'd have to check which drugs were appropriate for me.

'Herceptin is a new drug,' I persisted. 'There haven't been many babies born to women who're taking it.'

What if the treatment that had saved me made my child ill?

He remained unconvinced. 'Meningitis is present in the community,' he said. 'It's just bad luck to get it, I'm afraid. We have to treat people whom Holly has been closest to over the past few hours,' he went on to explain.

Oh God, the other babies.

'Scott, she was at Lorna's house with the other babies today,' I cried. 'I'll have to phone them. I'll have to warn them.'

I went outside to call. It was 6 a.m. and I knew I'd have to wake them. I called Nic, Sophie's mum. She was horrified.

'The doctor says the chances are no one else has got it,' I tried to reassure her, but I knew she was panic-stricken for her own baby. 'They're suggesting all the babies get checked out by their own GPs this morning,' I told her.

Nic said she would call the others and tell them, but

none of the kids had been ill to her knowledge. My phone soon started ringing.

'But Holly was in Callum's cot,' Lorna cried, 'and he's been sleeping in it all night.' She was angry and upset, and I understood, I really did.

'I'm so sorry, Lorna,' I said. 'I'm sure he'll be OK. Please take him to the doctor as soon as it opens. I'm sorry, but I need to get back to Holly.'

I remembered that Joseph had brought his little boy, Josh, to visit us a couple of days before. He would have gone home and played with his big sister, Olivia. Did that mean they were all at risk? The doctors thought it was best to be on the safe side, so I had to call Joseph and break the news.

'I think you should take them to get checked out,' I tried to tell him through my tears.

He rushed away to check his own kids for the telltale signs. It was excruciating.

Holly was moved to an isolation ward. Only immediate family could visit. The grandparents arrived. We didn't even have to speak to communicate our shared anguish. I knew what it was to be a mum, helplessly watching her child suffer. I'd underestimated my own mum, what she must have endured all the time I'd been ill. Of course I'd known my cancer was hard on her, but I had no idea how hard until I saw my own baby in pain. No wonder Mum had become an insomniac.

'She's so sleepy,' I said, gazing at my motionless baby. 'She must be using all her strength to fight it.' She'd survived a gestation from which no one had expected her to emerge. She'd fought for life then and she was fighting again. 'Keep on fighting, Holly,' I told her. 'You can do it.'

For three days she slept, awake for little more than a few minutes at a time. Tests had confirmed she had meningococcal meningitis with septicaemia, a killer combination that claims the lives of about twenty per cent of the babies who get it. There was also a risk that even if she recovered, she'd suffer some long-term side effects, deafness being the most common.

'As long as she makes it,' I said to Scott, 'we can deal with anything else.'

We slept by her bed, taking turns to go home and shower or collect a few belongings.

All the antenatal babies were treated with antibiotics immediately and their frantic parents went through a terrible wait to see if any symptoms would appear, but none did and, thank God, they were all fine. Josh and Olivia were fine too. Through our own misery, Scott and I could at least be grateful for that. I don't know how we would have coped if someone else's child had been struck down too. The sense of guilt that they might have caught it from Holly would have been unbearable. At least we could focus entirely on her now.

By the fourth day she was starting to show a bit of

faint interest in some of the toys we brought from home. She didn't have the energy to play with them, but they caught her eye when we held them to her and she reached out to touch them.

'I think she may be getting over the worst,' the doctor said.

We wept with cautious relief.

On day five she was sitting up in her cot, still being drip-fed antibiotics and fluids, but she was alert for the first time. She was even smiling. Two days later, as we struggled to keep a lively, demanding baby confined to her cot, the doctor told us he was preparing to have her discharged.

'Just keep an eye on her,' he said. 'If you have any concerns at all, bring her back immediately. If you notice any problems with her hearing, let us know about that too. But she seems to have recovered beautifully.'

My daughter the fighter. She gets it from her mum.

After just over a week in hospital, we got to take Holly home. She seemed to be back to normal. Her family, on the other hand, were nervous wrecks, too scared to let her do anything. As if I wasn't uptight enough, all my worst fears had been confirmed.

'At least I'll know to trust to my instincts in future,' I told Scott.

'Don't let this feed your insecurities,' he said. 'She has to live her life without being mollycoddled.'

Yeah, right. Mollycoddling would be the order of the day from now on. Nothing else was going to happen to my baby.

We decided to celebrate Holly's first birthday with a family holiday to Majorca.

'Let's go with Mum and Dad,' I suggested to Scott. It was a cunning plan that would suit us all. 'They won't mind babysitting on the odd night if you and I want to go out for dinner,' I said, 'and they'll love spending time with Holly. Everyone's a winner.'

So off we went to Palma Nova, where we could all chill out together, playing in the pool with Holly for a while or going for walks round the shops. Mum and Dad would take her back to the hotel room for a nap in the afternoon so Scott and I could laze around together. It was idyllic, just what we needed.

'You know, this is the healthiest I've been since I was diagnosed,' I remarked, as we lay by the pool one day. 'From the day I found out I was pregnant right up till now, I've not had any health problems. That's sixteen months.'

Dr Hendry had noticed too. The three-weekly Herceptin treatments certainly seemed to be holding things at bay. Dr Hendry also thought the high-dose radiotherapy I received after the recurrence on my breast may still be working on my body, even though I had it in 2003, three years before.

'It stays with you for quite a lengthy period of time,'

she'd explained. 'It's not unusual for radiotherapy to last for years.'

I was climbing out of the swimming pool when I noticed my swimsuit had moved a little and I could see an area of discoloured skin on my reconstructed breast. It was exactly at the site of the recurrence.

That looks a bit odd, I thought.

It was brownish in points, as if it had been singed. It might have been a reaction to the sun, but I remembered something that Dr Hendry told me.

I wonder if that's what she means when she says the skin can look a bit scarred after radiotherapy.

That seemed like a highly probable explanation.

I should have known better than to think I was in tranquil waters.

Chapter 18

'There's a chance that your skin won't heal properly after this biopsy,' Dr Hendry was telling me, though I was hardly listening. 'The radiotherapy has left a lot of scarring,' she went on. 'The skin is so thin there I'm not sure there will be enough to close over again afterwards.'

I was hearing, just not paying much attention. Her words were washing over me as I sat in front of her, too saturated by bad news to absorb them. I'd seen the look on her face as she examined me. Here we go again, I thought. The other details weren't important.

The brownish tinges on my reconstructed breast were the tumour's work. The skin had started to bubble too. I'd had sixteen months without any cancer developments, more than a year with Herceptin as my only official treatment. Motherhood had become my additional therapy in the meantime and I'd foolishly allowed myself to think that maybe, just maybe that would be enough. Now, though, the merciless tumour deep in my chest appeared to be literally popping up to the surface. The skin at the site of the original recurrence looked like a piece of bubblewrap.

'No, that doesn't look good at all,' Dr Hendry sighed, when I arrived for an examination shortly after our return from Majorca. 'This area of ulceration should definitely be investigated further.'

As her voice drifted in and out of my head, I was going over the possible implications: the Herceptin was no longer working; the cancer had spread; I'd run out of treatment options; the game was up.

It was July 2006. My daughter was a little over a year old. She'd just survived meningitis. She'd just started walking. Somebody somewhere must have been having a laugh.

'I'd like to have a core biopsy carried out nonetheless,' Dr Hendry was continuing. 'It will be a bit different to the last core biopsy you had. We'll need to take a larger sample of the tumour away and see what's going on. It'll be done under general anaesthetic. We need to establish whether the tumour has become active again.'

I already knew it was. We were going through the motions.

'It could still be the radiotherapy causing the problem,' she added, more in hope than expectation, I thought. Throwing me a scrap.

I'd seen problems at this patch of breast skin before, on my honeymoon, in fact. It was all too familiar.

'I'd like to get it done as soon as possible,' was all I said.

Two days later I was in Stobhill Hospital again, and Mr Hansell was removing a wedge-shaped section of my reconstructed breast. I wish I had listened more closely to Dr Hendry. Maybe I should have asked more questions when she'd said there was a chance the biopsy site may not heal over. It's probably just as well I didn't know I'd spend the next year with a huge gaping hole – eventually six inches long – in my chest. That, at its worst, I'd be able to see right inside my body if I dared to look and that I'd never find any substance – manmade or natural – that could soak up what leaked from its depths. That, ultimately, the surgery I would need to repair my damaged body would be life-threatening in itself. To be fair, Dr Hendry couldn't have guessed that either, but if I had known what was in store, I would never have gone ahead.

The cancer in my chest, which had been lying dormant, had reignited and was now growing with renewed vigour. The wedge biopsy proved that beyond doubt, so it was worthwhile in that respect. Just as Dr Hendry feared, there wasn't enough skin to close over the 'bullet-hole' wound it left in my breast, so it seemed utterly resistant to healing.

I caught sight of it for the first time when the nurse arrived to change the dressing.

'Oh my goodness, it looks like I've been shot,' I gasped. 'Will it go away eventually?'

The nurse was busy packing the hole with some kind of surgical cotton wool, but she seemed to be using a hell of a lot of it and it was taking ages to fill.

'We'll just keep it nice and clean until it starts closing up,' she said brightly.

Dr Hendry thought the Herceptin was still working, as the tumours in my neck and armpits hadn't grown and there was no sign of a spread to any other sites, but the cancer in my chest was unbelievably stubborn, so I'd have to start chemotherapy again: a four-month course of a type called vinorelbine this time. The memory of my Taxotere nightmare was still all too fresh but I wasn't about to turn anything down, not now, not since I had Holly to fight for. This was my third round of chemo, so I was really ploughing through all the different ones available. Dr Hendry chose a chemo type by considering things like the stage of my cancer and the state of my health. She would have started with what she thought was the best option, hoping to get rid of the cancer as quickly as possible, but my previous two courses had clearly failed to blast the tumour away, so it was a matter of trying to find something that would.

'We'll have to give you it through your left arm,' Vicky, the nurse, explained when I arrived for my first session. 'You've had so much chemo through your right arm that the veins aren't strong enough there.'

God, I was even running out of arms. I knew they were reluctant to give chemo on the same side as the surgery, as it can cause lymphodoema (painful swelling of the arm), but they didn't seem to think there was any other way.

'At least you shouldn't lose your hair this time,' Vicky added with a smile. 'Vinorelbine doesn't tend to cause hair loss.' Small mercies, gratefully received.

Holly was my solace, my shining light, the one thing that made it all worthwhile. She was becoming such a little character, toddling around the house on her unsteady legs, clutching her favourite cuddly toy, Lumpy the elephant.

Scott accused me of spoiling her rotten. 'You're not doing us any favours here,' he'd say as I went through the nightly routine of bringing her into our bed to sleep with us. 'None of us gets a good sleep and she'll never want to go back to her cot.'

I simply loved to have her close. I'd lie cuddled up beside her and watch her sleeping, stroking her soft blond hair and pressing my face against her little head so I could almost inhale her.

'You love it as much as I do,' I teased, and he did. We were absolutely suckered by our daughter. No night was so uncomfortable that we wouldn't want her in beside us. She was so much more than I had ever hoped for. At least we had Holly. Even if the Herceptin had stopped working, it had given me the chance to have her.

She'd been examined by paediatricians before being released from hospital as a baby and they continued to check her over every couple of months, just in case she developed ongoing problems that may be connected to my treatment. No one had any idea what those potential problems might be. Every specialist I spoke to was quite insistent that there was no connection between Holly's meningitis and my use of Herceptin. Then, just as her mum embarked on yet more cancer treatment, Holly developed breathing problems.

I'd only got the first chemo session under my belt when we were rushing back to A&E at Yorkhill Children's Hospital, another panicked late-night race across the city, clutching Holly to my chest.

'This can't be a coincidence,' Dad raved, as he drove like a madman. 'This has got to be the Herceptin. Don't forget to tell the doctors about Herceptin.'

Like I would. I couldn't get it out of my head.

'She doesn't sound good,' I said. 'Please just hurry, Dad. Her breathing is terrible.'

I'd thought she just had a cold. How come she couldn't breathe? What was happening to us now?

Mum and Dad had warned me she seemed to be sickening for something. They'd been babysitting during the day and had thought she didn't seem quite right.

'Holly's been a bit breathless,' Dad had said when I arrived to pick her up. 'Keep an eye on her tonight.'

I was fairly confident it was nothing. Since the meningitis trauma, Mum and Dad were even more cautious than Scott and me. The merest sniffle and they had her whisked off to the doctor.

'I'm sure it's just a wee cold,' I'd told them before fastening my baby into the car to drive her home.

'If you need to take her to the emergency doctor, just give me a phone,' Dad called after us. 'I'll drive you there if you like.'

Now there was an offer. Another one of my dad's famous road trips.

Yeah, I'll try and avoid that, I thought, as I smiled and waved.

As I was getting her ready for bed that night, Holly sounded a bit wheezy and she seemed a little worse when I put her down in her cot. Scott was working late, so I was on my own.

'Come into bed with Mummy, then, sweetheart,' I whispered to her. 'Daddy will be home soon.'

She was coughing really hard, and the wheezing was becoming more and more dramatic. Her little tummy was rising and falling rapidly as she tried to catch her breath. She couldn't possibly sleep.

Oh, please don't tell me there is something wrong with her again, I thought tearfully. Couldn't she just have an easy time of it for a while?

A couple of hours later, though, at around 9 p.m., I was on the phone to Dad. 'Holly can't breathe properly at all, Dad,' I told him, panicked. 'I want to take her to the emergency service. Can you come round?'

Without a pause to tell me he'd told me so, Dad grabbed his jacket and ran out though the door to come and collect us.

The GP at the out-of-hours service gave Holly steroids to try and ease the wheezing, but it didn't seem to make much difference and as soon as I mentioned her meningitis, that was it.

'I think we'll send her to Yorkhill,' said the doctor. Not again. 'I'll phone A&E and tell them you're on your way.'

'What's wrong with her?' I kept asking. 'Why can't she breathe?'

She'd been fine the day before. In fact, she'd been fine when I left her at Mum and Dad's a few hours earlier. She'd deteriorated so quickly.

'Please tell me what can be causing this?' I pleaded. 'Is the meningitis back? Why can't you help her?'

I phoned Scott and told him to meet us at Yorkhill and we set off, Dad and me, to dash across the city. The nurses and doctors were waiting for us again, and for the second time in eight months my little girl was taken from my arms and carried away from me while they set about trying to save her. They were taking us to the same short-stay area where Holly had been treated for meningitis. It was surreal.

'I took a breast-cancer drug called Herceptin all through my pregnancy,' I tried to tell the doctor as we followed him into the treatment room, but he was concentrating on connecting Holly to a nebuliser to stabilise her breathing. 'I've got breast cancer, you see, and I got Herceptin even though it's a new drug and they didn't know how it might affect my baby.' He was nodding, at least acknowledging what I was saying. 'You don't think it could have caused this, do you?' I persisted. 'I mean, she's had meningitis too and she's only fifteen months old.'

The doctor was shaking his head. 'No, I wouldn't think there's any link,' he said, without looking up.

I was annoying him. He was trying to block me out. How could he be sure it was nothing to do with Herceptin? Had he even heard of it? Did he have any idea what I was talking about?

'You'll have to let us work with her for a while to see what's wrong,' he said, directing me away from the bed to make more room for the nurses.

All we could do was watch as they pumped oxygen into Holly's little body and she struggled for breath. Scott arrived, having abandoned his Chinese deliveries in mid-shift, and I fell into his arms.

'Why can't we stay away from hospitals, Scott?' I sobbed. 'Why can't we be left alone for a while?'

Scott looked like he'd been hit by lightning. First his wife, then his daughter. What had he done to deserve it?

'I think it sounds like asthma,' Scott said eventually, as we listened to Holly's rattling airways.

'It does, actually,' I replied, recognising my own wheezy symptoms. If I stroked Coco and Kia for too long, my eyes would stream and I'd start to sneeze, cough and splutter. The doctor had prescribed me an asthma inhaler and suggested I should get rid of the cats to avoid making my symptoms worse, but I hadn't even considered it. Scott's sister, Nicky, also had terrible asthma, now that I came to think of it. Scott had it himself when he was a child.

Holly must have asthma too, I thought.

I questioned the doctor.

'Well, we don't diagnose asthma in children under three years of age,' he said. 'Up till then breathing problems like this tend to be temporary and related to some form of virus. We call it a viral wheeze. It's probably a one-off episode.'

The oxygen was definitely beginning to take effect. Her breathing was getting easier.

'We'll keep her in till we're sure we've got it under control,' the doctor added.

One week later, when she'd finally managed to go for twenty-four consecutive hours without her oxygen mask, they discharged her.

Just three weeks after that she was in again.

This time I had been on a hen night. Scott was working late again, but Liz and Jackie had bravely offered to babysit Holly.

'Don't worry about a thing,' Liz had said, as I'd faffed around, reluctant to leave. Holly had had a bit of a cold again, nothing more, but enough to put me on edge. 'She'll be fine here with her aunties, won't you, Holly?' Liz insisted.

When I called during the course of the evening, the girls claimed she was settled and that I should go off and enjoy myself. So I did. The vinorelbine chemo gave me a terribly sore left arm but no more problematic symptoms. I was relishing being out and about with the 'hens' for a bit of distraction.

I got home at around 3 a.m., feeling not just happy but a little merry too – slightly the worse for wear, truth be told. Scott was sitting on our bed, cradling a wheezing, coughing, sneezing Holly.

'She's been sick,' he said anxiously. 'I think we'll need to take her in again.'

I sobered up instantly. 'Give me a minute to change my clothes,' I said, and then we were on our way again, me still fully made-up and battling with the sudden onset of a hangover. 'Everyone's going to think I'm an unfit mother,' I cried. 'How could I have gone out when my little girl was sick?'

She was kept in, hooked up to oxygen again, and for another week Scott and I prayed silently by her bed.

'They'll get her sorted out this time,' Scott said weakly. 'We can't go through this again.'

But we did. We went through it again and again until it seemed it would never stop. All in, Holly was admitted to hospital five times in less than five months, at which point I finally cracked and demanded they accept she had asthma – under three or not – and give me an inhaler to treat her at home.

'I cannot keep bringing her to hospital for emergency treatment,' I implored. 'I'm going through chemotherapy treatment myself. I know it's not policy, but if you gave me an inhaler, I could manage her situation on my own, I know I could.'

At last they relented and presented me with two inhalers – a blue one to relieve an attack and a brown one that was supposed to prevent them happening in the first place. I had to keep an asthma diary so they could work out a treatment plan for Holly that I could handle by myself.

'So, she does have asthma, then?' I asked, determined to make them admit I'd been right all along.

'It certainly seems she does,' was the best I could get.

Dr Hendry insisted that the paediatricians we'd been in contact with would have spotted something if there was a fundamental problem with Holly's health. 'Holly has contracted common childhood illnesses,' she said. 'That's unfortunate, but you have to stop thinking that everything she gets is in some way related to your treatment. Generally speaking, she seems to be a perfectly healthy child. Once you get her asthma under control, I'm sure things will settle down.'

There was nothing else for it – we would have to find a new home for Coco and Kia. I couldn't take the risk of them aggravating Holly's asthma, but I could barely look at them once I'd finally agreed to let Scott start searching for kind and caring owners. I was betraying the friends who'd comforted me through so much of my own illness, yet they had no idea I was giving them up for adoption, and they'd still leap on to my lap for a reassuring nuzzle whenever I sat down. We put up a card on the notice board at the local supermarket, we asked the vet if he knew of anyone who might be interested, and we placed an ad in a newspaper. No takers. On the very last day the advert was due to run, we got a call from a woman from Cumbernauld who seemed really interested. We organised a handover. Scott and I were to take them to her home. I tried really hard to be strong, but I still cried the entire day. It was the end of an era. Coco, Kia and I had shared so much, yet I was giving them away because I had a new baby to love. In true Siamese style, they turned up their noses, put their tails in the air and walked away huffily from their ungrateful owner. Former owner.

I finished the course of vinorelbine chemo in November and everything seemed pretty positive for a while. The treatment seemed to have halted the tumour's growth, although the external appearance hadn't changed much.

'Your wound is getting smaller,' said Scott, who'd bravely volunteered to change my dressings for me because I couldn't bear to look at it. I'd seen a lot of horrors in my dealings with breast cancer, and I'd learned to face many of them, but this was too much for me. Scott insisted he could stomach it and took over the gruesome routine. 'It's taking less and less packing than it did before. It must be healing from the inside out,' he said, and pressed a dressing into place.

Dr Hendry was pleased enough with my progress to give me the all-clear to fly out on a dream holiday to Disney World in Florida just a couple of weeks after chemo ended, but the day before we were due to leave, we were back in Yorkhill A&E while Holly had treatment for yet another attack. It was touch and go whether we'd be able to travel at all. For a while it looked like we'd have to cancel, another dream shot down. The doctors thought Holly could cope with the trip, however. In fact, a couple of weeks away from a damp Scottish winter might actually do her some good.

We left for Florida more concerned by Holly's illness than my cancer, but as she splashed in the pool at our villa and whooped with delight at the sight of Cinderella's castle in Disney World, she seemed a glowing picture of health.

'The sun is definitely doing her good,' I beamed at Scott. 'This is the best she's been in months. Maybe it's the Scottish weather that's been making her ill.'

The Florida sunshine wasn't helping me, though. Around ten days into the holiday I realised my tumour must be growing again. The breast hole was getting bigger. In the shower, I would point the shower head at my chest while turning my own head away to avoid seeing anything nasty, but when I dried myself, I couldn't help but notice new bubbles of skin had appeared on the breast. Grudgingly, I had to concede the effects of the chemo had worn off already.

'I've been off it for less than a month and the cancer's already growing again,' I told Scott that night. 'Could this tumour be any more aggressive?' I was so despondent and really struggled to try and enjoy the rest of our holiday, not wishing to spoil it for everyone else.

What was next for me? I couldn't be on constant chemotherapy. How on earth were they going to get the cancer under control? Had it just become impossible to contain?

'Don't panic, Mandy,' Scott tried to placate me. 'There will be something else to try. We'll find out when we get back.'

Things were going seriously wrong, I just knew it.

I went to see Dr Hendry as soon as we got home from the States.

'We'll try you on capecitabine,' she said, like she was choosing a chocolate from an assortment. 'It's a tablet form of chemotherapy.'

I'd recognised the name as soon as she said it. A couple of women I'd met at the Beatson had been taking it. Sick women. People who knew they were on borrowed time. Did this mean I too had reached the bottom of the barrel? Was this my last chance? The side effects of capecitabine were usually less severe than other chemos; significantly it didn't cause hair to fall out. To me, that made it sound weak. Did they think I wasn't strong enough to cope with anything else? Because I would soon tell them differently if that were the case.

'I don't really have a lot of confidence that capecitabine will work for me,' I told Dr Hendry. 'I don't mind having another treatment block of liquid chemo again if you think it will help.'

She insisted capecitabine would be easier on me, and running alongside the Herceptin, it might just be enough to get things back under control. Might. I wasn't holding out much hope.

'You'll have to take ten tablets a day,' Dr Hendry continued. 'Five in the morning and five at night.'

I was also on regular bouts of antibiotics to stave off any infection in the open wound.

'I'm on so many pills that I rattle when I walk,' I grumbled to Scott.

By January 2007, about three weeks after I started on the capecitabine, the bullet wound began to leak, lightly at first, just enough to stain the dressings I was still wearing to protect it.

'I've got an infection in the wound, Scott,' I told him. 'I'm going to need more antibiotics, and Dr Hendry's not keen because she's scared I'll develop an immunity. I just don't think the capecitabine is making any difference.'

Scott was trying to stay level-headed: 'Give it a bit of time,' he said. 'You've not been on it long enough to make a decision.'

With every passing day, however, the weeping from the hole in my chest seemed to get worse and the dressings I needed got bigger and bigger. I started stuffing the hole with Aquacel ribbon, a very absorbent type of surgical tape that could be packed deep into the wound, but the liquid still continued to seep out.

'Nothing else is getting any worse,' Dr Hendry would tell me every time I complained the capecitabine wasn't working. 'There's been no further spread of the cancer. That means it probably is working.'

I was unconvinced.

It was Mum's birthday in March and we had arranged to mark the occasion with a girls' trip to Galway. I'd been looking forward to it, not least because Liz and Jackie were coming along too, joining in with Mum's group of pals, but my chest wound was difficult enough to manage at home, where I had everything I needed at my disposal. I was worried about how I would cope with being away. At home, I could change whenever I wanted and I could get by on a wardrobe of casual cover-up clothing. Going off for a glam weekend needed so much preparation.

'I have to bring a whole suitcase full of surgical dressings,' I told my mum as I packed, 'and I hate all my clothes.'

Each top was carefully chosen to cover every inch of my chest, right up to my neck. Even then the dressings would somehow manage to work their way out and I was obsessed with checking my reflection in mirrors every few minutes, convinced white surgical pads were sticking out.

'You'll look great whatever you wear,' Mum said loyally. 'You always do – it's just that you're so aware of what's going on you think that other people are too.'

She was right to some extent. Fully dressed, I didn't look any different to any of the other girls on the trip, but it didn't stop me being mortified sharing a hotel room with Liz and Jackie. I'd try to hide from them when we were getting changed and I'd all but drown myself in perfume, convinced that the wound had begun to smell.

'Do you need any help?' Liz would ask, noticing that I turned my back whenever I had to change my clothes.

'Let me give you a hand with your dressings.'

I wouldn't hear of that. 'No, no, it's OK,' I said. 'I'm used to doing it myself.'

Then strange blotches appeared all over my stomach, angry red weals and spots that spread out along the scar where my tummy fat had been removed for the reconstruction. It couldn't be a good sign, I knew that, and Dr Hendry couldn't disguise her horror.

'That looks very suspicious,' she said slowly.

I pushed her to try and explain it.

'It may be a sign the cancer is in the skin there,' she said reluctantly.

Oh God, no. Not a spread. Please don't let it have spread. I wouldn't survive that.

'We'll do some biopsies on these lesions,' Dr Hendry said quietly, 'but I think we have to prepare ourselves.'

I couldn't prepare myself. I wasn't ready. I didn't even want to be ready. I wanted my life. I wanted to live. I wanted to stay with my family.

At home that night, while Scott and Holly were watching telly downstairs, I sneaked upstairs and lay on our bed, holding the little angels that well-meaning friends had given me. I felt a bit daft. This really is last resort stuff, I thought.

I'd seen an item about angels on the daytime TV show *This Morning*. According to someone claiming to be an expert in these matters, angels were everywhere and they'd look after us if only we asked for their help. Well, if ever there was a time to ask for some form of inexplicable, mystical assistance, this was it. No one else could help me.

I kept thinking about the woman I'd met in hospital a couple of years before, the one who'd told me I had an angel on my shoulder.

I could do with finding out that's true, I thought, toying with the fragile little figures. I just hope Scott doesn't hear me. He'll really think I've lost the plot.

The woman on *This Morning* who claimed she communicated with angels had explained you should speak out loud to them or write out your request for them. They were around you, so they would hear you or see your note.

I cleared my throat. 'If there are any angels out there listening to me, please help me,' I said. 'Please don't let the cancer have spread to my stomach. If you can't take it away, please don't let it have spread. I need to be here for my daughter. If you can hear me, please help me.' Then I added, for good measure, 'Thank you very much.'

In the still of the dark room, I waited for something earth-shattering to happen. It didn't. I could faintly hear the telly downstairs. I could hear the wind outside the bedroom window, but there was no thunderbolt. No flash of light. No sense of an otherworldly presence.

Oh well, it can't have done any harm, I thought,

carefully replacing my little angels on the shelf by my bed that Scott had put up for them.

As I arrived at Dr Hendry's office for the results of the biopsies, my heart was in a vice. This could be the beginning of the end.

Strangely, though, Dr Hendry seemed to be smiling as she beckoned me through. 'The tests have come back clear,' she said, quite obviously astonished. 'I have to admit I'm somewhat surprised myself,' she added, as I tried to pull myself together. 'But there's nothing suspicious there. The results are clear.'

I grasped the arms of the chair, suddenly light-headed.

'How are the lesions anyway?' she went on.

I pulled up my top to show her. 'They're practically gone,' I said. 'It must have been the angels.'

Dr Hendry stared at me. 'Sorry?' she said. 'What angels?'

Chapter 19

It was eight o'clock one Friday morning in December 2007 – a whole seventeen months since the wedge biopsy – and I was getting ready for my appointment with Dr Hendry. The day was beginning with the grisly ritual that had gradually taken over my life: cleaning out the gaping wound in my chest. First, a long strip of Aquacel tape went into the hole, on top of that went a bulky square dressing impregnated with silver, on top of that another one containing charcoal to control any smell, then a final huge one that went right round the reconstructed breast. The surrounding skin had become dry and damaged from this daily trial. My inflamed breast was never exposed to the air, so the skin never got a chance to dry out. I was now using creams to try and repair the sore, angry tissue, and the worst part of the rigmarole was the knowledge that the massive mound of padding would be soaked through by 11 a.m. and I'd have to start all over again. Then again a couple of hours after that.

I couldn't tolerate it any more and was planning to tell Dr Hendry so.

'I really can't smell anything,' Scott would say kindly. 'You must be imagining things.' But I knew the wound had begun to smell, despite my best efforts to disguise it with litres of perfume. Our relationship was suffering as a result. I was so disgusted by my body I couldn't bear to let him too close. I didn't want to show him my wound. I didn't want him to look at me and see something so repugnant, but he wanted to help me. In fact, he insisted, though it upset me every time.

Just stop mentioning it, I'd tell myself. Don't say anything about it and he'll think it's all right.

If he walked into the room while I was changing my dressings, however, he was confronted with the full, unedited horror of my body.

'I really don't mind,' he'd say as I told him to get out.

No husband should have to see his wife like that. He was supposed to fancy me, for heaven's sake.

Dr Hendry kept insisting there was nothing she could do. 'The other tumours in your neck and underarms are being controlled by the Herceptin and capecitabine,' she would say.

She assured me the pea-sized lumps in my lymph glands had not grown, despite the behaviour of the other tumour. I could only take her word for that. I hadn't dared touch the swollen lymph glands since the day I found the lump in my neck.

'I don't want to switch you to another type of

chemotherapy because we would be using up one more of our options which we might need later,' she explained.

She didn't want me to have further surgery to try and remove the breast tumour either. That would require a massive surgical procedure, she said, which would be made more complicated still by the fact I didn't have enough healthy skin to stitch back together afterwards. Basically, she thought I had no option but to live with the leaking and the smell, which, it transpired, was coming from dead tissue in the hole in my chest. The wound was getting worse and worse, spreading and growing before my eyes.

The year before, when the hole was about a couple of inches long, I'd been referred to Eva Weiler-Mithoff, a renowned breast-surgery specialist at Canniesburn Plastic-Surgery Unit. The newly built centre, attached to the Royal Infirmary, was a gleaming replacement for the dismal old Canniesburn Hospital, where I'd had my original mastectomy and reconstruction. Its bright and airy atmosphere gave me a little unexpected optimism at first, but Mrs Weiler-Mithoff ruled out an operation at that point because any surgery to take out the tumour would be so enormous. I should persevere a while longer with the chemotherapy to see if that worked. If it did, I'd be spared a massive operation. It didn't.

Since that initial meeting with Mrs Weiler-Mithoff, the ulcers on the surface of my skin had split and the wound was about six inches long. If I lifted my arm, I could see inside. It was like a video nasty and I just couldn't take it.

'I don't want to live like this,' I confessed to Scott. 'If this is the best that life can be for me, I don't think I can go on.'

My bum had just connected with the chair in Dr Hendry's office when I broke down. 'You've got to do something for me,' I begged her. 'I can't carry on like this. It's inhuman to leave me this way. I can't do anything, I can't go anywhere. It's absolutely disgusting.'

I was in floods of tears. Scott tried to comfort me, but I shook him off. I was too upset to be pacified.

'The capecitabine isn't working,' I cried, frustrated and frightened at the same time. 'I've been saying it for months. I feel like this tumour is taking over my whole body. Please do something for me.'

Dr Hendry clasped her hands and leaned forward on her desk. 'Mandy, I have spoken to Mrs Weiler-Mithoff and she has agreed to see you again.'

I slumped back in the chair and sighed. Finally. They were going to try it.

'I have to warn you, though,' she was continuing, 'the operation she is considering is huge and you will have to think about things very carefully.'

I didn't care. Nothing could be worse than what I was going through. I had no life. It had been ruined.

'Obviously you've got Holly to think about too,' she added.

Holly. My lovely Holly. She was the reason I wanted my life back so badly. The reason I hadn't given up. What kind of mother was I being to her? I was afraid to hold her close in case she got wet from my dressings.

Scott blurted out, 'You don't actually want to go through with this, do you? It sounds like it's going to be massive, Mandy, and there are no guarantees it will work.'

Scott wanted certainties. If I was going to die, if nothing could help me, he didn't want to see me go through such an enormous ordeal in the vain hope of postponing the inevitable. I knew what he meant, but if there was a chance, no matter how remote, that I could get through this and have something like a normal life again, I was going to grab it. I was scared, more scared than I'd been about any of my treatment.

'I'll go and talk to Mrs Weiler-Mithoff about it,' I said. 'If it seems too much, I don't need to go ahead with it, but I want to know the facts first.'

Mrs Weiler-Mithoff took a look at my wound as promised, but she offered no guarantee of surgery. 'I'd like you to see a colleague of mine,' she said eventually. 'The operation to remove this tumour would be a very complex procedure and he has much more experience in chest-wall reconstruction. I'd like to hear his opinion first.'

Scott and I said nothing. The slim hope was shrinking away again. How bad could the surgery be, for God's sake?

Stuart Watson was one of the country's leading plastic-surgery specialists and pretty much my only hope of finding someone prepared to take me on. I was terrified he'd reject me, write off my chances, and I was quaking with nerves when I arrived, with Mum, for my appointment.

'Just take off the dressings and I'll have a look at what we're talking about,' he said, leaving a surgical gown on the examination table beside me and returning to his desk to check my file. He was only away for a few minutes, but by the time he came back, the gown was saturated with leakage from the wound.

'Oh dear,' he said. 'It's that bad, is it?'

He spent quite some time examining me, prodding my neck, my stomach, my back, my legs.

'I'm sorry about the smell,' I said, embarrassed to be subjecting him to the nightmarish impact of my exposed breast.

'Not at all,' he smiled. 'Please don't worry.' Then he said I could get myself dressed and rejoin him at his desk.

He certainly didn't mince his words. 'I'm afraid I don't think there are many choices available to you, Mandy,' he said. 'If you don't have this surgery, the tumour is going to take over and it's not going to be pretty.'

He revealed the full horror of the operation. The reconstructed breast would have to be removed. I started to cry. Mum joined in. After everything I'd been through to rebuild my body following the mastectomy, my breast would be discarded like rubbish. What a waste of time. What a waste of me.

That was just the start.

Mr Watson carried on, 'I'll have to take away a couple of ribs to get right in at the tumour,' he went on, 'and I'll probably have to break your breastbone. I'll scrape away as much of the cancer as I can. Then I'll use some of your stomach tissue to pad out the chest a bit, and I'll take a graft of skin from your leg to cover the whole thing over.'

My chest would be dented inwards after the surgery, my remaining ribs visible through the thin layer of skin. I'd be breathless for a while afterwards because he'd have to deflate my lung during surgery to make more space to work.

Mum was crying like a wounded animal.

'I know you don't want to hear this,' Mr Watson continued, 'but I have to tell you the truth. This operation is not for cosmetic purposes. What you will have afterwards will not be particularly nice, but I think it's the only way.'

I was shaking uncontrollably. 'I'll be a freak,' I wept. 'I'm bad enough as it is, but this is horrific.'

Remove ribs, take away a section of breastbone, scrape away the cancer, patch me up afterwards using bits of my leg . . . it sounded like a Frankenstein experiment.

'Would you be able to do another reconstruction?' I asked through my sobs.

Mr Watson frowned. 'If it all goes well, we might be able to look at doing something to improve the appearance a bit in the future,' he said, 'but I'm afraid it wouldn't be a full reconstruction. You will have lost too much tissue.'

Mum got control of herself first. 'If you don't do this, you're going to die, Mandy. He's just told you that in so many words. What do you want? You don't want to die, do you?' She was desperate, imploring me not to give up. No matter how awful things got, no matter how petrified she was, she would never agree to me giving up.

Mr Watson sat watching us, waiting for my decision, knowing there really wasn't a decision to make. I'd been presented with the facts. Take it or leave it. Gruesome, disfiguring and dangerous surgery or a nasty death at the mercy of the cancer.

'When would I have the surgery?' I asked slowly.

Mr Watson checked his diary. Six days later.

'I've already asked Mrs Weiler-Mithoff to keep the day free so we can work together,' he said.

So that was it. He knew I would go for it.

'If you're agreeable, we'll go ahead next Thursday.'

Mum and I went for some lunch to try and get our heads round what we'd just heard. I kept catching myself staring into space, lost in images of what I would look like after the operation. Some kind of pieced-together monster.

'You have to think about Scott,' Mum was saying. 'How would he cope with Holly on his own? You've got to do it for their sakes.'

I was thinking about Scott and Holly, of course I was, but I was also thinking about myself. I was numb with fear. The risk that I may not open my eyes again after the operation was very real, but, ridiculously, I couldn't stop thinking about the loss of my reconstructed breast. How would I ever look normal again – even if I did wake up after surgery? If I was going to have to live the rest of my life feeling appalled by my own appearance, was it even worth the risk?

'I can't imagine what clothes I could wear to disguise my chest,' I said. 'I mean, I never thought of the recon-struction as a real breast, but at least it filled a bra. It fooled everyone. I'm not going to be able to fool anyone after this.'

I phoned Scott at work and he listened thoughtfully to my recounting of Mr Watson's words. I got right to the end of the details of the surgery without mentioning the fact I'd already agreed to have it done. Scott was silent for a few minutes, digesting what it all meant. For a second or two I thought he was going to tell me to forget it, beg me not to put myself through such an ordeal, make the most of whatever time I had left.

'So, when are you going in?' he asked.

I smiled. Of course he knew I'd do it.

'Mummy's going to be in hospital for a few days, Holly,' I tried to explain to her.

'Yes, I know,' she'd say, slightly annoyed that I'd interrupted her play with some mundane information she'd heard a hundred times before.

I would be in hospital for about two weeks, but I knew she wouldn't even be able to visit me for at least five days, the length of time they expected me to be recovering in the high-dependency unit. It would be strange and confusing for her.

'And do you remember why Mummy's going into hospital?' I persisted, in the hope that if I got her to parrot it often enough, some of the information might stick in her mind.

'Yes, I remember.' She sighed a huffy two-year-old's sigh. 'You are sick and the doctor is going to make you better.'

There. She'd retained some of it. Not enough to distract her from the toy garage she was playing with, but enough to make sense when Daddy had to tell her Mummy wouldn't be home that night. Sometimes I found it difficult to look at her. She was so innocent, so beautiful, so perfect. What worse pain could there be than the thought I might never see her again? It was like a knife in my heart, twisting.

Suddenly it was my last night at home. Holly lay in our bed, sleeping peacefully between us while Scott and I cried and talked and cried more.

'I need to talk about some things before I go in tomorrow,' I said.

'I know,' he replied. 'Me too.'

It all spilled out: how much we loved one another, how grateful I was to have met him, how confident I was in his ability to raise our wonderful daughter on his own.

'I need her to remember me, Scott,' I said. 'I know it won't be easy to talk about me if anything happens, but I need her to know her mummy and know how much her mummy loved her.'

I didn't think I was going to make it. The surgery was more than just daunting; it loomed up before me like an insurmountable mountain. It was bigger than I could cope with, and if I'm honest, I didn't expect to pull through. I had to say what needed to be said.

When Scott finally fell asleep, I slipped out of bed and tiptoed down to the kitchen. I wrote notes, which ended up stained with my own tears. I slid one under Holly's pillow, another under Scott's, and lastly I put one on my special angel shelf.

'Dear Angels,' it said, 'please get me through this operation, but if I don't make it, please look after my family.'

Chapter 20

Faces were swimming into view, but my eyes kept closing. I forced them open again. Scott. Mum. Dad. Then they closed and I was drifting. I felt someone squeezing my hand. Was I dreaming? My eyes flickered, then opened fully. I could see Scott, his face close to mine. He was smiling, and I remembered. I knew where I was.

'I've come through it,' I rasped through the oxygen mask I hadn't even realised I was wearing. 'I'm awake. I've come through it.'

Mum was there, Dad too. I'd survived. Scott kissed my forehead. He was crying.

'I feel great, Scott,' I told him. 'I've come through it.'

They started to laugh.

It was 8 p.m. on Thursday, 24 January 2008 in Canniesburn Plastic-Surgery Unit. I'd been in theatre for nearly eight hours. It would be a few more before the enormity of the surgery bore down on me: the unspeakable pain that enveloped my whole body, the breathlessness, the gastric tube down my nose, my stiff and heavy leg. For three days I was a zombie, a presence in a hospital bed unable to move or communicate. The world was going on around me. I could hear it. I just wasn't part of it.

Nevertheless I had made it. Mr Watson had scraped away most of the tumour. Not all of it, but most of it. And he'd created a new version of me. It was missing a breast and its body was a patchwork of scars, but it was still me. I was alive. Alive again.

When I could finally summon the energy to turn my head very slightly, I noticed three of my favourite angels sitting on my bedside locker. Scott must have brought them in. Mr Watson wouldn't approve if I credited the angels with my survival, but who would refuse a bit of extra help?

Holly came to visit, once I was moved out of high-dependency, and she bounced all over my bed, demanding to know when I was coming back to play with her.

'I'll be home very soon, Holly.' I kissed her. 'Mummy's coming home very soon.'

Delight

'I'll do it, Daddy,' Holly was shouting, frantically shaking a little bag of glitter as she ran across our garden. 'I'll make sure Rudolph knows where to land.'

Scott was laughing his head off as he chased her over the grass, while I watched from the front door. 'Put down plenty of that reindeer dust,' he was calling to her. 'Rudolph has to be able to see it from way, way up high in the sky.'

Dressed in her polka-dot pyjamas and dressing gown, Holly didn't seem to feel the night chill and was squealing with delight, so loudly that all the neighbours in the street were at their windows. Suddenly I took a step back to take in the bigger scene.

It was Christmas Eve 2008, almost exactly a year since my most terrifying surgery. Against all the odds, my life, our lives, had gone on.

'I want to see her when she first understands what Christmas is all about,' I'd said to Scott the year before, never really believing that I would. Yet there I was, giggling with her as she laid out some carrots on the doorstep for the reindeers to munch, while Santa had milk and biscuits indoors.

'When I wake up in the morning, will Santa have been?' she asked, taking my hand, her face shining with excitement.

'Yes, Holly, I'm sure he'll have brought lots of lovely presents for you,' I told her, leading her upstairs to her bedroom.

'Do you think he's got me some *High School Musical* things and some Bratz things?' she said. Her eight-year-old cousin, Olivia, had influenced her choice of Christmas gifts.

'Well, you wrote them on your list, so I'm sure Santa will bring them for you,' I said, tucking her under her pink princess duvet. 'But you'll have to get to sleep soon. Santa doesn't come till you're sleeping.'

I'm not above a bit of festive blackmail. Cancer doesn't make you a saint.

Epilogue

I've ticked off so many of the goals I set myself when Holly was born. At first I just wanted to make it to her first birthday; then I wanted to see her take her first steps, to hear her say, 'Mummy,' to see her second birthday. Each time I reach a target, I push another one back a little. My daughter is three now, and my ambitions grow along with her.

Holly knows her mummy gets sick from time to time, and she knows I've had some pretty radical surgery, but it means nothing to her. That pleases me.

She was watching daytime telly recently, snuggled up on the sofa with my mum. 'Nana...' she mused, in the thoughtful way she does when she's about to impart some words of toddler wisdom. 'That lady's got big boobies, hasn't she?'

Mum raised her eyebrows and sniggered. 'Yes, she does, Holly,' she said, aware that the little one's brain was still ticking over but not quite sure where it was going.

'And you have big boobies, don't you, Nana?'

Mum glanced down at her own cleavage and self-consciously adjusted her top over her 38G chest.

'My mummy only has one booby,' continued Holly, still watching the buxom TV presenter, 'because she was sick and they had to take one away to make her better,' she said, and idly popped another raisin in her mouth.

I'm entirely normal to Holly, and I love that. On a day-to-day basis, I am pretty much normal now. My unclothed body looks rather strange, there's no denying that. The skin on the left side of my chest rests directly on my ribs. It looks paper thin, and I do have to be careful not to bump it, particularly against an energetic three-year-old. I don't have any protection there. When I breathe in, you can almost see my organs at work. It's a bit freaky. With a prosthetic breast called a 'softie' popped into my bra, though, my boobs are even enough under my clothes. I have fabulous camouflage make-up to rub on my leg if I'm wearing a short skirt and it covers the skin-graft scars beautifully. Thankfully, the leaking has stopped. The operation sorted it out.

Holly's normal too. The health problems that I feared were going to plague her seem to have abated, at least. The asthma has vanished, outgrown apparently, but she does manage to pick up every single bug going, more than other kids her age. Maybe her resistance has been lowered by the treatment I had while she was in the womb. I'll probably always believe that, but I'll never know for sure. What I do know is that Herceptin gave me the chance to have her, so I can never regret it. She's tall for her age, she's got silky blond hair, and people say she's the double of my dad. She goes to the local nursery like any other ordinary kid, and no one knows that she's a wee medical miracle. But we do, Scott and me. He tells me off for spoiling her, but how can I shout at her? How can I resist buying her extra gifts? At some point I'll be a memory to her. I want to be a good one.

Recently Dr Hendry was a little concerned that the tumour was growing again, so I started some more chemotherapy – my fifth course to date. I'm having Taxol, and it has threatened to leave me bald for a third time, but I gave the cold cap another try and I've managed to hang on to most of my long hair, albeit a kind of thin and patchy covering. My stretchy headbands have covered the worst of the baldness. I've managed to keep working at Clippers three days a week, and I've got three holidays booked for the coming year. I'm off to Spain with my pals in a few weeks, in fact. Poor Dr Hendry must despair that I won't sit back and rest, but she understands. I have to be me. Well, life is for living, isn't it? Seven years of cancer have taught me that.

Now, at the ripe old age of thirty-four, my best hope is that I can manage breast cancer as a chronic disease, not a terminal one. I'll happily go through a bout of chemo every now and again if it keeps things in check. I'll stay on the Herceptin as long as the experts think it's still having some effect, and I'll keep my eyes peeled for the next wonder-drug. There's nothing more certain than that. Something else will come along. I hope it works for me, but if it doesn't, I hope it buys some time for some other woman in my shoes. I hope it gives them the chance to experience the happiness that I have, despite cancer. From time to time, like when I watched my daughter play in the garden with her dad on Christmas Eve, I realise just how lucky I am. I get to treasure every day.

In my bedroom I have a memory box I'm working on for Holly, my little Herceptin baby. I pop in mementoes of holidays or birthdays, photographs and newspaper cuttings, just in case. Perhaps she can read this book when she's older and understand how special she is, and always will be. I don't want her to feel sorry for her old mum, though. This could have happened to anyone. Why not me?

My new target now? I want to see Holly start school. So if there are any angels listening . . .